ADVERTISING FROM THE DESKTOP

*The Desktop Publisher's Guide
to Designing Ads
That Work*

Elaine Floyd & Lee Wilson

VENTANA
PRESS

Advertising From the Desktop: The Desktop Publisher's Guide to Designing Ads That Work
Copyright © 1994 by Elaine Floyd & Lee Wilson

Library of Congress Cataloging-in-Publication Data
Floyd, Elaine, 1961-
     Advertising from the desktop : the desktop publisher's guide to
designing ads that work / Elaine Floyd & Lee Wilson. -- 1st ed.
          p.   cm.
     Includes index.
     ISBN 1-56604-064-7
     1. Advertising copy--Data processing.   2. Advertising layout and typography--Data processing.
3. Desktop publishing. I. Wilson, Lee, 1951-   . II. Title.
HF5825.F58 1993
659.13'2'0285--dc20   93-37858
                                                                       CIP

Book design: Marcia Webb
Cover design: Marcia Webb
Cover illustration: Todd Gilmore
Editorial staff: Marion Laird, Diana Merelman, Pam Richardson
Production staff: Brian Little, Terri March, Midgard Computing, Marcia Webb
Proofreader: Jean Kaplan

First Edition 9 8 7 6 5 4 3 2 1

Printed in the United States of America

For information about our audio products, write us at:
Newbridge Book Clubs, 3000 Cindel Drive, Delran, NJ 08370

Ventana Press, Inc.
P.O. Box 2468
Chapel Hill, NC 27515
919/942-0220
FAX 919/942-1140

Limits of Liability and Disclaimer of Warranty

TRADEMARKS

ABOUT THE AUTHORS

Elaine Floyd is owner and president of EF Communications, publisher of newsletters and training materials on small-business advertising. Floyd began her publishing career in 1985, using PageMaker 1.0 on a Macintosh Plus. She is also author of *Marketing With Newsletters* and *Quick & Easy Brochures* and editor of a newsletter, *Newsletter News and Resources*.

In addition, Floyd conducts workshops on advertising, desktop publishing and newsletter design and production. She is a mentor trainer for Sierra Club publications, and she has written for the American Management Association's Small Business Reports. Other clients include the International Association of Business Communicators and Exxon Company USA.

Lee Wilson is owner and president of Graphic Witness, a Nashville-based advertising and multimedia firm. Graphic Witness specializes in digital graphics and prepress technology, 3D illustrations, package designs and multimedia presentations. Clients include Aldus Corporation, La Cie Ltd. (a Quantum Company), Empire Berol and Smith Travel Research.

Wilson created "Black & White Images: Quality Reproduction on the Desktop," a color scanning course for Color Across America. He is also a contributing author to Thomas Monroe's *The Desktop Color Reference Manual*. In a previous position as computer graphics specialist, Wilson pioneered in producing black-and-white and color publications entirely on the Macintosh.

Lee Wilson holds B.S. degrees in engineering and computer graphics.

Elaine Floyd can be reached at

EF Communications
6614 Pernod Ave.
St. Louis, MO 63139

Lee Wilson can be reached at

Graphic Witness
850 Stonebrook Blvd.
Nolensville, TN 37135

ACKNOWLEDGMENTS

As a soccer enthusiast, the intricacies of tournament play fascinate me. The teams that win these grueling two-day events filled with hours of sprinting up and down 200-foot fields are not necessarily the fittest or those who boast star players. It's those with the strongest teamwork—and the wind at their backs at strategic moments helps, too.

Here are some of the teammates who kept this book tournament going.

Coauthor Lee Wilson directed the project and opened my eyes to just how much day-to-day advertising and planning can be done on the computer. A group of 50 Sierra Club writers and artists provided inspiration and energy to get things off to a fast start. Graphic artist Barbara Conover shared ideas on how to convey movement in layouts.

Optometrist Laura Bondy verified the information on color and vision. Consultant Maurice Julien loaned from his extensive advertising library. Ad man Rick Blair uploaded lots of good ideas to America Online. Electronic designer Jan V. White graciously wrote the Foreword somewhere over the Atlantic on a whirlwind seminar tour of Europe.

All the software companies listed in this book were good sports. The most-valuable-player winners are Multi-Ad Services, S. H. Pierce, EduCorp, Eastman Kodak, Corel, MarketPlace Information, Aldus, Quark, Ventura, Pantone, PagePlus, IdeaFisher, Spinnaker Software and TimeWorks.

The action photos used in the visuals are from the Professional Photography Collection and Kids CDs offered by EduCorp. The clip art is from Multi-Ad Services, EduCorp and T/Maker.

Down to the final match, Ventana Press provided the gale winds and team spirit that sent the project flying to completion. Thanks and appreciation go to coach Elizabeth Woodman, halfback Marion Laird, captain Pam Richardson, sweeper Marcia Webb, stopper Brian Little, forward Diane Lennox and all the other pro players at Ventana Press.

Dedication

To M.T.

Contents

Foreword   **xvii**

Introduction   **xxi**

Section 1: Concepts & Campaigns

Chapter One

Madison Avenue Goes Desktop   **1**

A Coordinated Attack   2
   From Concept to Creation   3
Making a Marketing Plan   4
   An Automated Consultant   4
   Where Your Plan Takes You   6
Targeting Your Audience   8
   Targeting Through Graphics   8
   Narrowing the Target   9

Creating a Concept   12

Launching a Campaign   16

    Build Recognition   17

    Reinforce Your Image   19

    Provide Information   22

    Make It Easy to Buy   23

Developing Your Layout   24

Chapter Two

Your Desktop Toolbox   27

Visuals   28

    Photographs   30

    Illustrations   39

    Logos & Signatures   45

    Type as Visuals   47

Typography   54

    Personality of Type   55

    Setting Type With Your Computer   57

    Headlines   64

    Attention-Grabbers   71

    Body Copy   73

    Mouse Type   81

Organizational Tools   82

Chapter Three

Desktop Layouts That Sell   93

Getting Started   94

    Basic Publishing   94

    Power Publishing   95

    Choosing a Program   95

Start With Thumbnails   97
   How Shapes Affect Layout   100
Visibility   102
   Color Includes Black, White & Gray   103
   Shaping Your Layout   107
   Provocative Visuals   109
Clarity   113
   Build Around a Central Element   115
   Movement & Balance   117
   Unity   123
Response   125
   Variety   126
   Emphasis   127

Chapter Four

Turn Up the Volume With Color — 133

Color & Advertising   133
   Getting Started in Color   134
Color on the Desktop   135
   Color Systems   136
   Light Versus Print   137
   The Wheel of Color   138
   Other Qualities of Colors   139
   The Pantone Matching System   140
   Spot Color, Four-Color & Duotone   141
Visibility   144
   Red & Yellow & Visible All Over   144
   Color & Shape   146
   Color & Provocative Visuals   149
   Recognition & Association   150
   Easy Come, Easy Go   151

Clarity   152
  Legibility   152
  Clarity in Communication   153
  Balance, Movement & Unity   154
Response   155

Section 11: The Real Thing

Chapter Five

Display Ads   **161**
Choosing a Medium   162
  Placement on the Page   166
  Sizes, Rate Cards & Restrictions   169
Designing Display Ads   171
  Visibility   171
  Clarity   174
  Response   177
Ad Design Formulas   179
  "The Ogilvy" & Variations   180
  The Visual Reigns   184
  All the Advertising That's Fit to Print 189
  Once Upon a Time   193
  Apples & Oranges   195
  Price As King   198
  What's Cooking?   200
  Mirror, Mirror   201
  Two-Page Spreads   202

Chapter Six

Small-Space Ads   **209**

Visibility in Small Spaces   210
   Stand Out in the Crowd   211
   Guarding the Flanks   218
Clarity   220
Response   222
Small-Space Ad Formulas   222

Chapter Seven

Sales Materials   **239**

Sneaked-In Advertising   240
   Sales Receipts & Invoices   240
   Business Cards   242
   Envelopes   245
   Mailing Labels & Promotional Stickers 246
   Order Forms   247
   Coupons & Gift Certificates   249
Direct-Mail Pieces   250
   Sales Letters   250
   Brochures   254
   Flyers   257
   Postcards   261
   Card Decks   263
   Promotional Newsletters   264
   Reply Cards   267
Innovative Approaches   268
   Stickers   268
   Notes   269
   Advertising Premiums   270

Chapter Eight

In-Store Advertising　273

Banners & Signs　274
　Designing Banners & Signs　275
　Wave Your Own Banner　277
　Window Sign Language　279
In-Store Signs & Displays　283
Packaging　286
Shopping Bags　289

Chapter Nine

Advertising of the Future　295

Just the Fax　297
　Types of Fax Advertising　297
　Fax-Friendly Designs　300
News Releases on Disk　309
Customer Bulletin Boards　310
Audio Recordings　312
Multimedia Presentations & Catalogs　313
Until Next Time…　316

Section 111: Helpful Resources

Software & Services　319

Books & Periodicals　351

Associations, Consultants & Training   **363**

Catalogs & Print Services   **369**

Advertising Software Features   **373**

Glossary   **399**

Index   **411**

OREWORD

Have you ever watched what people do when they are writing postcards to their friends? The first thing is to put down the address...then they look up, staring vaguely at the sky, searching for inspiration—while they are visualizing their pal's face to find the right personal tone to speak in. That's right: they are defining their audience. A postcard is a personal message from one person to another. Even more intimate than that, it is one person talking to another by means of a substitute voice: handwriting. (Plus a ready-made picture which saves all sorts of time and effort.)

What is writing a postcard? Talking to a friend. What is reading a postcard? Listening to a friend. When you come down to fundamentals, typography is just a mechanized, formalized version of handwriting, and it is much easier to decipher than handwriting, given the sorry state of primary education.

When you want to tell somebody that something is important, you write it (or set it) in big, fat letters. When you want to indicate its relative lack of importance, you write it (set it) small and you place it on the foot of the page as an after-thought or footnote. What prompts you to make that distinction? Is it the prettiness of the composition and the way the type looks? Of course not. Who cares about that? No: the decisions about type are driven by the value of the ideas that the words represent. To whom? To you? No, to your listener/reader.

What is typography? The picture of the idea. Don't be afraid of type, but use it naturally. Don't concentrate on the type itself. It is not an artform. It is nothing more than a vehicle used to carry your thoughts from one place to another. It is the thoughts that matter, not the vehicle. So open your eyes and listen to your type talk.

What is color? Not black. It is special only by contrast to the expected black ink or toner. It is therefore logical to reserve it for special use. Never use color to decorate with, because that wastes its potential value. Use it to emphasize what you want to have noticed first. Use it to rank information. Use it to classify segments. Use it to link thoughts. Again, concentrate on the message, not the design.

Is the medium the message? No, the message is the message. Put yourself in the recipient's mode: as a reader, what do you bother to read? Only the stuff that interests you. You reject everything that has no immediately discernible "what's-in-it-for-me" value, because you have no motivation and even less time. Besides, there are too many messages beamed at you from all sides, so you have to protect yourself from getting involved. You cannot afford to invest time and effort in anything that is unlikely to pay off. But there's a chink in your armor: your emotions. They are much harder to control than your rational logic.

What are pictures? Fast shots to the emotions. Images evoke curiosity, nostalgia, sentimentality, familiarity, voyeurism...how can you resist a picture of a kid with his dog? You can't. (That's the other reason there's a picture on the other side of that postcard.) Use the right image and the viewer's attention is caught. Now you have the opportunity to tell them the nugget of information that you want them to know about and that they must have.

Successful advertising, like any other good human communication, is an amalgam, blending the ideas with technique, the content with form.

There's nothing more infuriating than being told that something is "easy." Sure it is, if you know how. If you don't, or if you are new to doing it (rather than merely absorbing it, like everybody else), then it isn't nearly so easy. The fact is that good advertising is complicated, technical, many-sided and difficult—until you get into it, and discover that if you proceed step-by-step, there's no magic to it. You can indeed learn to control the monster. Remember how daunting the computer was the first time you faced it? (It sure scared me to death when I came to it, but I confess to being a member of the older generation.) You conquered that monster, too. So go to it. Use this book. It is a compendium of essential stuff you need to know. May you sell a million!

Jan V. White

P.S. Be ready to forgive yourself if you goof up. You're bound to. Haven't you ever spoiled a postcard or two?

1NTRODUCTION

Nestled in a small Italian community just outside of Pittsburgh, PA, is a great little pizza place. It's not a franchise. This one-parlor pizzeria was founded by two German women. "German women starting a pizzeria in an Italian community?" you ask. These women assumed you'd wonder. They named their restaurant Pizza With a German Twist.

While I've been working on this book, I've thought often of the German Twist. The pizzas are similar to those made by Italian hands but with a few slight differences. The crust is rolled like a pie instead of tossed (the women call them *pizza pies*). And the toppings are put on after the pizza is cooked. But it's still pizza.

And just as *pizza* is *pizza*, the advertising you "knead" and shape using your desktop system is still *advertising*. The underlying principles discussed in this book are based on techniques that have been around since the early 1900s. It's only the computer and printer technology that's new.

WHO NEEDS THIS BOOK?

This book is written for desktop publishers faced with the challenge of promoting a business, a nonprofit organization, a school or an association. You may be creating advertising for the first time or refreshing your existing materials.

If you're running your own business, you'll gain the satisfaction of doing your own promotions. If you're not, you'll learn design skills valued by today's employers.

Of course, good design isn't all that's required for effective advertisements. It's part of a three-step process that also includes copywriting and targeting an audience. This book assumes you've had some experience in writing advertising copy. It includes information on targeting your prospects but assumes you already know why this is important. (If you're interested in finding out more about writing and producing ads, flip to the listings in the resources section in the back of this book.)

ADVERTISING WITH A DESKTOP TWIST

Whether you use computer-aided or traditional methods, your challenge when creating advertisements is the same— winning attention and a response from your prospects. Luckily, you have all the tools you need right on your desktop.

Your mouse contains a concentrated chunk of "Madison Avenue." This book shows you how to extract it. It lets you in on secrets known to design gurus and advertising agency executives since the turn of the century. It takes what could be called basic advertising information and gives it a new turn. If my dear German ladies would forgive the play on words... it's advertising with a *desktop* twist.

TRENDS IN ADVERTISING

Desktop advertising is changing at a dizzying pace. Technology is responding to the "doing more with less" theme of the '90s. Ads are now produced in hours instead of days. Clip art and clip photo services take the place of subcontractors. Brainstorming software does the work of a conference table full of "idea people." And a desktop ad campaign can be carried off at a fraction of the time and cost of methods employed just a few years ago.

Staff and budget cutbacks mean that you must do more with less in a shorter period of time. The computer helps. Your own market is probably changing just as fast. New markets and uses for your products are opening all the time. The techniques of the '50s can no longer compete—gone are the general advertisements and publications of yesterday. Market fragmentation and target marketing are here to stay. You must speak to specific markets with targeted benefits and targeted graphics.

Your advertising dollars are scarce as well. You need more mileage from every promotion you do—from large ads, brochures, letters, receipts, signs, packaging and so on.

While prices for ad space, postage and paper are rising, many other prices are falling. The prices of computers and laser printers, for example. The prices of printing setups such as plates are also decreasing.

Lower prices on color are coming soon. In the not-too-distant future, you'll be able to get four-color flyers and signs printed at your neighborhood quick-print shop. You'll have a color laser printer and monitor (if you don't already). Alternate advertising media, such as computer bulletin boards and multimedia catalogs, are right around the corner.

These are tools that you and I—regular ole' U.S. business people—will soon be comfortable creating and using.

HOW TO USE THIS BOOK

Advertising From the Desktop is organized into three main sections:

Section I—Chapters 1 through 4: These chapters give you an overview on how design decisions are guided by your concept and campaigns. Chapter 2 describes all the desktop tools you'll be working with. All the elements come together in Chapter 3, with the focus on effective layouts. In Chapter 4, these general principles are expanded to include using color to spice up your advertising designs.

Section II—Chapters 5 through 9: In these chapters, you'll see how these design principles translate into all of your promotional materials. You'll see examples of all sorts of advertisements, from large- and small-space ads to sales materials you hand out to prospects, and in-store signs that help sell when you and your customers meet face-to-face. In Chapter 9, true to the concept that good design principles apply regardless of the media, we look at new adventures in advertising. New technology such as self-service faxes, multimedia, three-dimensional graphics and animation will soon be at your desktop. Finally, we take an enlightening look at advertising in the future.

Section III, at the back of the book, contains five resource collections—listings of desktop publishing, illustration, clip art, bulletin board, multimedia and other software, as well as books and periodicals, associations, consultants, training opportunities, catalogs and printers. The last of the resource sections is a special bonus—an evaluated listing of the advertising features of the top-selling Macintosh and PC desktop publishing programs.

Those readers familiar with advertising concepts and the latest in desktop technology could skim the first two chapters and dive into Chapter 3. Those new to desktop publishing should read the book from beginning to end.

REQUIRED EQUIPMENT & EXPERTISE

The techniques shown in this book apply to all types of computer systems—PCs, Macintoshes and others are all welcome. (For information on available software, see the resources section.)

Chances are, you've had your computer for a while. You bought it to automate your accounting and customer mailing list. You use it to write letters, and you've slowly ventured into the desktop publishing arena.

You may not be an artist. You don't have to be to use the ideas in this book. All that's necessary is a good grasp of how to operate your computer and your favorite desktop publishing or full-featured word processing program.

Here's a basic shopping list for color equipment:

- Color calibration; 230mb hard drive; Minimum of 8mb RAM

- 24-bit color monitor and video card

- Desktop publishing program that supports color

- Illustration, paint and photo retouch program supporting color

- Access to desktop color printer for proofs

- Color scanner (optional)

- Color service bureau

LET'S GET STARTED

According to the American Association of Advertising Agencies, each day consumers are bombarded with more than 1,600 advertisements. Only 80 are consciously noticed and only 12 create a reaction. Come with us now and learn how to create ads that will take their places among those enviable few.

Elaine Floyd
St. Louis, Missouri

SECTION I

Concepts & Campaigns

Promise, large promise, is the soul of an advertisement.
—*Samuel Johnson*

CHAPTER 1

Madison Avenue Goes Desktop

The desirable thing in advertising, as in life, is a nice balance between civilization and a state of nature.

—W. A. Dwiggins

Throughout this book the word *product* means a product, service, idea or cause.

This book concentrates primarily on desktop design. But when you're preparing advertising materials on the desktop, design cannot be separated from audience appeal and concept. It must enhance them. Advertising is more persuasive when you follow a coordinated plan.

Set out on the right foot with a marketing plan. Target your customers. Position your products and company through your advertising concepts. And let these concepts guide your campaigns and advertising design.

Desktop advertising pushes your publishing capabilities to new heights. In the spirit of persuading customers and prospects, your computer can help you produce eye-catching newspaper ads, brochures, circulars, newsletters, window signs and multimedia presentations.

In this book, space ads in newspapers and magazines are referred to as "ads" to distinguish them from other types of advertising. Other terms that relate to ad components include *visual, headline, deck, subhead, body copy, border, call to action, signature* and *starburst*.

Figure 1-1: We've added callouts to show the names of elements usually found in an advertisement.

A COORDINATED ATTACK

Professional agencies and large corporations approach advertising and marketing in a very methodical way. They develop plans of attack and painstakingly implement them. Their staffs brainstorm concepts, write copy, create visuals and design layouts.

Instead of an agency staff, you have your own creative powers and a desktop computer. In this chapter you'll learn how your desktop computer can help, in all areas of advertising—marketing plan, target audience, concept, ad campaign and layout. Other chapters in Section I cover your design tools, layout and use of color. Section II moves into how to use these tools for specific types of advertising.

Today, desktop publishing is no longer the "wave of the future"; it's the "wave of the *now*."

From Concept to Creation

Many advertisers use programs like IdeaFisher for help with developing concepts and marketing plans, targeting prospects, planning campaigns and implementing promotions. Though millions of dollars and 12 years of research went into the program's development, it's available to us average folks for around $100. That's less than you'd spend for one hour with a good design consultant.

> **Tip:** IdeaFisher, a brainstorming program for both the PC and the Macintosh, is a useful tool for any do-it-yourself desktop advertiser. The standard IdeaFisher package includes queries that step you through the marketing plan process.

The more visuals you have to choose from , the better your chance of a perfect fit for your concept.

A CD-ROM drive is also a useful accessory for desktop advertising. It allows you access to disks containing thousands of ready-made images. In the future, many software programs will be shipping on CD-ROM. Multimedia—the new wave of the future—relies heavily on CD technology. With multimedia, you can combine the targeting benefits of direct mail with the dynamic benefits of television and radio by putting your sales presentation or catalog on CD.

Figure 1-2: Having many images on CD-ROM disks lets you find the right visual for your concept—sporty, old-fashioned or casual.

MAKING A MARKETING PLAN

*€*ffective advertising is composed of three inseparable parts— audience, concept and copy, and design.

Why take the time to develop marketing plans and concepts? Why not just create a graphically pleasing ad? Because even the most creative advertising can't help your business if you don't have clear goals. Clear goals result in simple, persuasive advertising. Look at Nike's "Just Do It." Or Wendy's "Where's the Beef?" These campaigns tied together real benefits with entertainment value. Such simplicity requires a clear-cut plan.

An Automated Consultant

It's often said that a consultant is someone you pay to tell you what you already know. An automated version of a marketing consultant is a program called IdeaFisher. Through a series of questions, this program helps you put what you know into a useable marketing plan.

IdeaFisher's question bank helps you plot a course of action, anticipate market changes and deploy your full advertising capabilities. In the process of creating a plan, you gain insight into your customers' operations and anticipate their needs. This helps you synchronize your advertising campaigns and develop graphic uniformity throughout your projects.

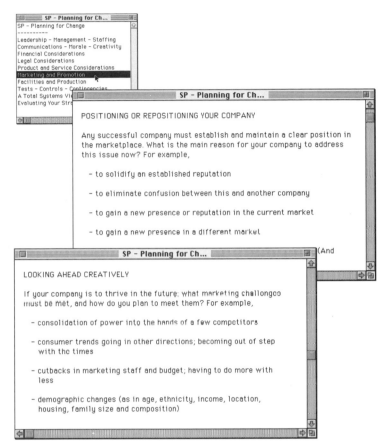

Create marketing plans with strategic planning.

Figure 1-3: The Strategic Planning module is an IdeaFisher add-on product that explores marketing plans and strategies in greater depth.

Always a Bridesmaid...
Because of their simplicity, many good advertising slogans become part of popular culture. We've long forgotten the Listerine campaign, but we still use the saying "Always a bridesmaid but never a bride."

Where Your Plan Takes You

Your marketing plan guides many important graphics decisions, such as logo design. A well-thought-out plan helps you establish what you want people to think of first when they see or hear your name. An effective logo and company signature can firmly entrench a positive impression of your company in your prospects' minds.

Figure 1-4: Most advertising is "signed" by its sponsor.

*G*ive your prospects good "visions of you" with a catcy logo design.

For a company that's trying to change its direction and image, graphics are the most immediate way to communicate the change. An updated logo and colors will be a great step forward.

Figure 1-5: A financial planner updated her logo to make it more attractive to corporate clients.

Part of good market planning is focusing on prospective customers. Your graphic techniques may be different for keeping customers than for attracting new ones.

*S*tepping through
the planning process
fills your marketing
basket with options.

**Get Your Hands on
Brochures & Newsletters, Too**

iLorem ipsum dolor sit amet, con sectet adipsicing
elit, sed diam nonnumy nibh nod tempor inci.
Sunt ut labore et dol magna ali quam erat volupat.
Duis autem
vel eum irure dolor in henderit in vulputate velit
esse consequat. Sunt ut labore et dolore.unt ut
labore et dolore magna ali quam erat volupat. Duis
auuisnod tmpor inci. Sunt ut labore et dolore
magna ali quam erat volupat. Duis autem vel cum
irure dolor in henderit in vulputate velit esse con-

Advertising Studio, Ltd.
Handmade ads crafted by computer
(800) 555-1212

**Stretch your advertising dollar
with Advertising Studio.**

iLorem ipsum dolor sit amet, con sectet adipsicing
elit, sed diam nonnumy nibh nod tempor inci. Sunt
ut labore et dol magna ali quam erat volupat. Duis
autem ure dolor in
henderit in vulpu-
tate velit esse con-
sequat. Sunt ut
labore et dolot ut.

"Thanks to Advertising Studio,
my business is booming.
—Charles President"

**Winner of
10
Antonio Awards**

(800) 555-1212

Advertising Studio, Ltd.
Handmade ads crafted by computer

Figure 1-6: When advertising to existing customers, you may be simply
reminding them of your services. Advertisements to new customers will
need to spell out benefits.

Marketing plans help you see your options for possible
promotions and how to coordinate your efforts. For example,
you might include brochures, coupons and newsletters in
your product packaging. Or you could create posters and
signs along with your ad campaign.

Your media mix for each promotion reflects how your
prospects find and buy your products. For example, the best
way to reach these customers may be with banners and
direct mail. Or perhaps newspaper ads are the first place
they're likely to look.

Tip: Planning ahead saves money. You may save
printing charges (not to mention time) by producing
several postcard mailings or banners at once.

TARGETING YOUR AUDIENCE

A narrow target covering the highest concentration of prospective buyers produces economical and effective advertising. The more you know about a group of prospects— age, gender, education, income, marital status, location, occupation, title, and so on— the better you can attract the attention of those prospects with headlines and visuals.

Targeting Through Graphics

Your target audience also has what's called a *psychographic profile.* Use the traits included in the psychographic profile for your particular target group to create enticing graphics.

For example, people in high-tech industries are usually well-read trendsetters that adapt easily to new technology. They also tend to be science fiction and "Star Trek" lovers. They will respond well to space graphics and cutting-edge techniques like 3D visuals and textured backgrounds.

The target audience for an environmental organization may be conservationists, nature lovers and hikers. They may also be vegetarians and interested in health and fitness. Graphics for this group would be calm, soothing and peaceful—images that represent the values and preferences of this target market.

Know your prospects so you can court them with visuals.

Figure 1–7: Nature lovers would relate to this photograph.

Within your defined target, the largest percentage of the audience must identify with your graphics. Advertising research has shown that ads containing visuals familiar to the target audience will outpull those ads with less familiar graphics. For example, an ad showing playing cards will outpull one with dominoes, since more people play cards.

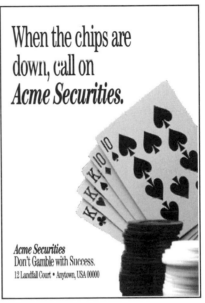

Figure 1-8: When you pick advertising visuals, choose those that are sure to interest the majority of your target audience.

*f*ine-tune your call to action based on your prospects' buying habits.

Narrowing the Target

Advances in targeting psychology have led many advertisers to leave mass media methods such as newspaper ads in favor of more narrowly targeted media—neighborhood journals, direct mail and hand-delivered circulars.

With the help of demographic databases and your own surveys, you can determine buying habits such as how long it takes to make a purchasing decision. This helps you plan the frequency of your promotions and lets you know if you should highlight fast-response items like an 800 number or operators on duty 24 hours per day.

The 80/20 Rule
Save advertising dollars using the "80/20 rule of sales": 80 percent of your sales come from the top 20 percent of your customers. The better you target your customers, the more add-on products you sell.

You may also be conducting surveys and analyzing data as part of targeting your audience. Software packages that automate this process include popular spreadsheets and databases such as FileMaker, Lotus 1-2-3, Microsoft Excel and Panorama.

Customer Type	Publishing?	PageMaker	Quark	Ventura	Software	Mac	PC
Government	Y	Y		Y	Y	Y	Y
Graphic Design	Y		Y			Y	
Graphics	N	Y		Y	Arts & Letters		Y
Health Care	Y	Y					Y
Health Care	N						
Healthcare	Y				Word Perfect		
HMO	N	Y		Y			Y
Hospital	Y	Y			MS Word, MS Works	Y	
Hospital	Y				Lotus, Harvard Graphics,		Y
Independent Writer	Y				MS Word	Y	
Industrial Distributo	Y	Y			MS Word		Y
Industrial Engineeri	Y				Word Processing	Y	Y

159 visible/159 total

Figure 1-9: Databases such as Panorama (shown here) help you store customer data along with addresses and phone numbers.

*S*ave direct-mail dollars by labeling with ZIP+4 and bar codes.

Also investigate mailing-list management programs authorized by the post office for bar coding and ZIP+4 that qualify you for postal discounts. Call the information desk at the post office for more about this and how to submit your mailing list on disk for address verification.

MarketPlace, a CD-ROM package, provides business-to-business marketers with data collected by Dun & Bradstreet. MarketPlace contains the addresses of seven million U.S. businesses on CD-ROM and lets you compile and purchase your own list from this huge database. Automated features help you target prospects, analyze markets, print mailing lists and export the data to other programs. Businesses are classified by business type, number of employees, location and annual sales figures. Quarterly updates of addresses are sold individually or on a subscription basis. The price of the program includes the first 3,000-name list from the database. After that, the cost is 10 cents per name with no minimum purchase necessary.

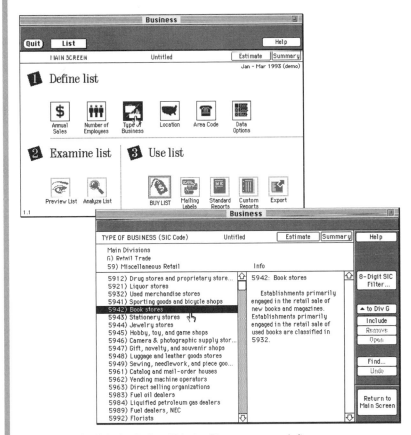

Figure 1-10: With the help of MarketPlace, you can define your own targeted list using annual sales figures, number of employees, business type, location and area code.

*D*on't have Saman-
tha and Endora
around? Try one
of the creativity
packages.

CREATING A CONCEPT

Remember the Daryn Stevens character on the TV program
"Bewitched"? He often needed magical powers to find the
right concept for a client's campaign. You probably won't
have a supernatural source to help you with your advertising
concepts. So you'll need to depend on your own knowledge
or business experience and your desktop computer.

Concepts are themes, ideas or key words that tie your
products, company name or slogan to your advertising
campaign. They hold your campaign together by guiding
your choices in copy, visuals and layout.

To arrive at a concept, draw from the following sources:

- Images associated with the product

- The product itself

- Benefits derived from using

- Losses suffered from not using

- Uses of the product

- Uniqueness of the product

- Personality of the product

Once you have a general idea of what you'd like your
concept to be, brainstorm. Develop key words by listing
what your customers are really buying when they choose
your product. With your key words, IdeaFisher can generate
other word and pictorial associations.

IdeaFisher provides lists of questions and key words to
help trigger your thoughts. The software doesn't come up
with ideas for you but stimulates you to come up with your
own by jogging your memory.

My coauthor and advertising mentor, Lee Wilson, works
with a manufacturer of hard disks. When people buy hard
disks, they buy storage space, speed, a disk drive and so on.
Some of his campaigns have included offering the potential

buyer a "test drive" of the product and a contest to win a Porsche. Recently he was working on a campaign with a "space" theme.

The persuasive effects of advertising are born in the conceptual stage.

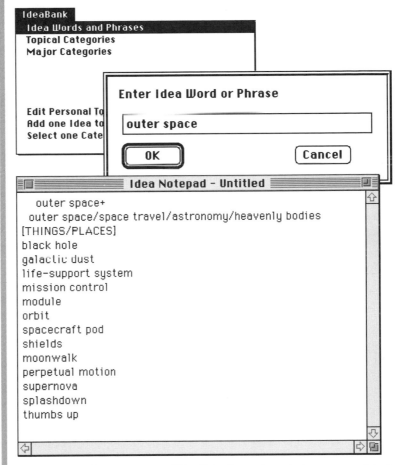

Figure 1-11: Here are some of IdeaFisher's words and phrases associated with outer space.

These suggestions can give you ideas for visuals. They can also provide other ideas that help you tie together your copy and your concept.

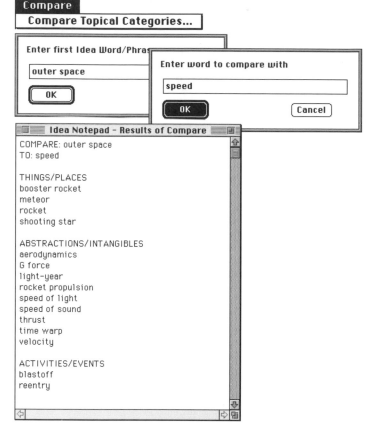

*B*rainstorm at the speed of light with IdeaFisher.

Figure 1-12: IdeaFisher also lets you compare words. Here's part of the result when *outer space* and *speed* are compared.

Brainstorming Pays Off
Linus Pauling, Nobel Prize–winning American chemist, said that the more ideas you come up with, the more likely you are to find a good one. Creativity research proves that the best, most original ideas are the last 50 percent of all the ideas you generate. The least original, obvious ones are in the first half of the brainstorming.

POE'S COUSIN, MOE

*O*nce upon a midnight dreary,
While I pondered weak and...
sorry... merry... furry...
ferry... weedy... weenie...
wheezy... really... reeky...
wacky... tacky... sake...
sappy...

Figure 1-13: The more open and playful your spirit, the easier it will be to generate lists of ideas.

*S*et the scene for your creative spirit with these simple steps.

Here are some tips to help you as you pursue those elusive great ideas:

- Start with a clean slate—no preexisting bias.

- Pretend you have all the time in the world.

- Think in terms of solutions, not problems.

- Have fun.

- "Translate" key words into actions or images of things.

- Dream up as many ideas as you can.

- Doodle.

- Think of things that appeal to sight, smell, taste, sound, touch.

- Take a break and come back later.

- Think about the project the last thing at night.

- Write down several ideas early in the morning.

- Bounce ideas off of other people.

- Role-play, with one person playing your prospect.

- Use brainstorming software.

Entire books have been devoted to single facets of advertising—creativity, marketing plans, targeting customers, surveys and so on. If you need more background information on any or all of these areas, please see the books listed in the resource section in the back of this book. Other sources to help you with word and picture associations include thesauruses (stand-alone volumes or those bundled in word processing programs) and encyclopedias on CD-ROM.

Tip: Successful concepts that reflect the positive aspects of your business can work for you over and over again. Adapt and coordinate concepts from one campaign to the next. Develop new slants for successful concepts to keep your advertising fresh.

LAUNCHING A CAMPAIGN

Successful advertising is an ongoing effort. A uniform advertising concept and design increases the performance of every promotion you do.

A campaign is a connected series of advertisements and promotions designed to accomplish specific sales goals set in your marketing plan. Many campaigns have a specific length—usually 10 to 13 weeks.

Decide on a time limit for your advertising campaign.

Marketing experts say you must reach your prospects between seven and ten times with the same message before you can assume people know who you are and what you provide. Places to repeat your message include window signs, displays, brochures, banners, sales letters, package labels, catalogs and order forms.

Figure 1-14: Advertising promotions can be built around holidays, seasonal events and clearances, endorsements, new products, anniversary sales or trade shows.

You must lead buyers through four graphical stages before they'll become customers:

1. Build recognition.

2. Reinforce your image.

3. Provide information.

4. Make it easy to buy.

Build Recognition

You recognize certain local or national ads at a glance. These advertisers use the same general design for each of their ads. Design continuity creates and builds on the power of repetition and familiarity.

Roll In For a Spring Cleaning.

Roll into springtime weather with a professional auto detailing. Includes wash, vacuum, interior protection, windows in & out and protective exterior coating.

Great for prom gifts, Mother's Day presents or just if your ride needs a lift... Done while you wait. No appointment needed.

Most cars
$ **18**⁵⁰

OPEN
MON-SAT
8 AM - 6 PM

Good thru May 15.

R IVERSIDE
TIRE & AUTO

1001 N. MacFarland Blvd.
at Rice Mine Rd. near Speedway

Postcard

Auto Detailing $ **18**⁵⁰

Banner

Figure 1-15: Reinforce by repetition. Keep the same look and message but place the message in different types of media.

To develop recognition in your advertising, be sure that the design elements in the list that follows are the same or at least recognizably similar for every ad you place:

- Borders and white space
- Typefaces for headlines and body copy
- Style of illustrations
- Your logo
- Colors (including screens)

Tip: Save time by developing standard designs for all campaigns. Save the designs as templates in your desktop publishing program. Or save a master file and make a working copy for each promotion. If you're a QuarkXPress or PageMaker 5.0 user, you can store frequently used graphics in a "Library" for quick importing into a page layout.

Reinforce Your Image

Before your prospects start reading, they draw their first impression of your company and what you have to offer. Your design sets you apart and helps people get to know you.

*A*dvertising design is your first chance to make a good impression.

Figure 1-16: To create a standard look for your campaign, set standards for headlines, borders and body copy to graphically reinforce your campaign.

Decide whether your customers prefer formality or informality. Then, use designs that create this image. For example, attract older buyers with traditional designs and younger buyers with informal ones.

*W*olves do it by howling. Advertisers attract with design.

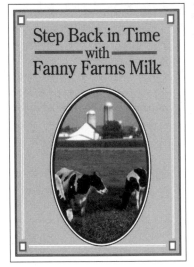

Figure 1-17: A dairy products company could attract older buyers with a formal ad and younger buyers with a more dynamic one.

Target Desired Buyers

While attracting attention to your ad is wonderful, you want to attract your desired *buyers*. People have become aware that advertisements for expensive products usually contain a lot of white space. They know if an ad is crammed full of prices, it's likely to be for a discount store.

*D*esign communi-
cates your position in
the marketplace.

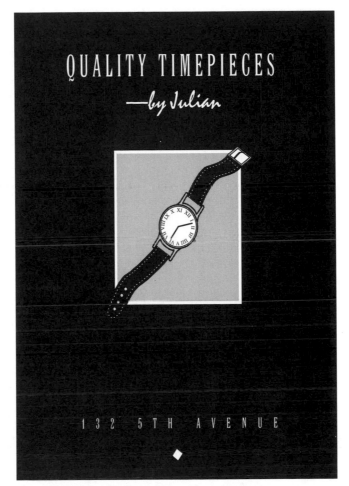

Figure 1-18: Lots of white space in an ad usually signals an expensive or exclusive product.

The look of advertising for an off-price store will be different than that for a store that's trying to build its image and awareness of its products. Don't dump a box of starbursts into your ad unless you want calls from price shoppers. It's better to let your advertising preselect and screen your customers. You'll receive fewer calls but more of the callers will turn into repeat paying customers.

Figure 1-19: The discount hotel highlights its low prices while a bed-and-breakfast opts for elegance.

Provide Information

For technical products and high-ticket items, buyers want information before they purchase. Other buyers, such as those looking through the Yellow Pages, may assume you don't offer a specific product or service unless you list it. This information can be graphically presented in a numbered list, a check list, a bordered inset or any other format that fits in with your design.

Feature One Product
According to advertising research findings, ads featuring only one product sell better than those promoting an entire product line.

Figure 1-20: Layout formats such as lists and figures help pack an advertisement full of information.

Make It Easy to Buy

Offer more than one way for people to place orders. Graphically show these in your ads through credit card logos, phone icons, maps and so on. Highlight your 800 number, include a coupon offering a brochure, draw a clear map of your location, tell your extended store hours and so on. Offer multiple ways to make a purchase.

Figure 1-21: Use logos, icons, maps and phone numbers in your ads to make it easy for potential buyers to reach you.

Let the concept be your layout guide.

DEVELOPING YOUR LAYOUT

The core idea of your campaign—the concept—will guide you in choosing visuals, type styles and layout formats for each advertisement. Dynamic layouts emphasize the headline, visual and response.

Depending upon your concept, you may be highlighting the problems your product promises to solve or the benefits people will derive if they use it. Or the emphasis may be on the call to action—your phone number, address, sale date, special pricing while supplies last and so on. In Chapter 3, "Desktop Layouts That Sell," we'll focus more on techniques to guide readers' eyes through your advertisements.

If you use similar layouts for each ad you create, you'll build recognition from one ad to the next. The placement of your illustrations, headlines and logo can integrate your

entire advertising campaign. In Chapters 4 through 8 you'll
learn ways to create large and small ads, brochures, postcards, signs and more—these are the building blocks of your
campaigns.

Figure 1-22: A one-shot approach (shown in the first version of the ad)
draws much less curiosity and attention than a well-thought-out sequence
(shown in the second and third versions).

Future chapters will detail the desktop design tools used
for all of your advertising layout. These include items you
buy, such as typefaces, ready-made backgrounds and clip
art, to combine with your page layout, illustration and
editing programs' boxes, rules, screens and other elements.

SUMMARY CHECKLIST

- Develop a marketing plan.
- Let your plan guide your advertising designs.
- Generate a targeted list of customers.
- Use IdeaFisher to help you create concepts.
- Let your concepts guide your campaign layouts.
- Choose visuals that attract your target audience.
- Strive for design consistency within your campaign and among campaigns.
- Design advertising to build recognition, reinforce your image, provide information and make buying easy.

MOVING ON

You may be tempted to bypass the planning steps discussed in this chapter. After all, if your computer makes it so easy, why not dive right into the layout process? The answer is, that same computer can make it easy—right from the beginning—to help you develop concepts and implement a strategy that will result in sales far beyond those produced with haphazardly created advertising.

For each promotion, you'll be working with visuals, headlines and copy. Tools found on the desktop can whip these elements into shape. The next chapter shows you how.

CHAPTER 2

YOUR DESKTOP TOOLBOX

W.A. Dwiggins coined the term "graphic artist" back in the 1930s. Paul Brainerd gave us "desktop publishing" in the 1980s.

Desktop publishing tools greatly influence modern advertising design.

In the early days of desktop publishing, it was easy to spot computer-made advertising. Boy, has life on the desktop changed. No longer design's stepchild, now desktop publishing tools not only influence but increasingly play a dominant role in modern advertising design.

In this chapter, we'll focus on using your desktop advertising software features to create eye-catching visuals and easy-to-read copy. We start out with visuals—photographs, illustrations, clip art and logos. Then we move on to typefaces, headlines and other typographic components. Finally, we look at the smaller but nonetheless important graphic features that help to separate and organize the elements of your advertisements: borders and boxes, shadows, screens and shapes.

Four Ways to Improve Your Designs
1. Develop and follow your concepts.
2. Invest in typefaces.
3. Use high-resolution output.
4. Expand your sources of visuals.

VISUALS

Good visuals arouse curiosity, emotion and interest. They persuade by appealing to the senses. Visuals used in advertising include photographs, illustrations, charts and diagrams, clip art and logos. In an all-text advertisement, the headline or copy itself may be the "visual."

€ffective visuals that show your concept halt scanning eyes.

Figure 2-1: Pictures of food can make you hungry.

Figure 2-2: Three-dimensional graphics look real enough to touch.

Figure 2-3: A photograph of a grandfather with his granddaughter evokes pleasant emotions.

Photos of people always draw attention.

Figure 2-4: A drawing of a telephone urges you to call.

The types of visuals you choose for your layouts will depend on your concept and the options open to you. For example, if you're building suspense for an upcoming product announcement, you could use a photograph with the object covered by a cloth or in a shadow. Or you might use a conceptual illustration.

Simple illustrations usually work best. Most advertising visuals highlight only one object or person. It's easier for the reader, or viewer, to identify with one person than with a crowd. This also allows the highlighted item to appear as large as possible in the advertising layout.

Tip: Match the look of the visual to the tone of the text: a serious visual with a serious message, a light-hearted visual with a cheerful message. And place captions under all visuals. According to David Ogilvy (founder of one of the world's largest advertising agencies, Ogilvy & Mather), four times as many people read captions as read body copy. Therefore, your caption should include the brand name and the promise.

Most advertising visuals are created using draw, paint, illustration or photo retouching programs. You can create them yourself from scratch, hire someone to create them from scratch, use existing images, such as clip art and/or photos, or modify existing images to suit your needs. The advantage of creating your own visuals is that you can match your concept to a "t."

Photographs

For many concepts, black-and-white or color photographs provide effective visuals. People associate with photographs because they appear lifelike. This lends credibility to your advertising. Readers are more likely to notice a *photograph* than an *illustration* of a person. For product advertising, consider showing people using the products instead of product-only photographs.

Figure 2-5: Show people using your products

If you're selling durable goods—such as an automobile—and want people to recognize a particular model when they see it on the showroom floor, use a photograph of the product. You can show the benefit of using a product with a before-and-after visual. If you're selling goods or services such as food or travel, you can show the delicious casserole made with your brand of chicken or show people who bought your vacation package lounging on the beach.

Figure 2-6: This photograph could help you promote a scuba-diving vacation package.

Up Close & Personal
You might want to show a close-up of one portion of a photo instead of showing the entire image. For example, you could open the hood of a car and show only the valves instead of the entire car. It depends upon what your copy says. Use clean illustrations rather than montages (a photograph merged with another photograph or illustration), and focus on one product at a time. Ask suppliers of products you carry to provide photographs on disk, preferably in TIFF format.

Pets and kids give readers the "warm and fuzzies."

Figure 2-7: Photos of children are sure eye-stoppers. The only thing better is a photo of a child with a dog.

Figure 2-8: Choose crisp, lifelike photos that include a wide range of tones—blacks, whites and many shades of gray.

1n direct-mail advertising, photographs outpull line art.

Photographs From the Desktop

Desktop tools available for helping you work with photographs include paint and photo retouch programs that let you crop, flop and silhouette. Photo editing programs also let you edit, alter brightness and contrast, adjust the screen density, change the screen angle and create other special effects. Your concept and the type of advertisement you create will guide the way you edit your photographs.

To highlight a specific feature, use your photo editing program to crop out all but the essential part of the image.

*E*dit your photo to
match your concept.

Figure 2-9: Television has trained our eyes to expect large, zoomed-in, in-your-face images.

If your photograph points in the wrong direction when placed in the layout, make a mirror image of it with a technique called flopping.

Figure 2-10: Flopping is a technique used to change the direction of an image in a photograph.

Unless you're creating a formal layout (more on this in the next chapter), you can silhouette the photographs you use in your advertising. Few images in life are exact geometric squares or rectangles. Add zest to your photographs and illustrations by giving them lifelike shapes.

Retouching programs greatly simplify the process of creating silhouettes. To silhouette, remove the background and leave the desired image. You can create a full silhouette or just a partial. Depending on the form of the photograph, a partial silhouette may create a more dynamic form than the full one.

*S*ilhouetting makes your artwork come alive.

Figure 2-11: A full silhouette emphasizes the shape of the subject.

Figure 2-12: A partial silhouette leaps out of the constraining rectangle.

If the silhouette doesn't create the shape you need to make an interesting layout, you can always "mask" the photograph (cover certain portions of it) to create a customized shape such as an "amoeba" or a vignette. These treatments can give your advertising a 1940s or '50s look.

Mask your photo to create an amoeba or a vignette.

Figure 2-13: You can mask portions of a silhouette to create a customized shape for your layout.

Other capabilities of most photo retouching programs include altering brightness and contrast, and changing halftone dots to lines, diamonds or other shapes.

Figure 2-14: Examples of photo editing: brightness and contrast levels are altered and halftone dots have been changed to lines.

Many page layout programs can also set the line screen.

When a photograph is prepared for printing in a publication, the image is broken into small dots (halftone screen). This helps the photograph reproduce better and give the desired effect in printing. Halftone screens for most newspapers give an 85-line screen (in other words, 85 lines of screen per inch); for printing on uncoated paper, 100- to 110-line screen; for printing on glossy paper and most magazines, 130-line. Other high-quality publications may support line screens up to 150 lines per inch.

Photo Editing Programs

Popular photo editing programs include Adobe Photoshop, CorelPHOTO-PAINT, ImageStudio, Digital Darkroom and Kodak PhotoEdge. An exciting new service from Kodak is film developed directly onto CD-ROM. Instead of having to make negatives and prints then scan in photos, you get the image into your computer through a CD-ROM drive. You can view the photographs in thumbnail size, choose the image you want and import it directly into your photo editing program. The other images can be cataloged and indexed on your computer using Kodak Shoebox or Aldus Fetch.

Figure 2-15: The newspaper standard 85-line screen (left) is coarser than the 130-line screen (right) used for magazine photographs.

Six Tips for Good Scanning

To use your computer to modify a photograph or artwork, first store the image electronically. You can either scan it yourself or take it to someone who has a scanner. To obtain the best final results, follow these steps:

*F*irst, run your images and scanner through the "white glove test."

1. If you have several selections of the same illustration, choose the one with the best contrast and crispest focus. Visuals printed in black ink on white paper scan best. If you have your logo printed in several different color combinations, try to find black-and-white.

2. Remove any dust or smudges from the surface of the artwork; some scanners have trouble with glossy photographs. If yours does, spray the surface of the photo with dulling spray (available at art supply stores).

3. Clean the glass of the scanner (if using a flatbed), warm up the scanner, preview the image and check to make sure it's aligned vertically and horizontally.

4. Select the portion of the image you want and the resolution, mode and type of file you want the image saved to. Now scan the photograph.

5. Leave the artwork in the scanner while you check to make sure the scan was successful. Re-scan if necessary.

6. Repair or modify the image with a paint or image retouching program. Silhouette or add a background to the image, if desired.

Illustrations

Illustrations also work well to emphasize product detail and function. They are sometimes created to show ideas, abstract concepts, or services and products that don't yet exist. An architectural drawing is an example of such an illustration.

If your concept is quality, choose an image associated with quality. For years, Cadillac was used in this way.

Sometimes illustrations reproduce better than photographs.

Figure 2-16: Some images immediately communicate a tone: this one says "quality and elegance."

Depending on the quality of the printing press, illustrations are sometimes used because they reproduce better than photographs in newspaper ads. Before creating illustrations, ask your newspaper, magazine or printing sales representative which line screens and percentages work best. Shading of under 10 percent screen may not show up in a magazine. Shading of over 10 percent may be too heavy for newspaper copy. In some cases, hairline (very thin) rules may drop out when the newspaper is printed; a half-point rule (line) is usually the thinnest you can use and still be sure it will show up properly.

Figure 2-17: Match the look of the illustration to your advertising concept: a bicycle rental service would use a relaxed look for pleasure cruisers (left), a sportier image when targeting racers (right).

*D*evelop illustrations around concepts, not concepts around illustrations.

Create Your Own

You can create your own illustrations using paint, draw or illustration programs. Or, you may prefer to hire an artist to create them for you and store them in a format you can import into your layout.

Most drawing and illustration programs—like Adobe Illustrator, Aldus Freehand and CorelDRAW—create graphics in outline format, such as EPS and PICT. In outline format, a line is defined from its two endpoints. Paint, scanning and photo editing programs use bitmap formats, including TIFF, RIFF, GIF and MacPaint. Bitmapped graphics are stored as dots or pixels. A line in bitmapped format is composed of all the dots used to form the line. When you scan an existing artwork image, the result is a bitmapped rendition of that image.

*W*atch out for
jagged edges in
bitmapped graphics.

The disadvantage of a bitmapped graphic is that curved edges get jagged as you enlarge the image. On the other hand, an outline image can be scaled without getting jagged edges because of the way the object is defined in the computer.

To get around this problem, many drawing and illustration programs let you import a bitmapped graphic and use a tracing function to create outline format. Specialized programs such as Adobe Streamline convert bitmapped TIFF images into scalable outline graphics.

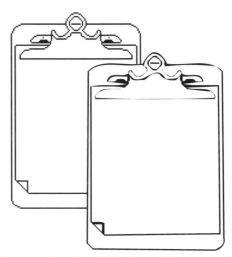

Figure 2-18: Rid your advertising of "the jaggies" by converting bitmapped images to EPS or PICT format.

Many desktop publishing programs also feature simple illustration tools. Shapes like squares, rectangles, circles and ellipses are available in all popular programs. More advanced programs offer freehand drawing tools, starbursts, triangles and polygons.

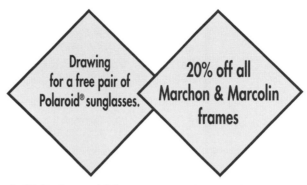

Figure 2-19: Desktop publishing programs alone can be used to create simple illustrations.

Tap Into Clip Art

For advertisers in a hurry or those with time but without expertise in creating original artwork, clip art can be a best friend. CD-ROM technology allows thousands of images to be cataloged and stored on one disk.

Several sources of clip art are listed in the resource information in the back of this book. Some illustration programs include clip art. For example, current versions of CorelDRAW include a library of 18,000 images. When you purchase clip art, make sure a printout of the images comes along with the disk.

The CorelDRAW package includes 18,000 clip art images.

Clip Art on CD-ROM

Extensive collections of clip art are now available on CD-ROM. These, coupled with a cataloging program, can put thousands of professionally created illustrations on your desktop. Software programs such as Aldus Fetch, Kodak Shoebox, Multi-Ad Search and CorelMOSAIC can help you catalog and retrieve your visuals.

Formats for clip art include TIFF, EPS, CGM and PICT. You can easily modify clip art using illustration, paint or draw programs. Other programs, like Aldus's Gallery Effects, let you drastically change the look of colored TIFF images using only one or two commands.

Figure 2-20: You can modify clip art to suit your needs.

Use clip art as is, or customize it with your own personal touch.

The illustration in Figure 2-21 was created in an illustration program for an account executive of an insurance and investment company. It was designed to calm prospective clients' fears about putting their future prosperity in her hands. It works with the company's concept, "We see the future in a different light."

Figure 2-21: This crystal ball graphic was created using a 3D illustration program.

In another scenario, what if after coming up with a concept the company has no means to create an illustration for it? Clip art is the first and most accessible source to turn to.

Figure 2-22: Here are three different crystal balls from CorelDRAW's clip art collection.

Logos & Signatures

A logo is an integral part of your advertising signature. In addition to your logo, the signature includes your company name, address and phone number and any other information that is standard in all of your advertising.

*B*uild recognition with your logo and signature.

If you're just getting started in business, a good-looking signature is your best step forward. For existing businesses, an improved graphic image helps solidify your presence in the market. It sends a message to the world that you're on the move.

Use your advertising signature as part of the image and recognition you build. Develop a standard way to represent it and stick with it. When developing your standard, keep in mind the shape it will form in the layout. Probably the most popular shape for advertising signatures is the oblong rectangle.

Create or scan your logo and store it in your computer. The computer can reduce and enlarge the image to exactly the size you need (you can make it less than one-inch high). This minimizes the size of the file. Make positive and negative versions of your logo to give yourself more flexibility when using it in your layouts. Make sure that the white version is stored as opaque white, not transparent (if the white is transparent, it won't show up against a dark background).

Figure 2-23: Create a positive version (black on white) along with a negative version (white on black).

Trace Your Logo

Make an EPS version of your logo using the automatic tracing feature of a PostScript drawing program or Adobe Streamline. This allows for more flexibility with sizing, and it usually produces a crisper image. Also, the file is smaller, if it was scanned in a resolution above 300 dpi (dots per inch).

Type as Visuals

Let your keyboard do the drawing.

Features found in many desktop publishing programs make it easy to design with type. Sometimes you can illustrate your concept through the shapes of letters and numbers. You can use the inherent forms of type characters to add graphic appeal to a key word. Large numbers and letters, as well as rotated and distorted type, can link words with their pictorial representations.

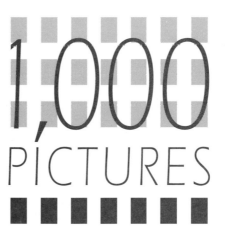

Figure 2-24: With the right typography, a word is truly worth a thousand pictures.

However, a quick caution is in order: Don't let your enthusiasm for designing with typography get you into trouble. The more you manipulate type, the harder the words are to read. Most of the techniques shown in the following figures only work well for small amounts of type.

Drastic distortions of type, such as 3D extruding and creating shapes with words should be reserved for logo design. Too many special effects can make an advertisement look cheap and gimmicky. And remember that these unusual designs require plenty of surrounding white space to make them stand out.

Extruding: You can "extrude" type into a third dimension using programs such as Pixar's Typestry and StrataType 3D from Strata. These programs also let you add textures, patterns and shadows to the text.

Too many special effects make an advertisement look gimmicky.

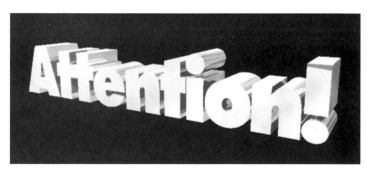

Figure 2-25: Extruded type creates a third dimension.

Letters as graphics: Study key words you're using in your advertisement. See if the form of a letter can be used to create a graphic that communicates your concept.

Figure 2-26: Use the shapes of letters to form graphic representations in your advertisements.

Numbers instantly communicate benefits.

Numbers: If your advertisement includes an itemized list, you can use large numbers as part of the headline and copy. In Figure 2-27, the circular form of the zero effectively draws the eye to the text in the center of the ad. Another example: the headline of an ad titled "Six ways to save on office supplies" could include a large image of the number 6 and an attractively designed numbered list.

Figure 2-27: Numbers are also good graphical elements for concepts that include itemized lists.

𝒜 variety of graphic symbols are "All in the Family" of dingbats.

Dingbats: Dingbats are graphic symbols stored as a typeface and are accessible via the keyboard of your computer. You can use dingbats in place of bullets in lists, as illustrations or as a way of separating sections of text.

Note: When the illustration used exists as a letter, number or dingbat, you can modify it just as you would any normal type by kerning, condensing, expanding and so on.

Figure 2-28: Dingbats provide another means for creating art using typography.

Decorative typefaces: Sometimes decorative typefaces are used in small-space ads when there isn't enough room for an illustration and the headline must do double duty.

Figure 2-29: A typeface called Sonata can be used to create "musical" graphics for your advertisements.

Figure 2-30: An office supply store could use the Stencil typeface to advertise packing materials.

Decorative caps: For editorial-style advertisements or to communicate stability and class, use initial caps. Initial caps and drop caps were discovered by hard-working monks as a way to decorate hand-drawn pages in the Middle Ages. Since you don't have the free time of a Middle Ages monk, use the decorative drop caps offered by clip art manufacturers; or you can create one using your desktop publishing program.

We Need Our Space
Treat decorative typography as visuals, not type. Leave adequate white space around the following elements:

- Extruded type

- Letters used as graphics

- Decorative numbers

- Dingbats

- Decorative type

- Decorative caps

- Type manipulations

In a small ad, use only one drop cap. In a newsletter or brochure, use no more than three per page. Make sure that sequential drop caps don't spell something embarrassing if they're read together as a word.

Figure 2-31: According to advertising guru David Ogilvy, initial caps increase ad readership by an average of 13 percent.

Type Manipulations: To highlight a key word in your advertisement while also separating elements, you can adjust the letter spacing of a word within a bar. Tall sans-serif faces work well for this effect.

Figure 2-32: Use this graphical separation device in ads, brochures, flyers and newsletters.

Another typographic manipulation you can use to illustrate the concept of your advertisement is to set type into a simple shape. Or the copy can be run within an outline, such as a goblet. You can create weird shapes using features that distort, wrap, rotate and curve. But take care not to create clutter or clash by using too many shapes in your ad.

Saw
Tooth saw blades
are guaranteed to remain razor
sharp for the life of your saw. Saw Tooth
saw blades are guaranteed to remain razor sharp
for the life of your saw. Saw Tooth saw
blades are guaranteed to
remain razor sharp for the
life of your saw. Saw Tooth saw
blades are guaranteed to remain razor sharp
for the life of your saw. Saw Tooth saw blades are
guaranteed to remain razor sharp for the
life of your saw. Saw Tooth saw
blades are guaranteed to
remain razor sharp for the life of your
saw. Saw Tooth saw blades are guaranteed to
remain razor sharp for the life of your saw.
Saw Tooth saw blades are
guaranteed to remain
razor sharp

Figure 2-33: Consider fitting type to create a certain shape.

TYPOGRAPHY

A large selection of typefaces is the desktop designer's horsepower.

You're working on your advertisement. You type in your copy and go up to the menu (the Fonts menu in many programs) to choose your typeface. What do you select?

The most powerful feeling you can have as a desktop designer is to have a large selection of typefaces. If you have only a handful, invest in more.

On a Deserted Island
With Only 10 Typefaces

I asked Lee Wilson, expert typographer and coauthor of this book, which typefaces he would choose if he could have only 10. Here are his choices:

1. Goudy
2. Garamond
3. Futura
4. Bauer Bodoni
5. Minion
6. Fritz Quadrata
7. Helvetica
8. Galliard
9. Eras
10. Stone Sans

Typography lends personality to the headline, body copy, prices, call to action, names, titles, locations and other identifying text in your advertisements. The shapes and sizes of the letters instantly communicate an image. Some typefaces are formal, others are friendly.

Personality of Type

Typefaces can be broadly classified into *serif* and *sans-serif* (*sans* is the French word for *without*). Serifs are the finishing (usually horizontal) strokes at the ends of letters. In general, sans-serif typefaces are considered more informal and are good for headlines and small amounts of body copy. Serif faces are more formal and are generally considered to be easier to read in longer blocks of copy.

Sans-serif typefaces are also simpler; they're often used in ads for health and beauty products because of their clean look (none of those dusty serifs!).

But these distinctions only begin to describe the character and uses of the face. One of the most important features of a typeface's design is its *x-height*, which is the height of a letter like *a*, *o* and, yes, *x*, as compared to an *h*, *l*, or *f*. The part of the letter that extends below the line is called the descender (*g*, *j*, *p* and *q*). The part that extends above the "body," or x-height, is the ascender. Modern (informal) typefaces have taller x-heights than classic (formal) typefaces.

The x-height of a typeface determines whether it's modern or classic.

> **Modern or Classic?**
> These are popular classic typefaces:
>
> - Times
> - Goudy
> - Bodoni
> - Galliard
>
> These are popular modern typefaces:
>
> - Stone Sans
> - Helvetica
> - Fritz Quadrata

Some typefaces are designed to be used in large sizes, as in posters, headlines and banners. These are called *display faces*. Others are designed as *text typefaces*. These faces work well for body copy.

Figure 2-34: In the early days of desktop typography, Helvetica (top) was the standard desktop sans-serif face. Times Roman (bottom) was the standard desktop serif.

Bodoni and Optima, shown in Figure 2-35, are classic typefaces. In both of these faces, the x-height is short compared to the more modern Stone Serif and Helvetica.

Create your own typefaces with a font utility program.

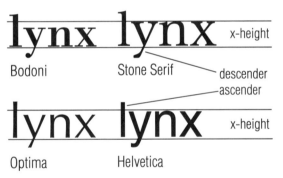

Figure 2-35: Bodoni, upper left, and Optima, lower left, are classic typefaces that have shorter x-heights than the modern Stone Serif and Helvetica faces.

Note: You can also create your own typefaces or modify existing ones using programs like Fontographer.

Setting Type With Your Computer

You buy typefaces with basic characteristics—serifs or lack of, x-height and so on—already in place. But the ways you use your desktop typesetting functions can drastically affect how the type appears in your advertisement. These functions, provided by desktop publishing, word processing and graphics programs, give you choices as to point size, leading, type style, condensing or expanding, tracking and kerning.

Type Sizes

Type is measured in points. In one inch there are 72 points. Therefore, a 72-point headline is one-inch tall. No hard-and-fast rules exist for type sizes in advertising. In general, most body copy type is between 9 and 14 points, and headline type ranges from around 14 points and beyond, depending upon the advertisement's size.

For most advertisements, keep the type size as large as possible to attract readers. Sixty-five percent of people over the age of 35 either wear or need to wear glasses.

Figure 2-36: Type sized at 72 points is one-inch tall.

Type Styles & Type Families

Common appearance variations found on the desktop include bold, italic and underline. Because underlining cuts through descenders, it is not recommended.

Boldface makes the strokes of the type characters heavier, and the result is blacker-looking type. Most headlines and emphasized sections of body copy are set in bold. Italicizing slants the type 12 degrees to the right. Italics give type a formal and graceful look. They're also used for emphasis.

*€*ven Helvetica is
available in light, black
and ultra weights.

As you add to your type library, consider purchasing typefaces in "families." This gives you many options for creating "color" and variety in your ads using type, so that you don't need to mix lots of different typeface designs and run the risk of creating a junky ad.

Type weights are distinguished by such names as book, light, medium, black and ultra. Even our tried-and-true Helvetica is available in many different weights.

Italic or Oblique
What is called *italic* on most publishing software is actually *oblique.* According to designer Jan White, true italics must come from a completely separate version of the typeface that has been designed with different, more graceful, letterforms.

Figure 2-37: The same typeface can look very different when used in different weights.

Leading

The leading is the amount of space between lines of type. Most desktop publishing programs have a default leading that is usually 2 points greater than the type size. For example, the default leading for 12-point type is 14 points. This means that the lines of type are separated from each other by 2 points (14 less 12) of white space.

The look of a type block can be changed drastically by adjusting leading. If you increase leading, the added white space between lines causes the text to appear lighter. Reducing the leading causes a block of text to appear blacker. The addition of leading can also make some typefaces easier to read.

> *Reduced leading causes text to appear darker. Reduced leading causes text to appear darker. Reduced leading causes text to appear darker.*
>
> *Increased leading causes text to appear lighter. Increased leading causes text to appear lighter. Increased leading causes text to appear lighter. Increased leading causes text to appear lighter.*

Figure 2-38: It is often recommended that sans-serif and italic type should have more leading to enhance readability.

Type Manipulation

In all advertising, space is at a premium. Type manipulation in desktop publishing and other graphics programs allows you to condense or expand existing typefaces. Some programs call this horizontal scaling.

*W*hen space is at a premium, condense your typefaces.

Condensing allows you to pack more information into a small space. It creates a modern look without sacrificing legibility. How much condensing is too much? Let common sense and the squint test be your judge. Hold the page at arm's length and squint. If you have trouble reading the text, you may have condensed it too much. The amount you can condense depends on how pudgy the typeface is.

Though most modern advertisements take advantage of condensed type, there are times when you may want to do the opposite and expand a typeface. This is usually done when you want a headline to take up more horizontal space.

*T**ip:*** Condensing type: For most typefaces, you should condense body copy no more than 70%. And if you do condense the maximum 70%, be sure to add extra leading to ensure readability. Headlines can be condensed up to 50%, depending on the typeface.

Headlines With Impact
Times Roman, 26 point, no scaling

Headlines With Impact
Times Roman, 52 point, horizontal scaling at 50%

Even a typeface like Times Roman—one that everyone associates with the "desktop published" look—gets a quick face lift when condensed.

Some programs call this horizontal scaling. By selecting a number less than 100, your typeface is condensed and given a new, taller look.

Times Roman, no scaling

Even a typeface like Times Roman—one that everyone associates with the "desktop published" look—gets a quick face lift when condensed.

Some programs call this horizontal scaling. By selecting a number less than 100, your typeface is condensed and given a new, taller look.

Times, Roman, horizontal scaling at 70%

Figure 2-39: You can change the look of your typefaces by condensing, or scaling, them.

*W*atch out for space-hogging pudgy typefaces.

You probably own a few typefaces you'll never use—ones that are too bulky to work with effectively. In body copy, they take too much room to say the same thing another typeface design can say in less space. In headlines, they take too much horizontal space (the width of an ad, for example) without being bold enough to attract attention. If you want to use a pudgy typeface, consider condensing.

TIFFANY sets a
feminine mood but
is a space hog.

AVANT GARDE
needs a good diet.
Replace with
Futura.

Figure 2-40: Tiffany and Avant Garde are examples of pudgy typefaces.

fine-tune your
ad typography
with kerning.

Letter & Word Spacing

Kerning means adjusting the space between the letters of a word. Automatic kerning is designed into the type characters in some typefaces. Some layout programs also have default settings for kerning letter pairs such as "To" and "We."

Sometimes, though, you may want to override the default kerning. For headlines in larger type you will most likely want to take away even more space between letters. On the other hand, body copy in smaller type may require more space. *Tracking* automatically adjusts the kerning of several lines of type.

Word spacing can also be adjusted in many page layout programs. It is commonly reduced to fit more body copy on a line or in a given space; it is often increased to improve readability or to stretch out a headline to make it more noticeable.

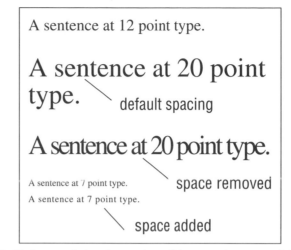

Figure 2-41: Automatic kerning works well for type sizes around 12 points. Larger sizes need less kerning, smaller sizes may need more.

Tip: Most desktop publishing programs have quick keyboard commands to adjust kerning pairs. On the Macintosh, to add space, place the cursor between the letters and press Command-Shift-] in Quark or Command-Shift-Delete in PageMaker. To take away space, press Command-Shift-[in Quark or Command-Delete in PageMaker. Using Windows, to add space, place the cursor between the letters and press Ctrl-Shift-] in Quark or Ctrl-Shift-Backspace in PageMaker. To take away space, press Ctrl-Shift-[in Quark or Ctrl-Backspace in PageMaker.

 Add volumes of typefaces to your library.

Building a Type Library

For the price of what it used to cost to buy one typeface, you can now buy a complete set. Advances in electronic typeface technology have given rise to a number of different formats. These include bitmapped, TrueType, PostScript, Type 1 and the lesser-known Type 2. If you have a laser printer that doesn't support PostScript, use Adobe Type Manager to convert your typefaces. This program is bundled with Windows. Other font management programs also allow for conversions.

Adobe, Microsoft and Apple are three majors in the typeface business. They all sell typefaces in sets or volumes. Adobe offers a catalog on CD-ROM that lets you view individual faces and buy only the ones you want.

> **Tip:** If you want a document output on a Linotronic imagesetter, most service bureaus require that you provide a list of the typefaces you've used in the document. Some layout programs will create these lists for you.

*A*d headlines attract attention and arouse curiosity.

Headlines

The headline is often the first element noticed in your advertisement. An effective headline arouses curiosity, offers benefits and reflects the tone of the advertisement.

The headline attracts attention through its appearance (the typeface used, its size, the type style and the spacing around and within it) in addition to the way it's worded. Some headlines are set in all-capitals and stretch the full width of the advertisement. Others are set smaller with white space surrounding them. The kerning and tracking of most headlines usually need to be manually adjusted to give a professional, powerful look.

Typefaces for Headlines

The typeface you choose depends upon the mood you're trying to create. Many headlines are set in sans-serif type for a clean, easy-to-read headline. Editorial-style headlines are often set in serif type.

*S*et formal head-
lines with short–
x-height type and
informal headlines
with tall-x-height
type.

The x-height of the typeface you choose will also affect the image of the headline. Remember that tall-x-height type, in both serif and sans-serif faces, makes the headline look informal; short-x-height type looks more formal.

The more distractions you have in your advertisement, the stronger the typeface must be to muscle its way through the crowd. Choose tall, bold typefaces that will take up less width, allowing you to leave some white space to each side. White space attracts attention.

Goudy—elegance in serifs

Futura—good, heavy headlines

Figure 2-42: Compare the serif to the sans-serif headline; each has a different feel.

luscious headlines

luscious headlines

Figure 2-43: Note that a lowercase sans-serif *l* looks like a capital *I*.

Helvetica Condensed Black

Figure 2-44: Muscle your way through the competition with a tall, bold typeface for your headline.

Type Size

Though sometimes advertising headlines are small and surrounded by white space, most designers try to make the headline as large as possible without interfering with the layout.

Most headlines are no more than seven to ten words. With a short headline you can create typography that will take the reader by surprise. On the other hand, some concepts cry out for long, creative headlines. Advertising effectiveness studies show that including your company name or product name in the headline helps get results; however, this means you'll need a longer headline. Balance attention-getting typography with effective communication of your message.

Make your headlines as large as possible without interfering with the layout.

Figure 2-45: A one-word headline calls for different typography than a seven-word headline.

Capitalization

When deciding whether to use uppercase, lowercase or a combination of both, remember that people skim headlines by looking at the upper halves of the letters. It's difficult to distinguish letters set in all-capitals. It is somewhat easier when they're set in initial capitals (uppercase/lowercase).

The easiest of all to skim is the "downstyle" headline: in downstyle, only the first letter of the first word in the headline is capitalized.

That aside, the more important thing is to use the style that works in a particular ad design. For example, a revolutionary new product introduction could justify a full-page, all-caps headline. A one- or two-word headline would be easy to read in all-caps. An editorial-style headline works well in mixed upper- and lowercase. Informal layouts work well with downstyle headlines.

Capitalization affects the shape of the headline.

You can also select a headline style based on the shape it will make in the layout. Headlines with all-capitals create striking blocks of dark type. Uppercase/lowercase headlines make irregular forms; downstyle headlines make shapes that are even more irregular. Based on shape, all-caps headlines are formal, uppercase/lowercase headlines are less formal, and downstyle headlines are informal.

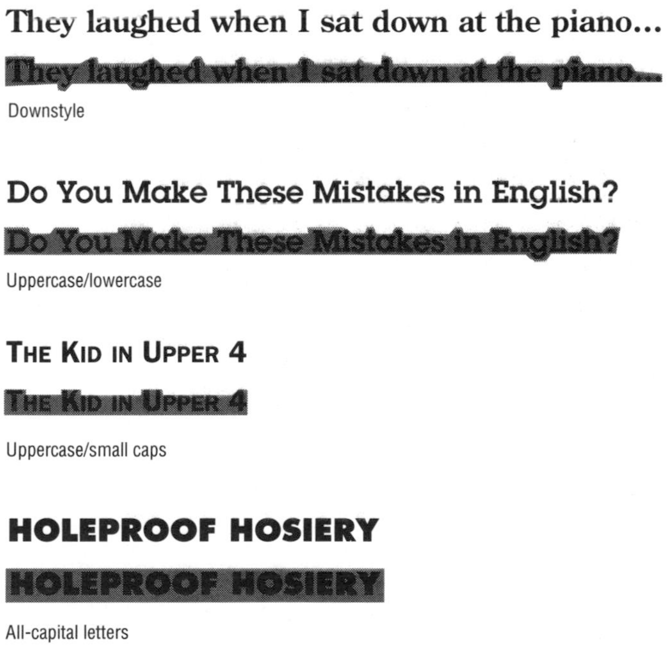
They laughed when I sat down at the piano...
They laughed when I sat down at the piano...
Downstyle
Do You Make These Mistakes in English?
Do You Make These Mistakes in English?
Uppercase/lowercase
THE KID IN UPPER 4
THE KID IN UPPER 4
Uppercase/small caps
HOLEPROOF HOSIERY
HOLEPROOF HOSIERY
All-capital letters

Figure 2-46: These are headlines from famous ads of yesteryear. Note how capitalization and punctuation affect the headline's shape.

Punctuation creates inflections, forces a pause, inserts another voice or leads readers into the body copy. Here are some tips on using punctuation marks in your headlines:

Periods: Currently, it's very popular to add a period at the end of a headline—even when the headline isn't a complete sentence. When the headline is set in downstyle, this gives the advertisement a personal, "chatty" feel. The only potential problem is that a period signals a stop. You may not want to create an interruption that causes readers to pause between your headline and your body copy.

Dashes: Use an em dash (—) in the place of a colon or items in parentheses. An em dash creates a quick pause and signals a slight change in the subject or an afterthought. Spatially, it links two parts of your headline together.

Ellipses: If you want the sound of a voice trailing off, use an ellipsis (...). The three dots (ellipsis points) can lead the reader right into the body copy by creating an arrow at the end of the headline. However, the softening effect saps some of the headline's strength.

Exclamation points: Use exclamation points with care. When you add an exclamation mark at the end of the headline, readers will immediately wonder whether or not the statement is true.

Question marks: The question mark is a good device for getting attention because it creates a good inflection of voice. Use a question mark to pose a question (and supply an answer) about something that's on the prospect's mind. Graphically it holds your headline down with a hook.

Quotation marks: Quotation marks can be used along with italics to dramatize your concept—to emphasize and separate out a different voice. If your layout program doesn't convert quotes automatically, use the keyboard commands to get the "curly" type of quotes (" ") instead of "typewriter-style" quotes (" ").

"When you put your headline in quotes, you increase recall by 28 percent."
—David Ogilvy

The gift that keeps on giving.

The gift—it keeps on giving

The gift that keeps on giving…

The gift that keeps on giving!

The gift that keeps on giving?

"The gift that keeps on giving"

Figure 2-47: Punctuation gives life to your headlines.

*A*void automatic leading when setting headlines.

Line, Letter & Word Spacing

You may need to override the automatic leading setting in your software program when you create your headlines. The default setting often adds too much space between lines of a headline. Most headlines can be set "solid" (leading equals type size). For example, an 18-point headline would be set with 18-point leading. The amount of leading your headline requires depends upon the look you're trying to achieve and whether you're working around the descenders and ascenders of lowercase letters.

Gap Therapy

If your software allows, also adjust the letter spacing of your headlines to achieve a professional look. Take a critical look at your headlines: search first for excess space between letters; some character pairs need additional space while others need less. For example, in a headline set in a sans-serif face, you may need to add space between an i and an l (as in *headline*), and remove space between a W and an o.

In addition to adjusting the space between letters, you may need to adjust the space between words. The word spacing in most headlines should be tightened.

Condensing & Expanding

If you want to make your headline as large as possible without taking up too much room, condensing the type can make it look fresh and different. If you have a short headline and want to fill more horizontal space without increasing the vertical line space, you may want to expand the type.

Often a bridesmaid but never a bride

24-point Times Roman bold with auto
(26-point) leading.

Often a bridesmaid but never a bride

Change this to 23-point leading.

Often a bridesmaid but never a bride

Add −10 kerning.

Often a bridesmaid but never a bride

Throw in 90% horizontal scaling.

Figure 2-48: Note how kerning, scaling and adjusting the leading changes the look of the headline.

Attention-Grabbers

Attention-grabbers—phone numbers, prices and dates—are elements of your advertising that are vital to its success. You want readers to easily find and act upon this information.

In general, you apply the same rules to attention-grabbers that you apply to headlines. But because attention-grabbers often contain numbers, they require some special desktop techniques to make them look good.

$$800\text{-}555\text{-}1212$$

$$(800)\ 555\text{-}1212$$

$$800.555.1212$$

Figure 2-49: Here are three ways commonly used to represent phone numbers.

$$\$29.99$$

$$\$29.^{99}$$

$$\$29.^{\underline{99}}$$

*A*ttention–grabbers require special desktop techniques.

Figure 2-50: Creating prices in dollars and cents can be a challenge for desktop advertisers.

Some desktop publishing programs create fractions and prices automatically. When you have to do them manually, use superscript, or superior, for the numerator, decrease the type size of the denominator to match, and replace the standard slash mark with the keyboard command (on a Macintosh, it's Shift-Option-1). Adjust the kerning to remove space between the numerator and the slash mark. You can bypass creating fractions by using percentages instead.

1/2

½

50%

Figure 2-51: If your desktop program doesn't make fractions, you can create your own.

Body Copy

At first glance, especially if you squint at it, your body copy looks like a block of gray. It's amazing how vital these gray blocks are in evoking a response.

Your choice of typeface and the way you set it can make a difference in how your readers approach your copy—or even *whether* they bother to read it. The factors affecting its shape are the justification style (alignment to the margins), the amount of indentation, the paragraph breaks and the tabs set for lists.

Typefaces for Body Copy

Simple typeface designs that aid in easy reading are best for most body copy. This rule can be bent a bit for shorter copy.

For long copy—newsletters, brochures and editorial-style or informative ads—use typefaces commonly used in newspapers and magazines. These typefaces deliver soft-spoken, simply-stated text.

Advertisements with shorter blocks of copy—usually those with large visuals—can use more modern typefaces. In small quantities, a more modern type style won't impair reading as it would in larger blocks.

*U*se classical typefaces for long copy, modern ones for shorter copy.

TIMES ROMAN looks newsworthy and serious. You can fit lots of type in a small amount of space with Times Roman.

Body copy work is intellectual and respectful. Employ soft-spoken, simply-stated typefaces. Like good message carriers, the typeface shouldn't be noticed. It should blend into the background while clearly stating your advertising message.

GALLIARD is tall and elegant. The angles of the serifs on this typeface can make it harder to read than some of the others.

Body copy work is intellectual and respectful. Employ soft-spoken, simply-stated typefaces. Like good message carriers, the typeface shouldn't be noticed. It should blend into the background while clearly stating your advertising message.

GOUDY is classy and elegant yet approach-able. Its x-height is one of the shortest of this group giving it a formal, classical look.

Body copy work is intellectual and respectful. Employ soft-spoken, simply-stated typefaces. Like good message carriers, the typeface shouldn't be noticed. It should blend into the background while clearly stating your advertising message.

GARAMOND is the least formal with its tall x-height. Avoid using it in italics because the *b* and *h* look alike.

Body copy work is intellectual and respectful. Employ soft-spoken, simply-stated typefaces. Like good message carriers, the typeface shouldn't be noticed. It should blend into the background while clearly stating your advertising message.

Figure 2-52: Most typefaces used for large blocks of copy are classic faces with low x-heights.

OPTIMA works well when printing on low-quality paper like newsprint.	HELVETICA is easy to read in almost all point sizes. Good for captions, too.
Typefaces used in shorter blocks of text can exert more of their personality.	Typefaces used in shorter blocks of text can exert more of their personality.
STONE SERIF was designed to work with Stone Sans to create a uniform look.	STONE SANS was designed to work with Stone Serif to create a uniform look.
Typefaces used in shorter blocks of text can exert more of their personality.	Typefaces used in shorter blocks of text can exert more of their personality.

Figure 2-53: For short blocks of copy, you can use classic typefaces with low x-heights or modern typefaces with high x-heights.

Appearance Styles

The type style of most body copy is Roman, or "plain," in desktop terminology. Sometimes italic type is used to give the copy a formal feel. If italic type is used, increase the type size or add leading to ensure legibility. If the type will appear on colored paper, over a screen or in reverse (more on this in a minute), set the type in bold.

Justification

fully justified copy is formal. Ragged-right is informal.

Most advertising copy is fully justified (flush-left and right) or flush-left/ragged-right. The advantage of fully justified copy is that the text block forms a rectangle. Text set ragged-right creates an irregular shape. This is why fully justified type is considered formal and ragged-right informal.

Centered type often creates the form of a circle or ellipse and gives a formal look. Avoid centering more than six or seven lines of type. In long blocks of copy, it's hard for readers to find the beginning of the next line.

Formality at a Price
If you want the formality that justified type provides, be aware that this alignment scheme often causes distortions in word spacing and bizarre hyphenation. Remember that you always want white space around, not within, design elements.

Text alignment determines the shape of a text block.

Yes, Phoebe, I can now see why the praises of this road you cry. My gloves are white as when last night we took the road of Anthracite.

Yes, Phoebe, I can now see why the praises of this road you cry. My gloves are white as when last night we took the road of Anthracite.

Figure 2-54: When the type is set in justified margins, it creates a formal look but often includes awkward gaps.

This is the maid of fair renown
Who scrubs the floors of Spotless Town.
To find a speck when she is through
Would take a pair of specs or two
And her employment isn't slow.
For she employs Sapolio.

Figure 2-55: This is the text of an old soap ad. Centered type is often used for invitations and announcements.

**Acme's line of glue
sticks adhere even
to slick surfaces.**

Figure 2-56: Justified–right alignment is used when you want to "stick" a
short block of type to another element, such as a photograph.

Paragraph Spacing

To conserve space while signaling the beginning of a new
paragraph, either indent the first line or leave some extra
leading between paragraphs. It's not necessary to do both.
According to ad man David Ogilvy, using leading between
paragraphs increases readership by 12 percent on average.
(Also, it's not necessary to use an indent in the first paragraph of a section of body copy.)

*Extra space be-
tween paragraphs
makes body copy
less intimidating.*

Lorem ipsum dolor sit amet, consectetuer adipiscing elit, sed diam nonummy nibh euismod tincidunt ut laoreet dolore magna aliquam erat volutpat.

Ut wisi enim ad minim veniam, quis nostrud exerci tation ullam corper suscipit lobortis nisl ut aliuqip ex ea commodo consequat. Dius te feugifacilisi.

Lorem ipsum dolor sit amet, consectetuer adipiscing elit, sed diam nonummy nibh euismod tincidunt ut laoreet dolore magna aliquam erat volutpat.

Ut wisi enim ad minim veniam, quis nostrud exerci tation ullam corper suscipit lobortis nisl ut aliuqip ex ea commodo consequat. Dius te feugifacilisi.

Figure 2-57: Paragraph indents affect the shape of your body copy. You
can keep your perfect rectangles by avoiding indentation.

Start off your copy with a one-sentence (or even one-word) paragraph. This little bite is graphically pleasing and could contain your best benefit.

Lorem ipsum dolor sit amet, consectetuer adipiscing elit, sed diam nonummy nibh euismod tincidunt. And the Caesar salad is always tasty. Ut wisi enim ad minim veniam, quis nostrud exerci tation ullam corper suscipit lobortis nisl ut aliuqip ex ea commodo consequat. Dius te feugifacilisi.

And the Caesar salad is always tasty.

Lorem ipsum dolor sit amet, consectetuer adipiscing elit, sed diam nonummy nibh euismod tincidunt.

Ut wisi enim ad minim veniam, quis nostrud exerci tation ullam corper suscipit lobortis nisl ut aliuqip ex ea commodo consequat. Dius te feugifacilisi.

Figure 2-58: Capture page–skimmers' eyes with varied paragraph lengths.

Lists

Use lists to condense sentences into one or two words. These lists can be numbered or tagged with bullets or dingbats.

*A*lign items in lists with tabs.

If you include a list in your ad, use tabs to align the listed items. Hold the list together as a unit by minimizing the space between the bullet, or dingbat, and the text.

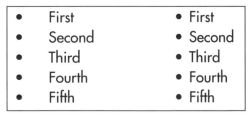

- • First
- • Second
- • Third
- • Fourth
- • Fifth

- First
- Second
- Third
- Fourth
- Fifth

Figure 2-59: To pack the most information into the smallest amount of body copy, use a list.

Leading & Tracking

The leading and tracking in your body copy affect the color of the piece as well as the readability of the typeface. Many designers claim that any typeface can be made easier to read with the addition of leading. Sans-serif and modern serif typefaces (those with high x-heights) look best when surrounded by white space.

Lorem ipsum dolor sit amet, consectetuer adipiscing elit, sed diam nonummy nibh euismod tincidunt ut laoreet dolore magna aliquam erat volutpat.

Futura 10/16; normal kerning

Lorem ipsum dolor sit amet, consectetuer adipiscing elit, sed diam nonummy nibh euismod tincidunt ut laoreet dolore magna aliquam erat volutpat.

Futura 10/16; space removed

Lorem ipsum dolor sit amet, consectetuer adipiscing elit, sed diam nonummy nibh euismod tincidunt ut laoreet dolore magna aliquam erat volutpat.

Futura 10/12; normal kerning

Lorem ipsum dolor sit amet, consectetuer adipiscing elit, sed diam nonummy nibh euismod tincidunt ut laoreet dolore magna aliquam erat volutpat.

Futura 10/12; space added

Figure 2-60: Change the "color" of the type by adjusting leading, kerning and word spacing.

Reverses & Screens

When reversing body copy (white type on a black background) or placing it over colored paper or a screen, use a strong, heavy typeface. Typefaces normally used for body copy are too light to show up well against most screens and reverses. A strong typeface is also needed when placing text on a dark-colored box or a dark screen.

The tall x-heights of most modern typefaces work well for reverses. The light serifs on a classic face like Bodoni are gulped up by any bleeding of the ink and are discouraged.

White on Background

Desktop designer Jan V. White recommends the following rules of thumb when placing white type over a solid black background or black type over a dark screen:

1. Choose a typeface with an even stroke or thickness.

2. Select a sans-serif or a serif with heavy serifs.

3. Find a face bolder than the body copy.

4. Use type one size larger than normal.

5. Shorten the length of your line.

6. Add line spacing.

7. Use reverses in moderation.

Readers quickly grow weary of reading reversed type.

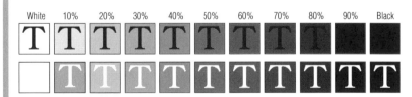

Figure 2-61: The screens on the far left (the lower percentages) work best as background for black type and those on the far right (the higher percentages) look better for white type.

Bookman takes up too much room when used for regular body copy but its bulk is good for screens.

Souvenir Gothic has a look some consider dated for use in body copy. But its breadth is good for reverses and screens.

Figure 2-62: Bookman and Souvenir Gothic are two modern typefaces that work well in reverses and screens.

Mouse Type

Disclaimers in advertisements, such as "...laws vary from state to state" or "Good only at participating restaurants," usually appear at the bottom of the ad in small, discrete "mouse" type. Certain businesses must by law include these disclaimers in their advertising, but the only requirement is that they be large enough to be "legible."

From a copy standpoint, this isn't the kind of stuff that makes customers rush through our doors. Your goal is to make this information *readable* but as unobtrusive as possible in the design of your ad.

Tip: Set mouse type in small point sizes (5 to 8 points) with reduced leading. Choose typefaces with light strokes that create a lighter shade of gray on the page. They can be shrunk down to small point sizes and still be read by the interested lawyers of the world.

This is 8-point Helvetica
Squeak, squeak, squeak

This is 8-point Stone Sans
Squeak, squeak, squeak

This is 8-point Futura
Squeak, squeak, squeak

Figure 2-63: Helvetica and other modern sans–serif faces are legible even in small point sizes.

Helvetica and other modern sans-serif faces are legible in even small point sizes. XYZ™ Brand is a trademark of XYZ Corp.© 1993 XYZ.

Usually mouse type matches the typeface used for body copy and is set either normally or in italic. XYZ™ brand is a trademark of XYZ Corp. © 1993 XYZ.

Usually mouse type matches the typeface used for body copy and is set either normally or in italic. XYZ™ brand is a trademark of XYZ Corp. © 1993 XYZ.

Figure 2-64: The typeface used in most mouse type either matches the face used in the advertisement or is a modern sans–serif.

Most electronic typefaces let you set copyright © and trademark™ symbols via your keyboard.

ORGANIZATIONAL TOOLS

Desktop publishing programs are rich in organizational tools. Borders, backgrounds and text-wraps help you "glue" headlines, illustrations and body copy together. Lines, boxes and screens help to separate and keep things tidy. Other tools bring attention to the layout. Some advertising layout packages let you create starbursts, graduated fills and automated drop shadows, and rotate, or tilt, graphics and text.

Borders

Borders help to group layout elements together. In small-space advertising, borders keep your ad from running into others on the page. Most borders are lines connected together to form a rectangular box. You can modify the shape of the box by rounding its corners, which makes it look less formal than a traditional square-cornered box.

The appearance of the border is controlled by changing the width and style of the line. Your borders can be plain lines or fancy shapes. Within your software options, you can choose from several line weights and multiline borders. Some programs even offer different box shapes.

*C*reate borders by combining various line weights and shapes.

Be Subtle With Borders
Don't overuse borders. Borders are meant to psychologically frame the ad. They should not call attention to themselves; if they do, they will detract from the message in your ad. Again, let the concept be your guide.

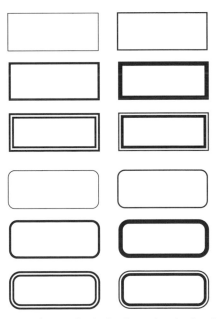

Figure 2-65: You can change the look of your border by changing the line style and line weight.

Figure 2-66: Border styles can be combined to form different shapes.

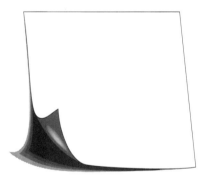

Figure 2-67: As an alternative to creating your own, many clip art makers offer border designs.

White Space

Misuse of white space is a common design problem.

White space also functions as a border; it's the gravitational force that holds advertising elements together. If too much white space appears between elements, the unit disintegrates, falls apart. White space also helps separate out a small-space ad from its competitors on the same page.

White space has an important place in advertising space. You may feel that since you've paid for the space, you should fill every bit of it with your promotional copy. But improper use of white space is the most common desktop publishing design mistake.

Figure 2-68: Left: Poor management of white space. The type floats randomly in the box. Right: This ad is much better. There's enough white space to invite readers in, but the elements still hang together as a unit.

Text Wrap

The ability of many desktop publishing programs to wrap type around graphics gives you a tool that helps unify your text and visual. Coming soon, in Chapter 3, we'll focus on unity as an important part of an effective layout.

Figure 2-69: Whenever possible, try to wrap to the right side of the text. Readability suffers when text is set with ragged left margins.

Lines & Boxes

While you want your design elements to come together, often you need subtle ways to keep them apart. Lines help separate items from each other. Your software allows you to create lines (rules) that vary in width from a hairline to several points thick.

Boxes also help separate elements. Boxes can hold such items as a satisfaction guarantee, notice of same-day shipping or a customer testimonial.

Lines and boxes help separate items.

Figure 2-70: These are line styles and weights commonly offered in desktop publishing programs.

Figure 2-71: Lines can be used to separate text in ads.

Figure 2-72: You can give your box a three-dimensional effect by combining two boxes.

Reverses, Screens & Drop Shadows

Reverses and screens set blocks of body copy apart from other elements in your ad. To add color behind your text, draw a box using your desktop publishing program and select the desired fill—from a 10 percent screen to a solid black.

The level of screening you choose will depend on the paper your advertisement will be printed on and what is appearing in the screen or reverse. For body copy appearing over a screen in newsprint, the maximum screen is 10 percent. The maximum for uncoated paper is 15 percent and for coated, 20.

If you add a fill and make the type white (or reversed), keep the screen 80 percent or above. You want the highest possible contrast between the type and the box.

*O*rganize and highlight text with screens and reverses.

White Sale

Stop by this Sunday & enjoy savings on the entire stock of—

Columns ♦ Leading ♦ Kerning
Tracking ♦ Scaling ♦ Space
Negative Space ♦ Letter Space
and more...

Sunday only. Shop early for best selection.

The Space Place
12th & Chestnut ♦ River Valley

Figure 2-73: Give color to an all-text ad with screens and reverses.

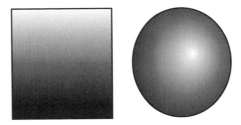

Figure 2-74: Some desktop publishing programs allow you to create boxes and circles with graduated screens.

Dynamic Devices

For some types of advertisements—such as newspaper—you only have a quick second to grab the reader. This is why auto dealerships, grocery stores and retailers use starbursts. These dynamic shapes attract attention to your ad. Unfortunately, overuse of such a device can wreak havoc in the organization of your layout.

Tilting graphics or type is another way to draw attention to your advertisement. You can tilt the text within a graphic, the graphic only or the entire unit (the graphic and the text).

Attract attention with starbursts and tilts.

Figure 2-75: A starburst adds drama to your layout.

Figure 2-76: Tilting is an effective way to attract attention.

These organizational tools help you meet your layout challenges and your three advertising goals—visibility, clarity and response. We'll discuss these goals in detail in the next chapter.

SUMMARY CHECKLIST

- Silhouette and add shapes to line art and photographs.

- Scan and store your logo in the computer.

- Select typefaces appropriate for the job at hand.

- Use formal serif faces for big blocks of copy, modern serif or sans-serif faces for smaller blocks.

- Be careful when choosing type for reverses.

- Make headlines tall, dark and handsome.

- Avoid pudgy typefaces.

- Try condensing your typefaces.

- Invest in typeface families.

- Select headline style based on shape and color.

- Keep headlines short and to the point.

- Use the effects of punctuation to your advantage.

- Set kerning and leading manually in all headlines.

- Choose justification and paragraph indent settings based on desired shape.

- Keep paragraphs short.

- Consider including a one-sentence paragraph.

- Organize with boxes, borders, lines and white space.

Figure 2-77: Use the tools you have on your desktop to create effective, professional-looking ads.

MOVING ON

Advertising layout involves attracting the attention of buyers, providing them with information, then inspiring them to take action. Your desktop tools come together in

CHAPTER 3

DESKTOP LAYOUTS THAT SELL

The more facts you tell, the more you sell
—Charles Edwards, Ph.D.
researcher, retail advertising

Newspaper readers decide in 2/3 of a second whether to read your ad. Shoppers glance at a grocery-shelf item for 1/25 of a second. Most people sort through the day's stack of mail while standing or sitting near a trash can.

You have a split second to shout your concept and benefits, to tell readers what you're selling and why they should buy it. Taking full advantage of that split second of time is the challenge of every advertising designer. In a quick glance, your prospects see only your headline and illustrations. The layout must attract them, entice them to focus on the piece, and inspire them to take action.

This chapter focuses on layout techniques that attract buyers. It shows you how to reflect the purpose and content of your advertisement through the placement of elements on the page. As the designer, you have to decide what you want your readers to look at first and where you want them to go from there.

Some general tips apply to all layouts. This chapter concentrates on these. Tips for specific types of advertisements—display ads, brochures, signs and other formats—will be presented later in Chapters 5 through 9.

Good layout takes planning. The desktop system makes it almost too easy to jump right into the mechanics of layout without pausing to think of your strategy. Start the layout

Today's advertising demands simplicity and a straightforward approach.

process by pushing specific details out of your mind. Make a series of quick sketches first. Concentrate on the shapes you'll be working with in your design. Throughout the layout process, strive for visibility, clarity and response.

Here is the "VCR" of desktop layout:

- **Visibility**—Make your advertising stand out from the crowd using color, shape, key words and visuals.

- **Clarity**—Organize your message by giving it unity and movement using desktop tools.

- **Response**—Use type and graphics to highlight where and how to buy.

GETTING STARTED

Gone are the days of Xacto knives and waxers. Electronic paste-up is as close as your computer keyboard. Before we go further into the layout process, I thought it might be helpful to mention some of the available desktop publishing packages in relation to their page-layout capabilities. Desktop publishing programs vary from simple to complex; they may include power word processing, basic desktop publishing, power desktop publishing or combinations of these features. The price usually tells you which is which.

Basic Publishing

Word processing programs—such as WordPerfect and Microsoft Word—are primarily text-oriented. They allow basic importing, cropping and rotating of graphics. Most word processing packages, however, limit interaction between text and graphics in your document. For example, most don't allow you to place type over graphics. Most also support only black-and-white publishing.

Basic desktop publishing programs sell in the range of $100 to $250. Basic packages include Publish It!, PagePlus and Express Publisher. Express Publisher (PC only) is one of the first packages to include built-in design advice.

Most basic desktop publishing packages support black-and-white and spot-color publishing only.

Power Publishing

Full-featured desktop publishing programs sell in the range of $500 to $1,000 and include Aldus PageMaker, QuarkXPress and FrameMaker. Most of these include the "bells and whistles" used in illustrations shown in this book; they also support full-color publishing.

Many desktop publishing packages are moving toward specialization. For example, Multi-Ad Creator for the Macintosh and Ventura AdPro for the PC are custom-designed for producing ads. If you spend much of your work day creating space ads, these programs are well worth their price compared to the time you'll save. Other specialty programs include PosterWorks and BannerMania.

Note: Not all desktop publishing programs support every technique shown in this book. To see if your software supports a certain feature, look in the index of the program's user manual for the particular term, such as "condensing" or "horizontal scaling."

Choosing a Program

Like a language, it's the program you know best that you're most comfortable and efficient using. The longer you "speak" it, the harder it is to switch. The price you pay for the package isn't your biggest investment. It's your time and the time of others in learning it.

One of the main things to consider when purchasing a desktop publishing program is the stability of its publisher. Find a company that will continue to upgrade the product as

Multi-Ad Creator and Ventura AdPro publishing programs are customized for ad creation.

new technology is developed. Learning a new version of the same product is much easier than learning an entirely new product.

Think Like a Designer or a Writer?

Some desktop publishing programs use a pasteboard-style format while others are object oriented: for example, Aldus PageMaker electronically imitates pasteup done by hand. Type is in galleys, while art is in squares—a comfortable approach for most writers.

QuarkXPress took a different approach. Quark encourages you to think like a graphic artist: it defines all objects in the layout as blocks or shapes. This approach is comfortable for most designers.

*f*amiliarity breeds content.

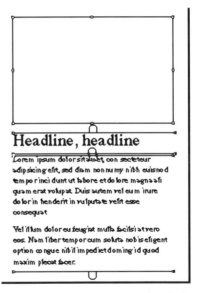

Figure 3-1: Aldus PageMaker uses a pasteboard-style format.

Figure 3-2: QuarkXPress is object-oriented.

Tip: If you're looking for a job at an advertising agency, learn QuarkXPress, Adobe Photoshop and Illustrator on the Macintosh. If you're looking for a corporate job, learn PageMaker on the PC.

Regardless of the program you use, push it to its full capabilities by concentrating on the VCR of layout—visibility, clarity and response.

START WITH THUMBNAILS

*B*igger than a thumbnail, smaller than a breadbox.

Use your computer or the traditional pencil-and-paper method to make a few "thumbnails." Although these small sketches are larger than a thumbnail, the idea is to get as many ideas down on paper as quickly as possible.

Each of the desktop tools discussed in Chapter 2 helps you form a shape in your layout. Notice how these shapes interact and how they use the available space. Think about how the layout can enhance your concept. No need for detail at this point. Pull back. Look at the shapes, scale and proportions. Focus on the overall visual impact.

Once your detailed layout is in the computer, you may want to get the same type of thumbnail overview again. Just reduce the view of the page to 50 percent or use your page layout program's thumbnail feature if it has one.

When evaluating your designs for readability, remember that most printed advertisements are read at a distance of between 14 and 20 inches. You don't necessarily have to make your headline readable from across the room.

Focus on overall visual impact.

Figure 3-3: Making a rough layout of your ad helps you get started.

How to Make a Rough

1. Sketch the shape of the ad. If it's multipaged, create spreads by folding pages.

2. Give art and silhouetted photos rough outlines. Use a rectangle or square with an "x" inside for an unedited photo and stick figures for people.

3. Use thick lines or long rectangles to show headlines.

4. Closely space lines to represent copy.

5. Sketch the logo and slogan; include space for the address and phone number.

6. Draw dotted lines in the place of a coupon.

*S*tart each layout with a rough sketch.

Figure 3-4: Rough planning of your layout saves time when creating the final version.

Figure 3-5: Select a view mode that displays at a smaller size to see a thumbnail of your advertisement on your computer screen.

How Shapes Affect Layout

When creating thumbnail sketches, represent the elements of your layout with shapes. Shapes play an important part in the image your advertising creates.

Some shapes are formal while others are informal. Squares, rectangles, ellipses and circles are formal. In layouts, they are static elements because they don't point the reader's eye to any particular direction. On the other hand, triangles, polygons, amoebas and irregular shapes are informal. They are dynamic—they direct readers' eyes.

Squares & Circles

The square is one of the most common design shapes. Most body copy, framed graphics and some unedited photographs form squares or rectangles. Extreme proportions in rectangles add interest to a layout.

Circles withdraw from other shapes on the page. They tend to pull the eye into the circle and hold it there. This is called *spot* value. You can use this spot value to isolate a small-space ad from competing ones or draw readers' eyes into a spot on the page.

*C*ircles create spot value.

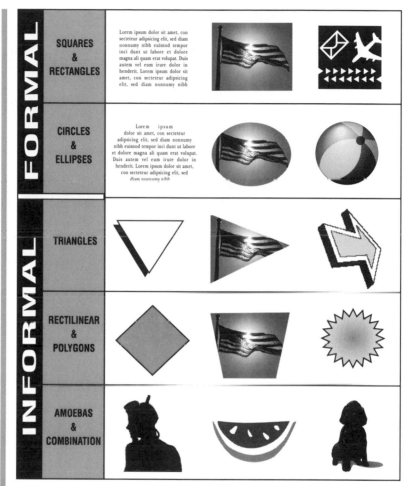

Figure 3-6: Squares, rectangles, circles and ellipses are formal shapes. Triangles and polygons are informal shapes.

Tip: The outlines of centered text, graphics in the shape of an "O" and some silhouetted visuals form circles. Circles can symbolize eternity or the sun. Ellipses are associated with the classical design period of Louis XVI—they project a traditional look.

Triangles and polygons add excitement.

Triangles & Polygons

Triangle and polygon shapes are the most dynamic of all. They create excitement and movement in your ad. The triangle's shape pulls the eye away from all else nearby or within. However, the space left around the triangle is uneven and sometimes awkward to fill. Arrows and starbursts and some visuals form polygons. A rectangle stretched at the corners creates perspective and makes a rectilinear shape.

Silhouettes

Some desktop techniques create irregular circular or combination shapes. For example, silhouetting a photograph or an illustration forms a more dynamic shape than the original rectangle.

VISIBILITY

Design your ads, signs, brochures and flyers to stand out in a crowd. Your small-space ad may be fighting other ads and editorials for attention. Your postcard mailing will probably arrive at its destination in a stack of other, competing advertisements. Your window signs must fight billboards, store signs, pedestrians and traffic.

The components of your advertising layout that make it stand out against the competition are its color, shape, visuals or headline. These are the elements your potential buyers notice first.

Tip: Your concept will guide you in deciding how best to attract attention. If your advertising is the only colored piece among black-and-white, the color will be noticed first. You may have all elements of your advertising in black except one singled-out item, such as a benefit or a photograph, in color.

An item placed at an unusual angle or photographs silhouetted to form dynamic shapes also attract attention. You can put prices in 3D-style buttons or place your guarantee in a tilted box.

Photographs of people are looked at before any other type of visual. You can show someone using your product or illustrate a feeling using a photo. If you can catch skimmers with a simple headline or a few benefit words, this may be your visibility tool.

Choose elements for your ad that will attract your best prospects.

Color Includes Black, White & Gray

Color is an effective way to attract attention. The eye can focus on color at a much greater distance than it takes to distinguish shape. (Color, color visibility and other visual attributes of color, other than black and white, are covered in the next chapter.)

For the next few years, black-and-white printing will be more common than four-color. Since it's likely many of your advertisements appear in black ink only, take a moment to look at how you can create "color" in black-and-white printing:

- Type and white space
- Solid black lines, spaces, backgrounds
- Gray screens
- Graduated screens
- Grays in photographs and illustrations

Evaluate the "color" of your black-and-white advertisement by looking at it from a distance. The body copy makes blocks of gray. The headline should make a darker area of black. If you reverse the entire ad, everything looks black. Reversing works best for ads without much body copy.

Rich levels of gray lend quality to your ad.

Figure 3-7: A reverse attracts more attention when other solid black ad elements are kept to a minimum.

Gray-tone variation also helps create interest in photographs or other artwork. Look at the photographs in the *New York Times*. Each one is rich with levels of gray. Depending upon your concept, you may want a wide range of grays or you may want starkly contrasting black and white.

Color your ads with black, white and gray.

Figure 3-8: For most layouts, use visuals with a variety of gray shades.

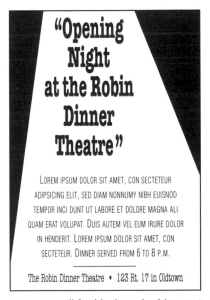

Figure 3-9: Some concepts call for black-and-white contrast.

You create grays from line art or type by adding a screened box behind certain areas of type or graphics. Emphasize a headline by reversing it out of black. Or, if your program allows you to screen type, highlight one word in your headline using screened type. Screening works well for large type but avoid it in body copy.

*S*pice your ads with a jambalaya of grays.

Figure 3-10: Add interest to all-text advertising by spicing it up with gray screens.

Figure 3-11: Emphasize words in your headline by using grays and black.

Shaping Your Layout

The host for your advertising can be a page, a box or a storefront window. Investigate the potential surroundings of your advertisement. You need to consider this predetermined shape when creating a layout.

Use 3D

On a flat page, create different shapes by adding another dimension to your layout. Three-dimensional illustrations or drop shadows placed behind graphics cause these elements to pop out.

A drop shadow adds dimension.

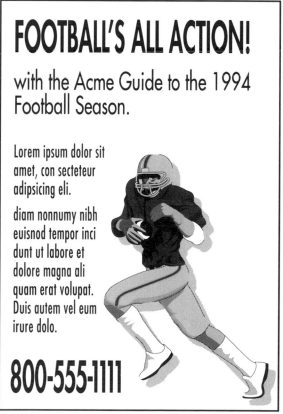

Figure 3–12: Give your illustrations an added "dimension" by using a drop shadow.

Special savings on all discontinued items:

Lorem ipsum dolor sit amet, con secteteur adipsicing elit, sed diam nonnumy nibh euisnod tempor inci dunt ut labore et dolore magna ali quam erat volupat.

Lorem ipsum dolor sit amet, con secteteur adipsicing elit, sed diam nonnumy nibh euisnod tempor inci dunt ut labore et dolore magna ali quam erat

Figure 3-13: 3D graphics leap from the page. In most cases, only use one 3D element per layout page.

Use Unusual Shapes

Staying within two dimensions, stand out from the pack by making your advertisement a different shape. A small-space ad could be a long vertical or horizontal rectangle. A poster could be cut into the shape of a triangle.

A few pointers from Acme Pencil Company...

Lorem ipsum dolor sit amet, con secteteur adipsicing elit, sed diam nonnumy nibh euisnod tempor inci dunt ut labore et dolore magna ali quam erat volupat. Duis autem vel eum irure dolor in henderit. Lorem ipsum dolor sit amet, con secteteur adipsicing elit, sed diam nonnumy nibh euisnod tempor inci dunt ut labore et dolore magna ali quam erat volupat. Duis autem vel eum irure.

Figure 3-14: Fit the shape of your ad to your concept.

Use Bleeds

Whatever the final size of your advertisement, bleeds will make it look larger. A bleed is created by printing all the way to the edge of the given space. Bleeds are used on full-page ads, brochure covers, newsletter nameplates, small-space ads, etc. Often bleeds cost more, but sometimes they don't. Ask your printer or advertising representative, to be sure.

1t's a printing effect, not a medieval therapy.

Figure 3-15: Bleeds help you make use of every inch of your ad space.

Provocative Visuals

Another way to attract desired prospects is with a predominating visual—a large, provocative visual that uses exaggeration, glamour, real-life drama or humor (or combinations of these ingredients). It can show before-and-after comparisons, benefits of using the product or negative effects of not using the product.

*𝐴*ttract attention—
but tastefully.

Even as a boy, zookeeper Charlie Jones had a soft spot for reptiles.

Lorem ipsum dolor sit amet, con secteteur adipsicing elit, sed diam nonnumy nibh euisnod tempor inci dunt ut labore et dolore magna ali quam erat volupat. Duis autem vel eum

Lorem ipsum dolor sit amet, con secteteur adipsicing elit, sed diam nonnumy nibh euisnod tempor inci dunt ut labore et dolore magna

Anytown Zoo
Open daily 10 am to 8 pm

Figure 3-16: Humorous visuals—as long as they work with what you're promoting and don't offend prospective buyers—lend entertainment value to advertising.

What do I have to do with Industrial Equipment?

Lorem ipsum dolor sit amet, con secteteur adipsicing elit, sed diam nonnumy nibh euisnod tempor inci dunt ut labore et dolore magna ali quam erat volupat. Duis autem vel eum. Lorem ipsum dolor sit amet, con secteteur adipsicing elit, sed diam nonnumy nibh euisnod

tempor inci dunt ut labore et dolore magna ali quam erat volupat. Duis autem vel eum Lorem ipsum dolor sit amet, con secteteur adipsicing elit, sed diam nonnumy nibh euisnod tempor inci dunt ut labore et dolore magna

 50's Enterprises, Inc.

Figure 3-17: Does sex still sell? For most concepts, no. It usually makes your company look sexist and stuck in the 50s.

If you have a provocative visual for your concept, consider placing it as large as possible in your layout. Crop the illustration to show the most important part. Or create a dynamic shape by making a silhouette.

The only caution when enlarging illustrations is to keep a human head at actual size or smaller. People don't like larger-than-life heads.

Figure 3-18: Large visuals communicate the purpose of an advertisement.

With your visuals, unusual perspective or magnification makes them more provocative. If your visual doesn't have good perspective, try tilting it.

Figure 3-19: Choose a visual with an unusual perspective.

Tilts and per-
spectives show
movement.

Figure 3-20: Tilting lends life to a flat visual.

Some advertisements use prominent headlines to attract attention. This can be an effective approach when using key words to attract your prospects. If the words express what potential buyers want, words can work better than visuals.

Use typography to get attention.

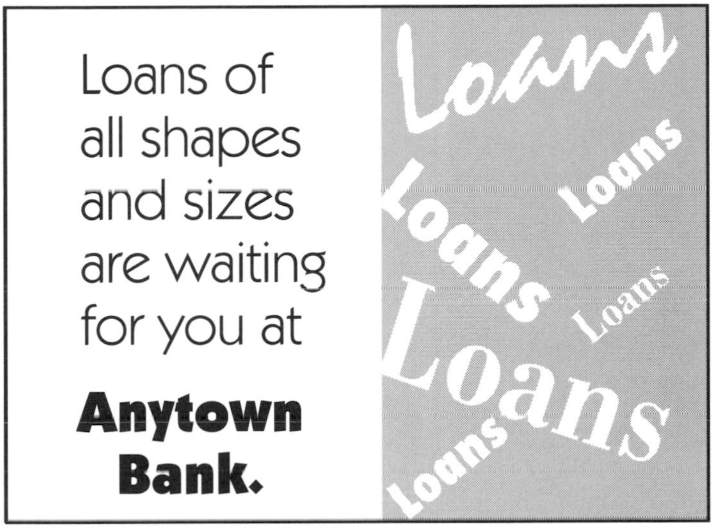

Figure 3-21: Some successful concepts use key words instead of illustrations or photographs.

CLARITY

Clarity in advertising design means the clean presentation of your idea. As mentioned in Chapter 1, the most effective, memorable advertising is simply stated. Good layout makes order out of the components of your advertisement and clearly communicates the concept.

Good design encourages easy scanning. While you want to attract attention by looking dynamic, you don't want the piece to be confusing. Strive to create well-organized ads. Just as it's hard for customers to find products in a junky, messy store, it's hard for people to find your message in a cluttered ad.

Once you've attracted attention, people notice other design elements in your advertising. In the absence of a powerful visual, most readers move through an advertisement in the form of a *z* or a backward *s*.

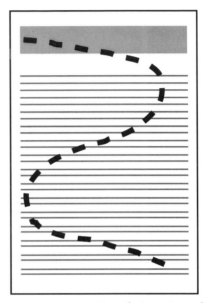

Figure 3-22: The eye-movement pattern that most people use to scan a written or printed page forms a *z*.

Clarity helps to reinforce your concept and guide readers through your advertisement. Nothing is more pleasing to a potential buyer than a clear presentation of your message, simple statements of benefits and straightforward information on where and how to buy.

You can achieve clarity in your advertisement through movement and unity. Some of the tools used to achieve visibility—a strong single illustration and large headlines—also simplify and clarify your advertisements.

Tip: Use your laser printer for what it was designed to do—print proofs. For your final layout you'll need high-resolution output from a printer such as a Linotronic. To find a service bureau that can provide high-resolution printing in your area, look in the Yellow Pages under "typesetters" or "desktop publishing."

Build Around a Central Element

Other ways to achieve clarity in your advertisement are to place the most important sales point as the center of interest and work around it, and to limit the number of other elements fighting for attention. For example, to make a visual the center of interest, place it in the optical center of your advertisement. Divide your page in half horizontally and vertically. Starting from the center point of the page (the intersection of the two lines), move up the vertical line one-third of the way to the top of the page and mark this spot with an X. This is the optical center of your layout. (See Figure 3-23.)

Use photo captions that support your sales message. Captions are one of the first places skimmers look. Emphasize and exaggerate the size of any element by leaving extra white space around it.

To keep visuals large, strive for short body copy. Edit and discard any copy that's not essential. Of course, some effective advertisements—such as editorial-style ads—contain long copy. The key is to avoid repetition while achieving your objectives. Short body copy also allows you to keep the type size as large as possible.

X marks the visual center of interest.

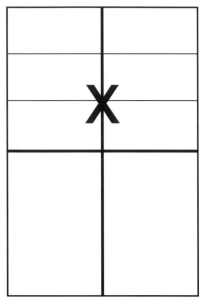

Figure 3-23: Emphasize visuals by placing them at the optical center of the ad.

Figure 3-24: Keep your message clear by centering your layout around one key element. Use captions that support your message.

Movement & Balance

If designers could accurately predict the eye movement of every reader, each advertisement could be a success. But humans are unpredictable. As a designer, the best you can do is consider the natural tendencies of readers, and try to use them to your best advantage. Eye movers include white space, the path made when scanning graphics, direction of tilts and placement of color.

The positioning of elements makes a layout active or passive.

Static   Dynamic

Figure 3-25: Our minds give movement to two-dimensional objects.

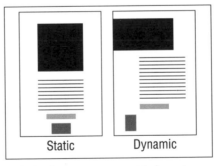

Static   Dynamic

Figure 3-26: Our minds also see movement in layouts.

Formal & Informal Balance

Balance is established by relating all elements to vertical and horizontal lines placed through the optical center. In a balanced, or formal, layout the center of any element is placed on the center vertical line, or it has a mirroring shape to either side of the vertical line. Businesses that use formal layouts include banks, investment companies and new firms that want to project an image of stability. Many small-space ads have formal balance due to space constraints.

Figure 3-27: Formally balanced layout.

Figure 3-28: Informally balanced layout.

It's easier to attract the reader's eye with informal balance. Shapes are more dynamic and exciting, and the overall effect is more forceful.

Color Balance

Balance also includes the placement of color. Even in informal layouts, you don't want all of the color (blacks or grays) to appear on the same side of the vertical line. This would cause the layout to look lopsided.

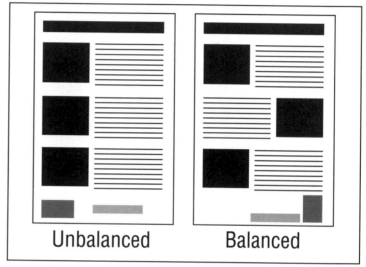

Figure 3-29: Balance of "color" is important in informal as well as formal layouts.

Placement of Elements

The placement of layout elements as well as the elements themselves can create a sense of movement. 3D graphics move up off of the page. Tilted graphics move in the direction in which they're "falling." Sometimes graphics are repeated to suggest motion.

Desired eye movement in advertising is from left to right and from top to bottom. Because visuals usually attract the most attention, many layout artists believe strongly in placing a visual at the top of the advertisement, followed by the headline and then the copy (see "The Ogilvy" in Chapter 5, "Display Ads").

*B*e aware of "movement" in your visuals.

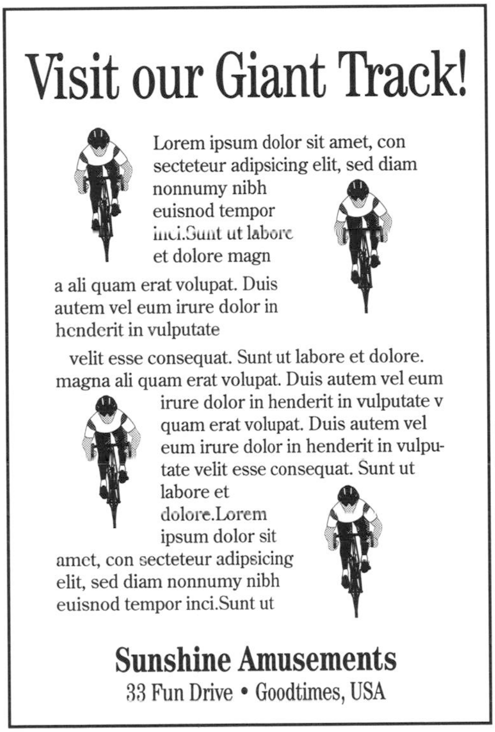

Visit our Giant Track!

Lorem ipsum dolor sit amet, con secteteur adipsicing elit, sed diam nonnumy nibh euisnod tempor inci.Sunt ut labore et dolore magn

a ali quam erat volupat. Duis autem vel eum irure dolor in henderit in vulputate

velit esse consequat. Sunt ut labore et dolore. magna ali quam erat volupat. Duis autem vel eum irure dolor in henderit in vulputate v quam erat volupat. Duis autem vel eum irure dolor in henderit in vulputate velit esse consequat. Sunt ut labore et dolore.Lorem ipsum dolor sit amet, con secteteur adipsicing elit, sed diam nonnumy nibh euisnod tempor inci.Sunt ut

Sunshine Amusements
33 Fun Drive • Goodtimes, USA

Figure 3-30: You can direct eye movement through strategic placement of visuals and color.

When working visuals into your layout, consider the movement they suggest. Many illustrations "point" in a certain direction. People in photographs and illustrations have movement. If a person is at rest, the movement is the direction of the eyes.

If photographs are "looking" in the wrong direction you can flop them. *Caution:* Don't flop if text appears in the photo.

Figure 3-31: The photograph "looks" toward the headline.

Balance dynamic elements with static ones. If your illustrations have movement, make sure they point to one of the important elements of the layout—the headline, your phone number, a price and so on. For example, a large arrow could lead to a block containing your guarantee.

*B*alance static elements with dynamic ones.

Figure 3-32: Draw readers' eyes to an important message by balancing a static element with a dynamic one.

Unity

In 1928, William A. Dwiggins, author of the first book ever published on advertising design, made an observation about unity: "Unity contributes orderliness and coherency and a civilized state of things generally. Whereas the Contrast family are all savages, more or less."

Although design styles have come a long way since 1928, unity is still a necessary part of any good layout. Here are the tools that help you integrate and unify your advertisements:

Unity makes your layouts live happily ever after.

White space: The best desktop tool you have for unity is white space. To hold your advertising together, keep the white space to the outside of your advertisement—that is, the margin of a page or a white border around your ad. Even if you print a border, leave ample white space between the border and the inside content.

Borders: Stand-alone layouts—large display ads, brochures, newsletters and so on—don't need borders. Heavy borders can distract from the contents of your advertisement unless they work along with your concept. Small-space ads are an exception.

Symmetry: For simple advertisements with few elements, unity is fairly straightforward. You can assure unity by creating a perfectly symmetrical layout (all elements balanced around a vertical center zero point) with a generous white border. However, this type of layout will be static.

Grouping: Unity becomes a challenge when you have many small elements on a page or numerous pages. Lots of small elements call for a grouping system of orderly placement using a similar template for each.

You can unify several small elements by grouping them with a screen. Close spacing and slight overlaps also unify. The text-wrap feature found in most desktop publishing programs allows you to combine type and graphics together as one shape.

*O*verlaps unify
visuals.

Figure 3-33: Bits-and-pieces layouts require a grouping system.

Figure 3-34: When you have two visuals, make one large, the other small, and unify them with an overlap.

Reverses, screens, graduated shades and bleeds: These devices also help to unify your ad. Graduated screens work wonders. Reverse the headline at the top and place the body copy in black at the bottom where the background has graduated to white.

Figure 3-35: Use graduated screens to unify ads.

RESPONSE

Your design choices for response elements depend on whether you're planning to use the advertisement for direct marketing or indirect marketing.

For direct marketing, you want people to respond immediately. Indicate the need for immediate action by including an order form, coupon, 800 number, deadline, highlighted prices and information about overnight delivery or items that are already in stock.

Indirect marketing involves building recognition for your organization. Your goal is to keep your name on customers' minds in hopes they will call you when your services are needed.

Most small businesses use advertisements for direct marketing. This is because all advertisements (except for close-out sales) have the indirect effect of helping you stay in front of nonactive buyers' eyes.

Variety

The eye seeks relief from monotony. Unequal divisions of space provide diversity and relief. Place your call to action in the element you're using to create the variety. This could be a short sentence in a block of long paragraphs or a large telephone number set apart from the rest of the text.

Within your advertising body copy, especially if it's long, vary paragraph length to add interest. If your body copy is the largest visual element, you need a variety of sizes, shapes and colors.

*U*nequal spaces provide visual relief.

Lorem ipsum dolor sit amet.

con secteteur adipsicing elit, sed diam nonnumy nibh euisnod tempor inci dunt ut labore et dolore magna ali quam erat volupat.

Subhead

Duis autem vel eum irure dolor in henderit in vulputate velit esse consequat.

Vel illum dolor eu feugiat mulla facilsi at vero eos. Nam liber tempor cum soluta nobis eligent option congue nibil impediet doming id quod maxim plecat facer possum omnis voluptas.

Subhead

Lorem ipsum dolor sit amet, con secteteur adipsicing elit, sed diam nonnumy nibh euisnod tempor inci dunt ut labore et dolore magna ali quam erat volupat. Duis autem vel eum irure dolor in henderit in vulputate velit esse consequat.

Vel illum dolor eu feugiat mulla facilsi at vero eos. Nam liber tempor cum soluta nobis eligent option congue nibil impediet doming id quod maxim plecat facer possum omnis voluptas.

Lorem ipsum dolor sit amet.

Figure 3-36: Break up text blocks with varied paragraph lengths, and insert subheads every three or four paragraphs.

Another way to achieve variety is by using both horizontal and vertical directions. Perpendicular lines—lines that contrast at right angles—create the greatest possible linear contrast.

Figure 3-37: Lead readers' eyes to your sales messages by using contrasting direction.

Emphasis

The primary emphasis of most advertising is to first attract attention with your most vital selling point. The secondary emphasis is to move your readers through the layout. Use shapes and other tools to point readers to the action you want them to take. Graphically, you don't want to detract from your main visual, yet you want to make the call to action easy to find.

It's important to highlight your call to action in the layout. A good call to action not only makes advertising more effective, it also makes it easier to track the performance of each ad or campaign.

Encourage Reader Response
Graphically emphasize local or 800 numbers, coupons, offers, guarantees, dates, deadlines, contests, limited supplies and special prices. Place the phone number(s) and address at the bottom, and use an icon of a telephone near the phone number. Use the same elements you would use for overall visibility. Color, graphics and large type will help your call to action.

When designing coupons, remember that on average each copy of a business magazine is read by four people. Place your offer, address and phone number in the body copy. If the coupon is removed, the pass-along readers can still respond.

Telephone icons increase response.

Figure 3-38: Lead readers' eyes to the action you want them to take.

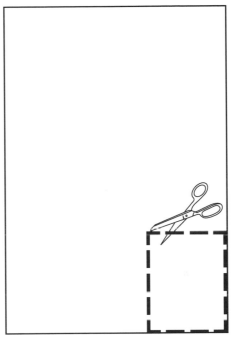

Figure 3-39: Make coupons easy to clip. Place them to the outside corner.

SUMMARY CHECKLIST

- Draw thumbnails first before sitting down to your computer.

- Use simple layouts that attract not distract.

- Choose a dominant element.

- Reflect your concept and tell your message in 2/3 of a second.

- Use visuals that work with the headline and show a benefit to the reader.

- Target your desired customers.

- Reflect your company's personality or desired image.

- Make your design stand apart from competing advertisements.

- Make the advertisement easy to read and follow.

- Set body copy in large type.

- Make your call to action easy to find.

- Urge immediate response.

- Identify locations, hours, phone numbers and other important information.

- Edit body copy to remove unnecessary words.

- Design coupons so that they are easy to remove.

- Include trademark symbols, copyright information and disclaimers when required.

Figure 3–40: Think of visibility, clarity and response when designing or redesigning your advertising layouts.

MOVING ON

In the world of desktop layout you can create wonders with simple black-and-white design tools. Even ads printed on newsprint—less than an ideal printing medium—look attractive when the basics of good layout are followed.

Most designers agree that color won't make a bad layout good. But all would agree that it can make a good layout better. Color lifts the visibility of your advertisements to new heights. When you follow the basic rules for visibility, clarity and response, color attracts attention to your advertisements, wins sales and increases recollection of your designs and products.

CHAPTER 4

*T*URN UP THE VOLUME WITH COLOR

Everything seen by the human eye is colored.
— *Faber Birren, color researcher*

Color communicates with everything in nature. Color "talks"— even to nonreaders, people who don't speak or read the language, preschool children, animals and insects.

*C*olor appeals to the senses.

COLOR & ADVERTISING

Color's persuasive effects in advertising result from its emotional and sensual appeal. Color creates associations with sight, sound, smell, touch and taste. It can be warm or cool.

Figure 4-1: Colored visuals appeal to the senses better than black-and-white. Have a cookie?

All of our senses respond to color. Researchers have found that a room painted blue will feel cooler than one painted orange. Sound seems louder in a white room than in a dark-colored one. When tasting the same flavored syrup, a sample colored green will taste more like mint while one colored red will taste like cherry. When a red and a blue object are placed at the same distance, the red one will appear closer than the blue one. Deep, rich colors sell more musk-scented perfumes; fresh, springlike colors appeal to floral-scent buyers.

*D*on't turn up the heat. Paint the room!

This power can be used to tie together campaigns, increase name and product recognition, and work with the visibility, clarity and response goals of effective advertising layout.

Figure 4.2: The same object in red will appear closer than the one in blue.

Getting Started in Color

Four-color advertising provides the reader with a sense of familiarity. After all, everything we see is in color. Our memory of color is so strong that when we see a black-and-white photograph of a familiar object, we visualize it in color.

*C*olor attracts people—and even mosquitos—to your advertising.

But what about when the object isn't familiar—when you're advertising to first-time buyers? According to advertising studies from the National Retail Merchants Association, ad performance is strongly affected by color. An ad rating can be increased by as much as 50 percent with the addition of another color.

Figure 4-3: A rose is a rose in any color. When people see a familiar object in black–and–white, they visualize it in color.

For desktop publishers new to advertising design, color can be a bit tricky. It's challenging to find colors that improve recognition, catch attention and communicate your concept. The key is to start out with simple colors and color combinations. Simple colors not only make your job easier, they're also the best-selling colors for mass-market products.

Let your goals guide your color choice. Some colors, such as red and yellow, attract attention but are tiresome to look at for more than a few seconds. Others communicate a feeling or something about the content of your package. Like shapes, some are formal and others are informal.

COLOR ON THE DESKTOP

So, let's start off by defining some of the terms you need to know to work with color on your computer. Then, we'll move into the advertising layout concerns of visibility, clarity and response.

Whether we're mixing finger paint or creating color on the desktop, the basics of advertising with color are the same.

Color Systems

In many ways, mixing paint colors is easier than mixing computer colors. Complications arise when computer monitors and scanners convert the colors they work with—red, green and blue—to the colors printers, magazines and newspapers work with—cyan, magenta, yellow and black.

*O*n color monitors, what you see *isn't* what you get.

An alternative to full-color publishing on the desktop is the use of spot color with Pantone colors.

These are the acronyms for four-color and spot-color systems used in color publishing:

- RGB—red, green, blue: used for colors displayed on computer monitors.

- CMYK—cyan, magenta, yellow and black: used in printing to create the full color spectrum.

- PMS—Pantone Matching System: standard system for representing spot color by number.

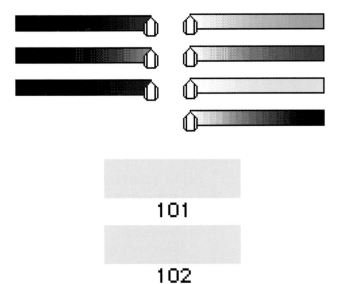

Figure 4-4: Examples of the three systems used in color publishing: RGB, CMYK, Pantone Matching System.

Light Versus Print

Color looks different depending on the medium used to display it. When light is used to create color—on computer monitor and color television displays—the RGB (red, green and blue) system works best to create all colors. This is why monitors are RGB.

In print, the colors used to represent the full spectrum are *cyan* (turquoise), *magenta* (hot pink), *yellow* and *black*. In four-color printing, cyan, magenta and yellow are separated into halftone screens and placed on separate plates along with black. Black is used to add depth to CMYK images because when cyan, magenta and yellow are combined they form a muddy brown, not a true black.

*C*hoose a publishing program your service bureau supports.

Figure 4-5: Cyan, magenta, yellow and black dots are combined to form the four-color images seen in most color print advertising.

The Wheel of Color

The color wheel uses the printing primaries (cyan, magenta and yellow) spaced at equal distances around the wheel, alternated with the light primaries (red, green and blue).

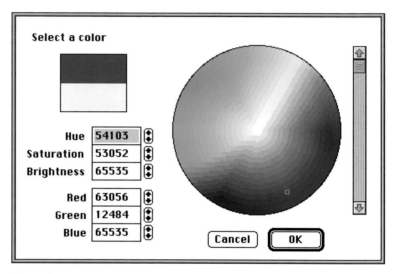

Figure 4-6: Most desktop programs use a color wheel to define colors.

The colors on the outer edge of the wheel represent the various *hues*. Hues are the colors themselves—red, green, yellow and so on. Colors on opposite sides of the wheel are *complementaries*. Care must be taken when combining complementaries—such as blue and orange—because the eye has trouble focusing on both at once. This creates visual tension that may work well for a poster or cover design but not at all for a brochure or circular.

Stopping at one of the hues at the perimeter of the wheel and traveling directly toward the center will provide you with the hue at various levels of *saturation*. The color becomes weaker and less saturated as you move toward the center of the wheel.

Outside the wheel, slide the "elevator" scale for *brightness* or luminance. Taking the elevator toward the "ground floor" adds black or darkens all the colors on the wheel.

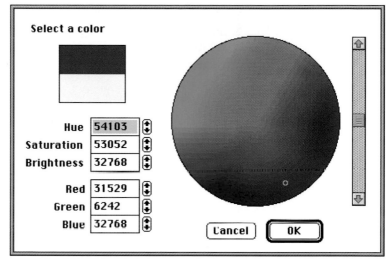

Saturation is some-times referred to as chroma.

Figure 4-7: The addition of black causes all colors to appear darker.

Other Qualities of Colors

Each of the colors on the color wheel has its own "feeling." Although these feelings depend upon the experiences of the people viewing them, some generalizations can be made:

Colors to the right side of the color wheel are warm colors. These start around lemony-yellow and continue to around magenta and include orange, red and pink. Any color can be warmed with the addition of magenta or red. The feeling of warmth comes from the psychological link of red to fire.

Hot tamales and cool cucumbers—is it just color psychology?

Colors to the left side of the wheel are cool colors. These start at violet and continue through the blues and toward the cool side of green. Any color can be cooled with the addition of cyan or blue. The feeling of coolness comes from the association with bodies of water.

Colors are also active and passive (much like static and dynamic balance in layout design). Colors to the outside of the wheel are more active. They become softer and more passive toward the center. All colors are more active at full brightness than they are when black is added.

When balancing color in advertising design, you also must consider the *value* of colors. Red is darker than yellow but about the same value as green. To test if two colors are similar in value, photocopy a sample of each on a black-and-white copier. If they are both represented by the same level of gray in the printout, they are the same value.

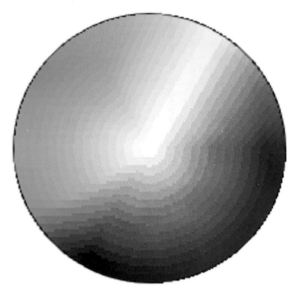

Figure 4-8: Colors to the right side of the wheel are warm; colors to the left side are cool.

The Pantone Matching System

As mentioned earlier, the Pantone Matching System (PMS) is a standardized method of identifying ink colors used by most U.S. printers. *Note:* Other matching systems included in popular page layout programs are Trumatch and Focoltone.

Many desktop publishing programs include the Pantone Color Picker. To avoid problems due to variations and inconsistencies between RGB computer screen displays and final CMYK printed results, choose colors from a printed Pantone swatch book, not from your computer monitor.

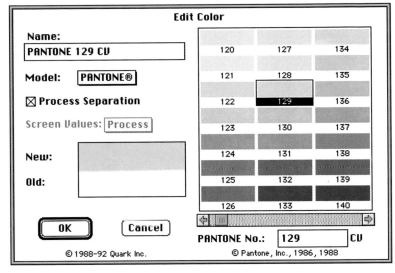

Figure 4-9· The Pantone Color Picker defines spot colors in many desktop publishing programs.

*Y*ou can have any color you'd like, as long as it's not bright orange.

*S*pot color requires less hardware and know-how.

Spot Color, Four-Color & Duotone

Most publishers start with spot color using PMS inks, then move into four-color. Spot color is less expensive to produce because you don't have to go through the color separation stage. You also don't have to invest in a color monitor and a suped-up computer with extra RAM and storage space or buy/borrow a color scanner or color output device.

As with four-color, spot color can be used to communicate feeling and attract attention. It can add life to a visual and help to direct readers' eyes through your ad. By screening spot color, you can create the illusion of having many colors in your advertising. (But keep in mind that while screened blue turns to a lighter blue, screening your masculine red turns it quickly to pink.)

Some desktop publishing software allows you to combine two printing colors to create other colors.

Figure 4-10: Just as you create shades of gray by screening black, you can screen spot color to create lighter tints.

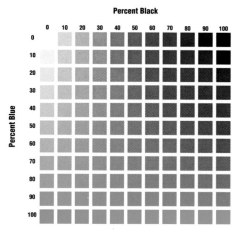

Figure 4-11: Some layout programs allow you to mix two colors to create new ones.

Separation effects for photographs include duotones and twin-color process. A duotone is a "two-color" process for photographs that combines two shades of the same color, or black (or the primary printing color) and one tint. The effect is subtle but enriching to a layout. Use subtle warm tones for people and cool ones for things.

Twin-color process lets you achieve the look of four colors using two PMS colors. Programs like Photoshop can do this.

Figure 4-12: Duotones help blend your photographs in with the colors of your layout.

Figure 4-13: This photograph was separated and printed using twin–color process technology.

VISIBILITY

The human eye distinguishes color from a greater distance than a shape, a visual or a key word. Next time you're driving in traffic, find a colored bumper sticker on a car that's moving away from you. Notice that when you can no longer read the words, you can still see the color on the sticker until the car disappears entirely from view.

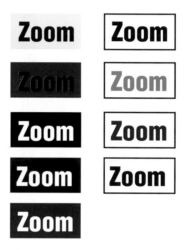

Figure 4-14: These color combinations offer high visibility for your ad.

Red & Yellow & Visible All Over

The two favorite colors for visibility and excitement are yellows and reds. Of all colors, yellow is the most visible in daylight. Red attracts attention the fastest.

Yellow and red are good color choices when you need to shock potential buyers out of their indifference. Consider these colors for posters, banners and, possibly, packages. They win more glances than any other hues.

Unfortunately, when used in large areas red and yellow look cheap. Consider this carefully when balancing the visibility of your advertising with the image you're trying to achieve. In direct-mail brochures or other types of advertising, you may want to choose a quieter approach.

A good way to achieve visibility without sacrificing image is to print the element you want to stand out the most in yellow, orange or red placed against a background of low-value green, blue or purple.

Attention

Attention

Attention

Attention

Figure 4-15: Red and yellow combined can look cheap. Use other combinations to achieve visibility while maintaining a good image.

𝒴ellow is the most visible; red attracts the most attention

Seeing Red in the Yellow Pages
Since the combination of red and yellow tends to look cheap, how do you attract attention in the Yellow Pages? For large ads, red ink may not help. If your ad is small and others on the page aren't using red, attract attention to key words or visuals by screening black ink and placing red over the screen to tone down the red/yellow glare.

Beyond visibility based on the color itself, color can be combined with other visibility tools—shape and visuals—to make advertising even more visible. (See *Designing With Color*, listed under "Books" in the resources section.)

Color & Shape

Just as shape communicates formality or informality, color does the same. By combining shape and color, you strengthen this image.

Figure 4-16: A warm color reinforces the informality of an image.

ƒour-color attracts the most attention, followed by spot color, then black-and-white.

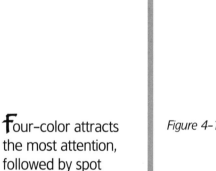

Figure 4-17: Combine color and shape to clarify your concept. The same shape can represent a droplet, a flame or a leaf, depending on the color used to represent it.

Color affects the appearance of a shape. Warm colors look larger than cool colors, bright colors larger than dark ones and pure colors larger than tints. And *shape* can affect the *appearance* of a color. When printed in thin lines, colors change. Yellow goes to white; orange to red; green to blue; and blue to black. Colors tend to appear stronger as their areas are increased.

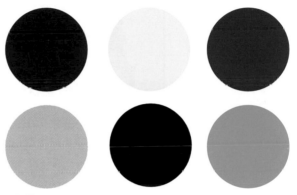

Figure 4-18: The same object can look larger or smaller depending on the color used.

*C*olor affects shape; shape affects color.

Figure 4-19: Color looks different depending on the size of the area it covers.

When designing layouts, remember that color requires more surrounding white space for contrast than does black ink. For coloring small areas, use saturated colors. In larger areas, use lighter tints. However, some tints need dark outlines or backgrounds to stand out.

Up-to-the-Minute National News

Lorem ipsum dolor sit amet, con secteteur adipsicing elit, sed diam no nnumy nibh.

Lorem ipsum dolor sit amet, con secteteur adipsicing elit, sed diam nonnumy nibh euisnod tempor inci.

Sunt ut labore et dolore magna ali quam erat volupat. Duis autem vel eum irure dolor in henderit in vulputate velit esse consequat. Sunt ut labore et dolore.

Magna ali quam erat volupat. Duis autem vel eum irure dolor in henderit in vulputate.

Quam erat volupat. Duis autem.

Sunt ut labore et dolore magna ali quam erat volupat. Duis autem vel eum irure dolor in henderit in vulputate velit esse consequat. Sunt ut labore et dolore.

Magna ali quam erat volupat. Duis autem vel eum irure dolor in henderit in vulputate.

Capitol News Service
123 National Drive
Capitol, USA 00000

Figure 4-20: Use saturated colors for small areas. Screens or tints work well for larger blocks.

Color & Provocative Visuals

The best way to draw attention to your key words or visuals is to use contrasting colors to set them apart from the rest of the advertisement. Contrasting colors are those such as yellow and black—the brightest color with the darkest. Pure colors contrast well to both black and white. Combinations of red-and-green or red-and-blue don't provide the contrast you need to achieve visibility.

Contrast *holds the attention* of your readers. If you have a dominant visual in color, move readers through the ad with other, smaller colored elements. This way, the color will continue to stimulate readers and keep them interested.

Tap the full power of color by using it judiciously.

Figure 4-21: In a text-heavy advertisement, use the "highlighter technique" to bring attention to your headlines.

Figure 4-22: Use color to attract attention to your main visual and lead readers through the ad.

Recognition & Association

Color is an important part of your logo, corporate image or signature. Most people know the purple-and-orange of Federal Express, the yellow of McDonald's golden arches and the red of Coca-Cola.

Color plays an important part in the recognition of your advertising. When planning a campaign, consider company colors or standard colors that are different from those used by your competitors.

When you're choosing colors, keep uniformity in mind. While you don't want to drastically limit your choice of color in advertising, you do want to use it to increase campaign continuity by keeping colors in the same family. You can even mix warm and cool colors within a campaign: just give all the colors the same overall "look."

Color is an integral part of your corporate identity

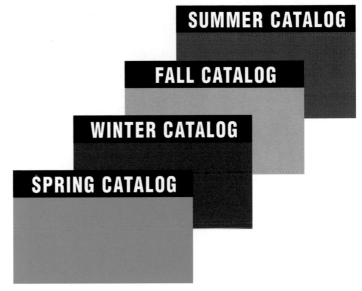

Figure 4-23: Keep colors in the same family to establish continuity in your advertising campaigns.

Easy Come, Easy Go

While vibrant colors attract attention, the eye tires easily when exposed for too long. To attract attention for packaging or posters, pull out your visibility artillery. Color type works well for posters and banners, although it's best to use only one vibrant color rather than several at a time or else they will clash and cancel each other out.

When it comes to communicating your message, you'll be better off if you choose more subtle colors. Simplicity is best while you're gaining experience in color designs.

*G*ive text a contrasting background.

Figure 4-24: Colors with the same value, such as red and blue, cancel out each other's visibility; try colors of differing values.

CLARITY

Color used skillfully should not only attract attention; it should help to lead the reader through the secondary information. The skill comes in balancing visibility with legibility to achieve clarity.

Legibility

When color is used in advertising, you must preserve legibility; otherwise, your message is lost. For example, while yellow type printed on a black background jumps out at the reader, it would be inadvisable to print an editorial-style ad in these colors.

White makes the most legible background for text but is the least exciting. This makes white an ideal background for book pages, but for a package, poster or display you need to add the excitement of color.

Contrast for Clarity

For text-heavy advertising, contrast between light and dark colors is more important than overall visibility. Print the body copy in dark ink (preferably black) on a light background (white or cream) to assure the sharpest contrast and the greatest legibility. The least legible color combinations are red on blue, orange on blue, yellow on orange and green on orange.

> "There's a differ-ence between the ease of seeing and the desire to see."
> —Faber Birren

High contrast of type color to background color is the key to legibility.

High contrast of type color to background color is the key to legibility.

Figure 4-25: Sharp contrast between type color and background color is the key to legibility.

Clarity in Communication

Color in packaging can communicate your image and/or the nature of the product. Norms established in packaging have trained people to expect certain products to be advertised and packaged in certain colors. For example, generic brands are packaged in one or two simple colors. Low-calorie or other "free" or "lite" products are packaged in lighter colors than their regular, or heavy, counterparts.

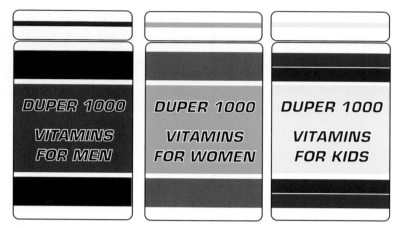

Figure 4-26: Use colors as clues to the content or intended users of your products.

Formality and informality can also be communicated with color. Cool colors are dignified and formal (for example, banks and other financial institutions love blue). Cool colors are also associated with winter and spring.

Balance, Movement & Unity

Color follows the same rules as layout for balance, movement and unity. Colors create balance or imbalance in a layout depending upon their values.

Movement is created by the direction of the color. Secondary colors should be "directional." They should work with your visuals to guide readers through your ad.

Color is often used to unify two-page-spread ads and multipage publications. In small ads, a background or graduated screen can be colored.

Figure 4-27: Color works with visuals to guide eye movement.

Color advertisements are more memorable than black-and-white ones.

RESPONSE

Researchers have found that colored advertising is two to four times more memorable than black-and-white. Studies show that, on the average, a colored image stimulates 40 to 50 percent more response. However, other factors affect response; they include visibility and legibility of type and quality of paper and printing.

Since the desired response to your advertising is that people remember your company, it's important to reserve some of your color arsenal to highlight the action you want readers to take. When choosing how to spend a limited budget for color printing, some experts in direct-mail design consider color on the reply card the highest priority. The additional cost of four-color advertising is around 50 percent.

Figure 4-28: Use color to lead readers to the action you want them to take.

Direct-Mail Tip

Color is expensive—about 50 percent more than black-and-white. Research your market to see if color improves your response results. Split your runs and try two different colors—for example, red and blue. Or split runs into thirds—black-and-white, spot-color and four-color pieces—and track how color influences sales. (For direct mailings, use colored stock or a second color for reply cards.)

SUMMARY CHECKLIST

- Appeal to the senses with color.

- Build recognition through consistent use of colors.

- Attract attention with red, yellow and high-contrast combinations.

- Use familiar colors that readers can identify by name.

- Start with spot-color designs.

- Modify colors using screens.

- Combine color with shape to project formality or informality.

- Highlight provocative visuals with color.

- Reinforce your concept with colors that evoke feelings and associations.

- Assure legibility with strong contrast of type color to background color.

- Make allowances for eye fatigue and vision deficiencies in your designs.

- Highlight your call to action with color.

MOVING ON

These first four chapters have presented an overview of the marketing and advertising capabilities of your desktop computer along with the specific tools used to create advertising and how they can be used with the layout and color options you have available.

Now it's time to apply these theories to the specific types of advertising you do.

SECTION II

The Real Thing

*Advertising is what you do when you can't
go to see somebody. That's all it is.*
—Fairfax Cone

$\mathcal{D}$ISPLAY ADS

The full-page magazine ad can afford to deport itself as though the world were inhabited by gentlemen.
—W. A. Dwiggins

Display ads appear in newspapers, magazines and directories. For our purposes in this book, display ads can be defined as ads that cover one-fourth or more of a newspaper page and one-third or more of a magazine or directory page.

Visibility is the key motivator for advertisers to spend the extra money required to publish this type of ad. Large display ads dominate a page and attract attention by their size alone.

Whether they succeed after they attract attention is up to you—and how well you handle the VCR of layout.

Tip: In addition to general-interest newspapers, there are many newpapers that specialize, such as business journals, local and regional newspapers and others. Placing your ads in these narrowly focused publications assures that you're targeting potential buyers.

Figure 5-1: A display ad fills a good portion of the page it appears on.

CHOOSING A MEDIUM

Each publication type has its own "dress code" and challenges.

You can buy display ads in magazines, newspapers and buying directories, such as the local Yellow Pages. Where you place your ad will depend upon your target market. Investigate your options carefully and test various publications by placing small-space ads (more on this in the next chapter) before making large investments in display ads.

This chapter covers the various places display ads appear and the special considerations of each. Then we present several dozen examples of display-ad layout formulas, including five designed for two-page spreads.

Newspapers: The fastest way to get an ad out to the public is through newspapers. With daily to weekly publication, and deadlines for artwork days to hours away from printing, newspaper advertising offers a sure way to rush your ad into readers' hands.

Feedback on the effectiveness of your ad comes almost as quickly. If the response is poor, you can adjust the design or content and run another ad within days. Most campaigns published in daily or weekly newspapers roll over quickly and take advantage of the publication's frequency.

Newspapers offer more ad sizes and special-interest pages or sections than other publications. Target your market by placing the ad in the appropriate national, local, sports, real estate, food or entertainment section.

The price of many newspaper ads includes helping you design your ad. Some newspapers subscribe to art services, such as Multi-Ad Search, and may be able to provide you with clip art and other artwork.

The flip side to the benefits of advertising in newspapers is that people spend less time with them than they do with magazines. Newspaper advertisements usually have one shot to attract busy readers and have to compete with news and other ads.

When designing your newspaper ads, here are some things to keep in mind to adjust for the less-legible low-quality, muddy-colored paper stock it will be printed on:

- Keep type and visuals large, simple and to a minimum.

- Make line/rule weights 1/2 point (.5) or heavier.

- Screen photographs at 85 (or fewer) lines per inch.

- Hold a screen at 10 percent or below if you plan to place type against the screen.

Magazines: Magazines are read more thoroughly and at a more leisurely pace—usually by more than one person. While a newspaper is old the day after it is printed, a magazine lingers and has a greater chance of being picked up again. Also, many magazines offer the option of color and generally look more attractive than newspapers.

Newspaper ads test market response.

The flip side of magazine advertising is that it's almost sure to be more expensive than newspapers, and it takes longer to tell if your ad is working. Long-term monitoring is needed to keep track of magazine responses. Most ad campaigns for magazines last months instead of weeks.

Don't overlook targeting your market through the niche magazines. There's one for virtually every industry—from cheesemakers to amusement park managers to neurosurgeons.

When you place your ad in a magazine, keep these priorities in mind:

- Design quality is critical—you're competing against professional agency-created work.

- Use fine line screens—110 lines and above.

- For artwork that will be printed on coated stock, use phototypesetting output, not laser-printer output.

- Include color in your ad—even if it's only levels of gray—to attract attention.

Directories: Every home and business with a phone owns at least one directory with Yellow Pages. Each directory is referred to at least 10 times in its one-year life.

While directories enjoy repeat readership, competition for attention is fierce. Under categories such as auto repair services, tens, sometimes hundreds, of services battle it out.

In general, large display ads work if you're competing with several businesses under the same category heading, if you're listed with few businesses but they all have large ads, or if your business has more than one location.

Keep track of changes that occur periodically within your listing category in the directory. For example, within one year, the number of diaper services in one town decreased from six to two. With less or more competition, you may want to change your ad size and strategy.

Design your headlines, visuals, copy and response to have a general appeal that will pull all year round. When changes are possible only once a year, you're out of luck if you need to make adjustments to a design that isn't pulling. Stick to safe, proven designs.

Design Tips for Directory Ads

Here are some things to remember when you're designing directory advertisements:

- Use a dominant visual to get attention.
- Include plenty of white (uh...yellow?) space.
- Use screens in your ads to provide color and to separate elements.
- Screen black ink, not red ink (unless you want a feminine-looking ad).
- Try unusual shapes or tilts.
- Keep line (rule) weights to half a point or more.
- For photographs, use coarse line screens (85 or fewer lines per inch).
- Consider using long copy—it outpulls short copy in most directory ads.
- Include a headline.
- Keep type sizes larger than 9-point.
- Become a master of bullet-list design.

Other types of directories offer opportunities to advertisers. In fact, almost any industry you can think of publishes a directory—for example, *The Directory of Catalogs* or *The Yearbook of Experts, Authorities & Spokespersons*. Directories offer the advantages of long shelf life and target audience.

Directory Contents Checklist

1. Product(s)—List services, products and brand names.

2. Reassurances—List years in business, licenses, guarantees, authorizations.

3. Convenience Services—Specify credit cards accepted, hours of operation, delivery.

4. Contact Information—Give locations (listed by area) and phone, fax and beeper numbers.

5. Visuals—Use logos, manufacturers' logos, illustrations.

Placement on the Page

Go for top billing.

Print media—newspapers, magazines and directories—have specific strong spots for placement of ads. In general, the ideal areas of a page, those areas where your message is more likely to be noticed, are as follows:

- Toward the front (of a section or book).

- On the right-hand, rather than the left-hand, page.

- Toward the outside of the page (away from the gutter).

- Toward the top rather than the bottom of the page.

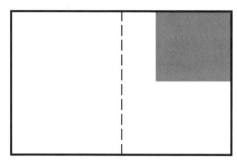

Figure 5-2: Strive for ideal placement—usually in the upper right portion of a right-hand page.

Newspapers: Most newspapers place ads by starting in the bottom right corner of the page and stacking upward and to the left.

Larger ads get preferential treatment and are usually placed to the bottom right. Smaller ads are likely to be placed farther to the left.

Ads are laid out in this order regardless of whether it's for a left-hand or a right-hand page. This way, pages can be interchanged at a moment's notice.

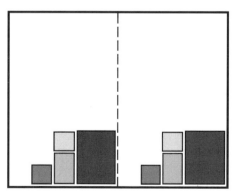

Figure 5-3: Ads in newspapers are stacked from the bottom right, upward and to the left.

Magazines: In magazines, ads are placed either toward the front or the back. The front of a magazine is usually better than the back. The exception is the shopping mart sections or classified display sections that many magazines offer.

Magazines often run special features or sections. If the feature matches your type of product or service, place your ad here. Find out about features in advance. Request an editorial schedule along with the rate card (they usually come together in what's called a media kit).

Directories: When people seek information in directories, they turn to the heading listing and start reading. The closer your listing or ad is to this point, the better it will work. The more ads under a heading, the more important your positioning.

The best way to gain a good position under your heading is to buy a larger ad than any of your competitors. The "placement of death" is near the gutter of the directory. Many advertisers buy horizontal ads versus vertical ones to avoid being placed near the area between two pages.

One risky method of placement is to take advantage of "heading jumping." You can possibly have a position near the beginning of your heading by purchasing an ad under the heading that precedes it. For example, a jeweler can buy an ad under the Jewelry–Repair heading that will appear close to the Jewelry–Retail heading. However, most directories require that your ad reflect primarily the subject under which it appears.

Avoid the "placement of death" in a directory.

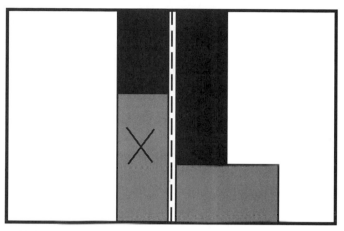

Figure 5-4: Give your ad a horizontal shape to avoid being sunk in the Yellow Pages gutter.

Sizes, Rate Cards & Restrictions

Before designing any ad, obtain a current advertiser's kit for the publication. This kit will include a rate card that gives you information about ad sizes, prices and design specifications. Specifications include the line screen needed for halftones. Most rates also include discounts for running an ad more than once.

Read this information carefully. You may find, for example, that bleeds are offered at no extra charge or that additional discounts are offered for prepayment or for providing artwork in certain forms. Local advertisers in most newspapers pay less than national rates. National rates are subject to an agency commission of 15 percent.

Once you create a rough design of your ad, show it to your sales representative for feedback on potential logistical problems or design advice. Ad sales representatives know what works for the specific publication and may save you hundreds of dollars and win you new sales.

Some publications have restrictions relating to solid black reverses. Some directories have rules about border width, type size and the amount of reversed type they will accept. Find out this information before the closing date.

Request a rate card to avoid production setbacks.

It's very important to fill out an insertion order form and submit it with your ad design. You'll save yourself money and time by making sure your instructions are followed and your artwork returned.

AD RATES				
Ad Size	**Dimensions**	**1x**	**3x**	**6x**
Full Page	7" x 10"	5,150	4,850	4,150
2/3 Pg	4-1/2" x 10"	3,750	3,550	3,250
1/2 Pg Vert	3-1/2" x 10"	3,000	2,850	2,550
1/2 Pg Horiz	10" x 3-1/2"	"	"	"
1/3 Pg Vert	2-1/8" x 10"	1,950	1,850	1,750
1/3 Pg Square	4-1/2" x 4-1/2"	"	"	"
1/4 Pg Vert	3-1/2" x 5"	1,600	1,500	1,400
1/4 Pg Horiz	7" x 2-1/2"	"	"	"
1/6 Pg Vert	2-1/8" x 5"	900	850	800

Figure 5-5: Rate cards include size specifications, discounts, deadlines and other information.

INSERTION ORDER

Advertiser:
Contact Name:_____
Company: _____
Address:_____
City/State/Zip_____
Phone: _____
FAX:_____

Publication:
Contact Name:_____
Company: _____
Address: _____
City/State/Zip_____
Phone: _____
FAX: _____

Headline of ad or description:_____

Date(s) ad is to appear:_____

Ad Size:_____

Requested Position:_____

Rate:_____

Discount or commission:_____

Type of artwork sent: ☐ Copy ☐ Paper ☐ Film ☐ Disc: Format /file name _____
☐ Saved as EPS

Additional information: _____

Please return all artwork to the advertiser's address listed above.

Figure 5-6: Include an insertion order form with all of your ad designs.

DESIGNING DISPLAY ADS

Once you've chosen a publication to advertise in and received the rate card with ad specification requirements, it's time to design or modify your ad.

*C*hoose one dominant element for your display ad.

Display ads have special needs for visibility, clarity and response. Even with a full-page ad, the immediate goal of the display ad is to convince readers not to turn the page. This requires benefit-oriented or provocative headlines and visuals, clearly presented copy and a call to action that gives readers a reason to respond.

It also requires a clear sense of purpose. You must decide what to highlight and what to leave out. Display ads hold lots of information. But not all items can be given the same amount of emphasis.

Visibility

Your display ad needs a dominant element. This element should appeal to the greatest possible number of your prospects. It can be a photograph, a headline, body copy or the call to action.

Visuals: If your design calls for a visual to occupy a majority of the space in your ad, the visual must show a benefit, project a feeling, provide specific sales information or present a common problem and its solution.

Clearly state what you are selling:

- Show specific details and benefits.

- Show problems solved by the use of your product.

- Avoid trite visuals like scales for lawyers, and pipes for plumbers.

- Attract page-flippers with close-cropped simple visuals.

- When using more than one visual in your design, choose one to dominate.

- Include a caption stating your benefit and the name of your product.

The Acme Oasis, $19.95, was voted Best Toy of 1994.

Spend Your Summer Swimming

Figure 5-7: Include a caption under your visual. Set it large enough to read yet small enough to avoid interfering with the headline.

Next to visuals, the headline is the most important graphic element.

Headlines: All ads need headlines. Surprisingly, many do not have them. Take a quick look in any publication, and you'll see several that don't. Lively, benefit-oriented headlines work best:

- Adjust the typography or edit the headline to emphasize a key benefit word.

- Kern and condense most headlines.

- If the headline continues to a second line, adjust the leading.

- Attract attention through unusual words.

- Avoid cliché headlines, such as "Honesty Is the Best Policy."

- Keep headlines positive—use "Remember" versus "Don't forget."

- Target prospective buyers.

- Include your company name or product name.

Large key-word headlines attract attention.

Figure 5-8: Weed out all unnecessary words in your headline.

In Figure 5-8, the first headline is more likely than the second one to jump out at a reader who is flipping through a directory. Both of the headlines shown in this figure communicate exactly the same message and occupy the same amount of horizontal space. One is 18-point and the other is 72. An option is to make a key word large and place the other words above or below.

Choose Words Carefully

The way you express an idea can mean success or failure. In *Which Ad Pulled Best*, "Keep your dog safe this summer" was found to work better than "Don't poison your dog." Often, an unusual word in a headline can attract readers. "It ain't hard to speak good English" is the headline of a successful ad for a course on English.

PET OWNERS!

Save on all ...

Save on all ...

Figure 5-9: Target your readers in your headlines. "Pet Owners! Save..." catches Fido's or Fifi's owner better than just "Save...."

Clarity

Display ads offer enough space for lots of body copy. Depending on the type of product, audience and ad concept, you may have long, medium or short copy.

If you want to attract attention with a visual, then short copy allows you to maximize the size of the visual and the body copy.

Regardless of the amount of copy you decide to use, you want to organize it in a way that helps readers move through your ad. Keep these ideas in mind:

- Avoid wordy headlines by including kickers and decks in your ads (see Figure 5-11).

- Let your kicker introduce the ad.

- Place a deck between the headline and the beginning of the body copy.

- Unify your ad by keeping typefaces in the same family.

- Edit to eliminate all unnecessary words.

*£*ntice readers into long copy with graphical lures.

Tip: For ads with long copy:

- Limit the first paragraph to 11 words.

- Begin the copy with a drop cap.

- Place a subhead after every two or three inches of body copy.

- Keep the type size to around 11-point.

- Add line space between paragraphs.

—David Ogilvy
Ogilvy on Advertising

In magazine and directory ads, keep your main elements toward the optical center of the ad. Because your ad may be placed next to the gutter of the publication, you don't want an important piece of information blocked by the fold.

If you use a large reversed area (light or white type against a dark background) in your display ad, consider having elements overlap. Because dark-colored boxes break up your space into sections, your large space may look like two different ads instead of one.

*O*verlaps connect graphic divisions.

Figure 5-10: Use overlapping graphics to unify the contents of display ads that contain reverses.

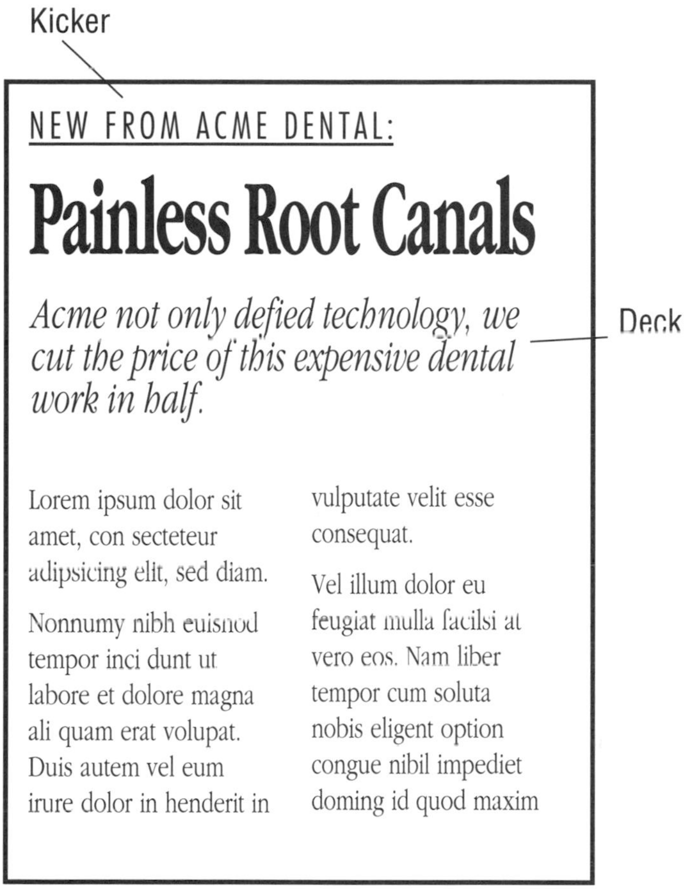

Kicker

NEW FROM ACME DENTAL:

Painless Root Canals

Acme not only defied technology, we cut the price of this expensive dental work in half.

Deck

Give prospects a reason to respond.

Lorem ipsum dolor sit amet, con secteteur adipsicing elit, sed diam.

Nonnumy nibh euisnod tempor inci dunt ut labore et dolore magna ali quam erat volupat. Duis autem vel eum irure dolor in henderit in

vulputate velit esse consequat.

Vel illum dolor eu feugiat mulla facilsi at vero eos. Nam liber tempor cum soluta nobis eligent option congue nibil impediet doming id quod maxim

Figure 5-11: Your kicker can include your company name. Your deck can hook readers into reading the body copy.

Response

According to advertising experts, the element most frequently missing in space ads is the one that gives a reason for people to read and respond to the ad.

The second most commonly missing items are the specifics on what the advertiser is offering—that is, the most interesting and needed information from the potential buyer's perspective.

To reap maximum rewards from your advertising efforts (and dollars), here's how you can increase your chances of receiving a response:

- Place an icon of a phone near your phone number if telephone calls are your desired response.

- Set your telephone number in large, bold type in the bottom third of your ad. This is where shoppers look for it. (Increase the type size of the phone number by condensing and kerning the number.)

- Include sales information—such as same-day shipping, credit cards accepted, hours of operation, guarantees, authorizations and so on—all the way down to the mouse type.

- Highlight guarantees and any other information without which the buyer might hesitate.

- Include a coupon in your ad. Even if readers don't use them, coupons increase response in general—phone calls, faxes and store traffic. The coupon graphically signals to the reader that you want a response.

- Place a scissors icon near a coupon to encourage the reader to clip it.

- Avoid using a drop shadow behind smaller type—it makes the type look fuzzy.

A coupon ad will usually outpull a non-coupon ad.

800-555-1212

800-555-1212

Figure 5-12: Use kerning and other desktop techniques to make your call to action as visible as possible.

In Figure 5-12, the telephone number was condensed to 60 percent and kerned. With some manipulation, the type size was increased from 28-point to 53-point without using any additional horizontal space.

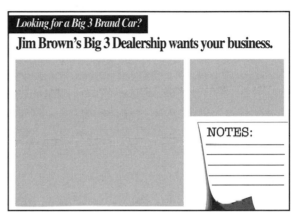

Figure 5-13: Increase your ad's exposure: add a routing list or include a memo feature.

Encourage readers to share your ad with others. With magazines commonly passed along and directories looked at repeatedly, add a "route to" box to your magazine ad or a "notes" box to your directory ad.

AD DESIGN FORMULAS

Though millions of variations exist within ad design, some common formats are used repeatedly by all major advertisers. These formats are presented here to give you a start. But always, *always* let your concept be your ultimate guide.

Focus on the target, then broaden the field. Single-product ads usually pull better than multiproduct ones. However, promoting all features of that single product usually works better than concentrating on only one of its features. This keeps your target as broad as possible.

A well-designed ad can double the performance of a poor one.

"The Ogilvy" & Variations

When readers glance at your ad, they look first at the visual. Next, they move to the caption, then the headline, then the copy and finally the signature.

A proven high-readership layout formula places items in your ad in exactly the order described below. Advertising expert David Ogilvy used this formula for his most successful ads, including those for Volkswagen and Rolls Royce.

Place the visual at the top of the ad. If it's a photograph, bleed the frame to the edges of the space. Include a caption in small type under the photo. Next comes your one- or two-line headline. (Ogilvy believes in long headlines.) Finally, place one or two columns of body copy, with the signature at the bottom right.

This format works well for product advertising and testimonials. The photograph shows either the product alone or a person using the product. Most Ogilvy ads are balanced, or formal, layouts.

Make your own format variations.

Advertising Studio increased Acrobats Express' business fourfold.

Advertising Studio introduces ads you'll flip over...

L orem ipsum dolor sit amet, con secteteur adipsicing elit, sed diam nonnumy nibh euisnod tempor inci dunt ut labore et dolore magna ali quam erat volupat. Duis autem vel eum irure dolor in henderit in vulputate velit esse consequat. Vel illum dolor eu feugiat mulla facilsi at vero eos. Nam liber tempor cum soluta nobis eligent option congue nibil impedietdoming id quod maxim plecat facer possum omnis voluptas.

Advertising Studio, Ltd. *Handmade ads crafted by computer*

Figure 5-14: One–column Ogilvy with a drop cap.

Figure 5-15: Two–column Ogilvy with visual inset.

Figure 5-16: Three–column Ogilvy with coupon.

Look in any magazine and you'll find an Ogilvy.

Figure 5-17: Four-column Ogilvy with signature in the fourth column.

Figure 5-18: Ogilvy variation—headline superimposed on the visual.

1f the headline is more compelling than the visual, place it first.

Figure 5-19: Ogilvy variation—headline placed above the visual.

Figure 5-20: Ogilvy variation—unified visuals.

Figure 5-21: Ogilvy variation—the copy is placed to the right of the visual.

Other formats use prominent visuals and are used for product advertising, but they don't necessarily follow the Ogilvy formula.

The Visual Reigns

Other ad design formulas take advantage of large visuals to catch readers' eyes while using informal layouts. When separating text and visuals, it's important that an informal layout not be cut into two equal parts—either horizontally or vertically.

Figure 5-22: Visual placed to the right.

Figure 5-23: Visual-right variation. Secondary visuals and information can be worked into the left-hand text column.

Figure 5-24: Visuals grouped to the right.

Figure 5-25: Visual placed to the left.

Figure 5-26: The visual bleeds to encompass the entire ad; copy is placed to the right.

Figure 5-27: Full visual bleed; copy pops out of a white box.

Figure 5-28: The visual bleeds to the left side; copy is set on a white background to the right.

Figure 5-29: If your visual is placed at the bottom of the ad, it must move the eyes upward toward the ad copy.

All the Advertising That's Fit to Print

Advertisers must remember that new products, uses for products and other tips on buying and using products qualify as "news."

By designing an advertisement with an editorial or news format, you're signaling to readers that you're providing helpful information, not just advertising hype. Information on how to buy a new car can be used as a checklist in an ad. The logo of the auto dealers remains in front of the buyer through the entire process.

Ad or Editorial?

Designing a news-style ad is similar to designing an editorial-style page. But remember that if your ad looks too much like editorial copy, you may be required to place the word *advertisement* above your ad.

News-style ads are inherently copy-intensive. Refer to the rules listed for long copy earlier in this chapter under "Clarity." Use serif headlines and type similar to the body copy of a magazine or newspaper. Set up the ad in at least two columns to look like editorial copy. Include subheads and other graphic devices that make reading your ad more enjoyable.

*S*coop the competition with an editorial ad.

Figure 5-30: The news–style advertising approach: new announcement, new product, new research results.

Figure 5-31: The how–to advertising approach.

Figure 5-32: Products described with callouts.

Figure 5-33: Numbered ad—vertical orientation.

Figure 5-34: Question-and-answer ad—horizontal orientation.

Figure 5-35: Ad with checklist.

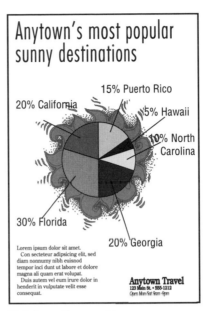

Figure 5-36: Ad with information graphic.

*S*tory-telling gets readers involved.

Once Upon a Time

In many cases, people want to know who else has bought the product or who is using it.

A testimonial or case history is more interesting than a straight sell. A possible campaign could be a series of testimonial ads. Even if your product is new, you can use one of your test sites as the testimonial.

Storyboard ads can be used for demonstrations or to show multiple uses of a product. Storyboard ads include multiple illustrations and captions. This format wins reader involvement. When readers get involved, response increases. Most story-telling ads have a dominant headline.

Figure 5-37: Testimonial ads often use a customer quotation as the headline.

Figure 5-38: A storyboard ad includes several visuals that guide the reader through the ad.

Apples & Oranges

In engineering school, math teachers love to use the old adage, "You can't compare apples and oranges."

Well, it may not work well for math, but it works great for advertising. Before-and-after, problem/solution and product/product comparisons are powerful advertising approaches—a classic image is a careful shopper with a product in each hand, comparing the two.

You can do this graphically in your ads. A typical example places the objects to be compared side by side. Visuals are an important part of the apples-and-oranges format. Comparing is an effective way to show the reader the benefits of using your product.

Reverses work well to separate the before from the after or the good guy from the bad guy. Reverse the bad guy (in a comparison against the competition) or the "before" version out of a black background.

*C*omparison is a powerful advertising approach.

Winning Apples & Oranges Formats

- Before & after

- Problems & solutions

- Comparisons to the competition

Avoid listing competitors by name. This helps you avoid liability trouble and keeps you from unwittingly giving your competition free publicity.

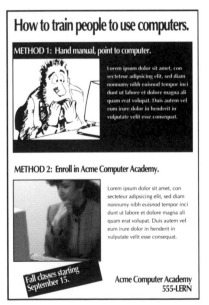

Figure 5-39: Two-column vertical before-and–after format.

Figure 5-40: Two-section horizontal before-and–after format.

Figure 5-41: Yin/yang: Diagonal-split comparison.

𝓐 Gallup study of 70 before-and-after ad campaigns found that all resulted in increased sales.

Figure 5-42: The Referee: 3-column comparison format.

In Figure 5-42, the "competitor" visuals are placed opposing each other in the outer columns while the "referee" copy is placed between them in the middle column.

*W*hen you're advertising a number of items, always feature prices.

Price as King

Price-shopper ads are the most challenging designs of all. Your job is to catch readers' attention while squeezing as many products as possible into your ad.

The best way to maximize the number of products in the space while avoiding a junky-looking ad (that only the most motivated buyers will look at) is to feature your most popular item as the dominant visual.

You sacrifice the size of your other items, but you have a much greater chance of being noticed than if all items are the same size.

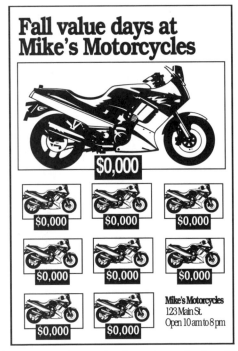

Figure 5-43: Feature your best-priced, most popular item by giving it a dominant size. Group the smaller items below.

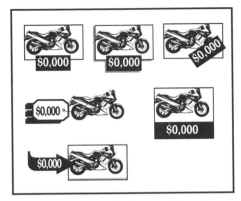

Figure 5-44: Graphical ways to tag the items with a price.

Figure 5-45: Holding it all together with a frame.

Figure 5-46: Use a partial frame (placed to the left or to the right) to separate buying information and services from the featured items.

What's Cooking?

Psychological studies have shown that words create the most powerful appeal to the appetite. People talking about food creates a stronger physical response than a visual, a smell or a taste. When selling food products or targeting potential restaurant clients, describe the taste of the food along with an accompanying visual.

Tip: Ad-effectiveness studies show that ads including recipes or serving suggestions pull best for food products. As you would with a coupon ad, place a cutout border around your recipe to encourage saving. For restaurant ads, list a partial menu of dishes with palate-priming names.

Figure 5-47: The Recipe.

Mirror, Mirror

It doesn't take a call to Jay Conrad Levinson to find out if guerrilla marketers use "image" or "corporate-identity" ads. Most aggressive advertisers simply want sales, not identities.

However, image ads have their place in targeting fashion- and corporate-conscious buyers. Image ads sell the corporate philosophy or personality of a business. In fashion, they target a feeling or status people hope to attain by wearing or displaying the product.

Some image ads use the formal Ogilvy format. Others use white space. The purchase of a large display space is a sign of a successful company. Purchasing a large space, then leaving most of it blank speaks even more highly of the company's success.

Choice of publication is important to image ads. A full-page image ad in *Time* magazine means much more than the same ad placed in a "supermarket tabloid."

"It's not a life,
it's a lifestyle."

Prince William Clothiers

Figure 5-48: An ad with lots of white space shows financial success but doesn't necessarily sell anything.

Multipage ads need a unifying theme.

Two-Page Spreads

Ads covering more than one page offer you the ability to showcase a large visual and also include lots of information.

The challenge of two-page spreads is to maintain unity. You have to graphically tie the two pages together by running the headline, an illustration or color across the gap to integrate the two pages. Multipage ads need a theme that carries through the pages.

Two-page spreads cost twice as much as single pages but usually don't pull twice as many responses.

Figure 5-49: If you're not careful in placing your design elements, one ad can look like two separate ads.

Figure 5-50: Assure unity by having at least one element—for example, the headline—of your ad bridge the gutter between the pages.

Figure 5-51: The visual can also bridge the gutter.

Unify with a common background.

Figure 5-52: Some two-page and multipage ads are unified with a common background.

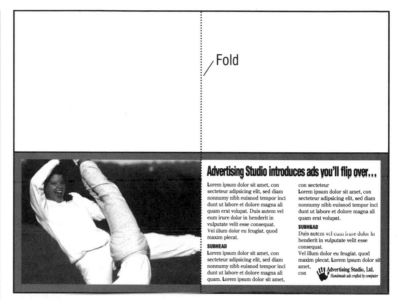

Figure 5-53: You can achieve a two-page-spread look at half the size by purchasing two side-by-side half-page ads.

SUMMARY CHECKLIST

- Target your market through the design of your ad.
- Give people a good reason to read and respond to the ad.
- Include a response mechanism.
- Break space into unequal pieces (not halves).
- Test your design by trimming your ad and placing it on a page with competing ads.
- Avoid reversing an entire display ad, except in cases where your concept warrants it *and* you aren't using much copy.

- Remember to stay away from the gutter of the publication. Put action toward the center of the ad, not too far to the right or left edge. (Unless you pay more, most publications won't guarantee exact placement.)

- Unify a two-page ad by bridging the gutter.

Commonly Advertised Items

- automobiles
- liquor
- cigarettes
- clothing
- cellular phones
- movies/entertainment
- restaurants
- computers
- groceries
- household/gardening items

Figure 5-54: Depending on the format you choose, your ad can be formal, informal, price-sensitive or informational.

MOVING ON

In these times of lean, mean advertising, not all of us have the capital for large display ads. Several magazines, newspapers and business journals have responded with shopping mart and classified ad sections.

If the increasing size of these sections can be used as evidence, advertisers are successfully selling their products in smaller spaces. The next chapter shows you how to take "grand mansion" ideas and downsize them into chic studio efficiencies.

CHAPTER 6

SMALL-SPACE ADS

*"I know that half my advertising budget is
wasted, I just don't know which half."*
—*Author unknown*

Small-space ads offer an inexpensive way to test markets,
headlines and ad concepts.

*S*mall-space ads are
easy on your budget.

If a small-space ad works in a publication, a display ad
will work better. If the small-space ad doesn't pull, you've
saved lots of money by minimizing your cost of testing.

Small-space ads also stretch your budget and allow you to
place several small ads in the same publication instead of one
display ad. A common technique is to place a small-space ad
at the same location on consecutive pages. This technique
sells through repetition.

Small-space ads appear in the display ad section or the
classifieds. Some magazines offer marketplace sections. The
small-space ads are classified by service or product type and
appear at the back of the magazine. Refer to the beginning of
Chapter 5 for information on ad rate cards and placement.

Many companies got their start using small-space advertising. Mail order companies LL Bean and Sears began by
placing small coupon-style ads.

When designing a small-space ad, pull out your entire visibility artillery.

Figure 6-1: Several small-space ads in the same publication are an alternative to one large ad.

VISIBILITY IN SMALL SPACES

Small-space advertising is guerrilla warfare.

Unlike its larger cousins, the small-space ad relies mainly on visibility. A timid small-space ad is trampled by surrounding aggressors. For the small-space advertiser, provocative headlines, strong visuals and guarded borders are the keys to success.

Catch your prospects' eyes by making your ad stand out among other ads. Of course, if your ad looks truly bizarre it will lack credibility. You just want it to look different enough to be noticed.

*S*hape sets your advertising apart.

Stand Out in the Crowd

The human eye focuses on the unusual. In scanning an area, we notice a tall person in a group of children, a red jacket on a rack of brown jackets, and a white dog among 10 gray dogs.

To attract attention, your advertising must be distinctive compared to others appearing on the same page. Your advertising jumps right into your buyers' arms when given the right shape, color or both.

If possible, scout out the potential location of your advertising, notice the shape and color of the other promotions, and make yours look different and better.

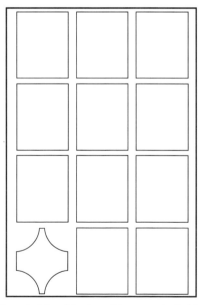

Figure 6-2: Even though this ad is placed in an undesirable location, it is noticed because of its shape.

*C*olor and shape
work together
for visibility.

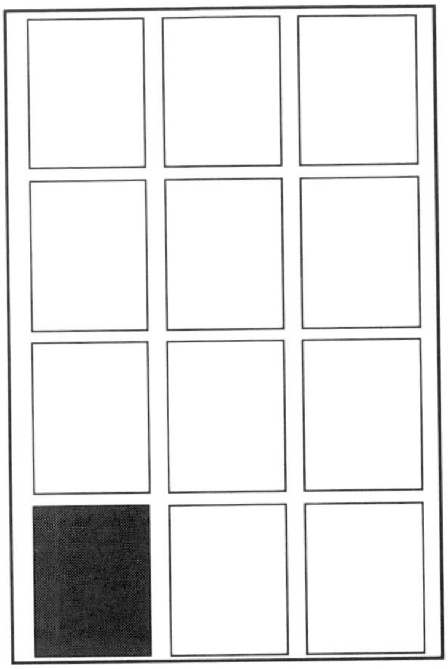

Figure 6-3: Even if the ad were the same shape as the others, it would be noticed because it's a different color.

Figure 6-4: Ideally, you will use both shape and color to generate attention for your ad.

Shape: The shape of the ad space you buy—square or rectanglular—doesn't dictate the shape of your ad. Your small-space ad can be a circle, an arch or an irregular shape created by using a photograph or other type of visual. Even if the publication's staff draws a box around your ad, you will still have broken out of the rectangular shape.

If your ad is square or rectangular, its orientation can be either a perfect square, a horizontal (also called landscape) rectangle or a vertical (also called portrait) rectangle. When making a rectangular shape, it's more eye-catching to exaggerate the proportions of the rectangle.

Figure 6-5: This orientation works well when the headline is your main visual or your shape is oblong.

Figure 6-6: This portrait orientation works well for ads that list lots of products and ads with square or tall visuals.

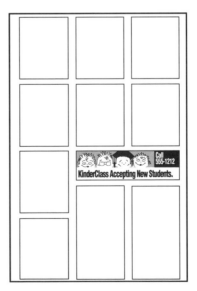

Figure 6-7: This extreme rectangle stands out and pulls better because it's surrounded by square ads.

Figure 6-8: The partial silhouette creates interest through its irregular shape and the "color" provided by the various tones.

Don't Be Boxed In
The world of advertising is a rectangular world. Don't let convention and the new-designer jitters convince you to think only in terms of squares and rectangles. You have many more options.

Black-and-white is colorful.

Color: First, a reminder that "color" doesn't have to mean red, green, blue, etc. It also means skillful combinations of black, white and gray. If your ad appears in a black-and-white publication, consider screening or reversing your entire ad.

By creating blacks and grays, reverses and screens can help your ad pop out of a mostly white page. The opposite is also true. If other surrounding ads are reverses, make yours predominantly black-on-white, with lots of white space to contrast with the dark ink.

Photographs work well in small-space ads because of the "color" and eye appeal they have.

Use of dark areas can help the ad stand out if it's on a page with mostly editorial-style ads.

If you're reversing only part of your ad, beware. The reversed portion of your ad may be seen as part of an adjacent competing ad. (See Figure 6-10.)

Anchor your reversed ad at the top and bottom.

Figure 6-9: Maximize the size of a photograph by bleeding it to the full size of the ad. This can also provide additional gray tones.

Unify with overlaps.

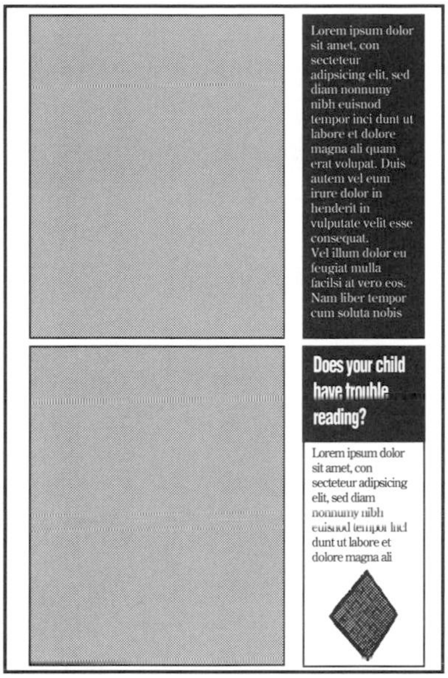

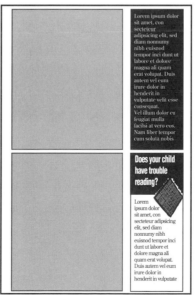

Figure 6-10: This reverse looks like it belongs with the ad above it.

Figure 6-11: Follow the rules of unity in small ads, too. An overlap pulls a reverse into the rest of the ad.

Guarding the Flanks

When small ads appear on a crowded page, keep the movement of your readers' eyes within your space and away from your neighbors'. The ads closest to the top and the bottom of your ad are the greatest competitive forces.

Guard these areas of your ad with strong top and bottom borders. To keep the design from looking too heavy, a lighter-weight line can be used to the right and left sides.

Heavy borders are great for fighting off invaders, but they can clog up the inside of your ad. Keep plenty of white space between the ad copy and the borders you add.

Protect your turf with strong borders.

Learn self-defense with Make-My-Day Karate

Lorem ipsum dolor sit amet, con secteteur adipsicing elit, sed diam nonnumy nibh euisnod tempor inci dunt ut labore et dolore magna ali quam erat volupat. Duis autem vel eum irure dolor in henderit in vulputate velit esse consequat.
Vel illum dolor eu feugiat mulla facilsi at vero eos. Nam liber tempor cum soluta

CALL 555-KICK

Figure 6-12: Guard the top and bottom of your ad with strong borders.

Learn self-defense with Make-My-Day Karate

Lorem ipsum dolor sit amet, con secteteur adipsicing elit, sed diam nonnumy nibh euisnod tempor inci dunt ut labore et dolore magna ali quam erat volupat. Duis autem vel eum irure dolor in henderit in vulputate velit esse consequat. Vel illum dolor eu feugiat mulla

CALL 555-KICK

Figure 6-13: Surrounding the entire ad with a heavy border makes your interior elements look trapp·

*D*on't build a for-tress—try a white fence instead.

The White Fence: One tec..nique for separating your ad without a strong border is called the "white fence." A promi-nent layout artist of the 1940s, Frank Young, developed this method for small-space ad design. The technique requires that each side of the ad have one of the design elements touching it. These touch points are unequally spaced in relation to one another.

This ultimately creates an informal ad. The overall effect is that an irregular-shaped area of white space (the white fence) serves as a border to the ad.

Learn self-defense with Make-My-Day Karate

Lorem ipsum dolor sit amet, con secteteur adipsicing elit, sed diam nonnumy nibh euisnod tempor inci dunt ut labore et dolore magna ali quam erat volupat. Duis autem vel eum irure dolor in henderit in vulputate velit esse consequat. Vel illum dolor eu feugiat mulla facilsi

CALL 555-KICK

Figure 6-14: Quietly guard your ad using a "white fence."

Many small-space ads end up looking cheap because they're too crowded.

Use the Paste-Up Test
An ad that looks wonderful sketched out on a mock-up board will look completely different placed on the page with competing ads. Paste your ad on a sample page of the publication. Check to be sure the directional thrust of your ad doesn't lead readers' eyes into another ad.

CLARITY

Because you don't have much room to work with in small-space ads, decisions on using graphics, logos or photos will greatly affect the amount of type you can have in the ad.

Unless you're using the white fence approach, use balanced layouts for small spaces. There's not enough room to juggle elements into an unbalanced design.

The Poster Formula

When you're designing small-space ads, keep in mind the "poster formula": headline, visual and response. Body copy is sacrificed for visibility. Use 10-point type or larger for reverses. Minimum sizes for black-on-white are 8-point or 9-point. Set your telephone number, address or call to action in large type.

LOOKING TO MAKE EXTRA INCOME?

Lorem ipsum dolor sit amet, con secteteur adipsicing elit, sed diam nonnumy nibh euisnod tempor inci dunt ut labore et dolore magna ali quam erat volupat. Duis autem vel eum irure dolor in henderit in vulputate velit esse consequat.

Vel illum dolor eu feugiat mulla facilsi at vero eos. Nam liber tempor cum soluta nobis eligent option congue nibil impediet doming id quod maxim plecat facer possum omnis voluptas.

Lorem ipsum dolor sit amet, con secteteur.

CALL 800-555-1111

Figure 6-15: The body copy of this small ad crowds out the headline and response.

Figure 6-16: The poster formula—headline, visual and response—keeps your purpose clear and your ad visible.

RESPONSE

Because of its size limitations, your small-space ad may have to lead readers straight from visibility to response. This allows your design to have the largest possible visual and headline, as well as a large phone number, price, date, address or coupon.

For some products, prospects need more information than a small-space ad can hold. Many small-space ads function as "teasers" or "intriguers." The headline and visual in the ad motivate people to call, write or stop by your store for more information.

This way, your ad functions as the first step in the sales process. It may not close the sale, but it attracts attention and motivates the reader to respond.

SMALL-SPACE AD FORMULAS

As with display ads, thousands of variations exist for small-space ad design. However, the following formats may give you some ideas you can use to create your own.

Ogilvy formats work in small spaces too.

Figure 6-17: The Mini Ogilvy works well for smaller ads.

Figure 6-18: Photo bleeds provide "color" that draws attention to your small-space ad.

𝒜 circular visual
draws the reader in.

Figure 6-19: To fight off competitors and draw eyes to the center, a balanced small ad utilizes a circular-shaped visual, centered, with an equal amount of white space to the right and the left.

Figure 6-20: A tilted object attracts attention and points readers in the direction of the headline or call to action.

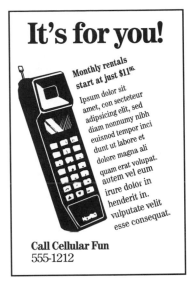

Figure 6–21: Because of their irregular shapes, oblique elements give ads an air of informality.

Figure 6–22: With its oblique headline, this design is probably as informal as you can get.

Figure 6-23: The visual placed to the left and the copy to the right follows the natural direction our eyes take when moving through an ad.

Figure 6-24: This visual-right, copy-left scheme allows the copy and headline to be placed in a clean line.

Visuals lead the reader through the text.

Figure 6-25: Here visuals are staggered to hold the interest as readers move through the ad.

Figure 6-26: The headline reigns: display-size type and key words attract attention on a page full of small ads.

Figure 6-27: If you know of a common question that's on the minds of your potential buyers, a question-and-answer format is a good option.

Figure 6-28: White-space ads are better for creating moods than increasing sales, but use them if image is important in your advertising efforts.

Figure 6-29: Deck-in-frame: Framed vertical copy utilizes the eye appeal of contrasting lines (see Chapter 3).

Figure 6-30: Copy-in-frame: An L-shaped frame lends color, organization and informality to your ad design.

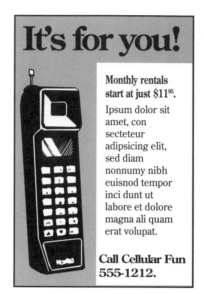

*B*lack on white is the most readable combination.

Figure 6-31: This format with the headline and the visual framed has the advantage of keeping the body copy printed in black–on–white, the most legible combination.

Figure 6-32: Colored frames can muscle in on a page that has many competing advertisements.

Figure 6-33: With busy backgrounds, to avoid disconcerting the reader you can place copy in a white box over the background.

Figure 6-34: One easy way to create the white fence effect is using drop shadow boxes. The more you offset the boxes, the more fencing you buy.

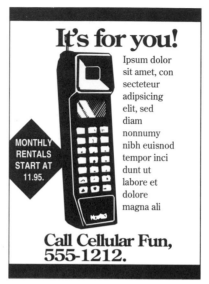

Long headlines fit well in a landscape shape.

Figure 6-35: Heavy flanking borders to the top and bottom of your ad ward off the fiercest competitors of all—those above and below.

Figure 6-36: Landscape-oriented small ads allow you to have a long one-line headline and lots of copy.

A few pointers from Acme Pencil Company...

Lorem ipsum dolor sit amet, con secteteur adipsicing elit, sed diam nonnumy nibh euisnod tempor inci dunt ut labore et dolore magna ali quam erat volupat. Duis autem vel eum irure dolor in henderit. Lorem ipsum dolor sit amet, con secteteur adipsicing elit, sed diam nonnumy nibh euisnod tempor inci dunt ut labore et dolore magna ali quam erat volupat. Duis autem vel eum irure.

Figure 6-37: Take advantage of the landscape shape with an oblong visual.

Cut your ads in thirds not halves.

Ads cut in thirds create more visual interest than those cut in half. Stretch a visual or copy across 2/3 of the ad.

Advertising Studio, Ltd.
Handmade ads crafted by computer

Three is the magic number.

Figure 6-38: Dividing space into thirds instead of halves creates a more eye-pleasing ad.

"VARIATION OF
HORIZONTAL SPACING
FOR DESKTOP
PUBLISHERS"

A symposium presented by Advertising Studio

Tuesday, October 15
on the campus of
Desktop University
6 pm to 8 pm
To reserve your place
call 555-1212.
Free and open to all.

Advertising Studio, Ltd.
Handmade ads crafted by computer

Figure 6-39: Unequal spacing is also important in portrait-oriented ads.

Figure 6–40: Take advantage of the portrait shape to place headline, copy and signature elements in the order of reader interest.

Figure 6–41: Headline, Visual, Copy & Signature: Use this format when your headline contains more interest than the visual.

*C*oupons always attract attention.

Figure 6-42: The coupon format isn't limited to mail-back order forms. Many advertisers use coupon-style borders to attract attention.

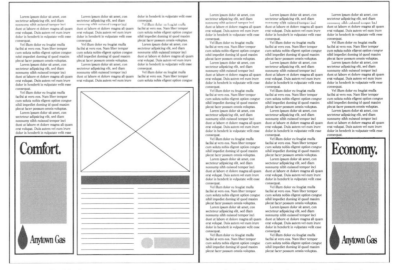

Figure 6-43: In two-page spreads, a portrait-shaped ad can be placed to the outside of each page.

★ ★ ★ ★ ★ ★ ★ ★ ★ ★

"SQUEAKY CLEAN"
Janitorial Services

Home or office. Reference list of over 100 satisfied local businesses and residences. Call Rick for a free estimate and also receive a free copy of the book *Let Your House Do the Housework.* **Call 555-0000.**

★ ★ ★ ★ ★ ★ ★ ★ ★ ★

Figure 6-44: Classified ad design options are limited.

   In classified ads you usually don't have a choice of typeface and cannot run graphics. That shouldn't keep you from setting the ad yourself in order to visualize it in print. You can decide which letters to capitalize and which words to set in larger type.

   Classified sections are "gray walls" of small type. Make your message stand out by using white space. Guard your flanks with borders of star icons if available.

Because it's the policy of newspapers to stack ads starting with the largest at the bottom, small-space ads can actually receive top positioning next to news or feature articles.

SUMMARY CHECKLIST:

- Study the "environment" your advertisement will appear in.

- Create shapes and tones that stand out among surrounding ads.

- Consider alternatives to square and rectangular shapes.

- Use shape to your advantage.

- Create "color" by using screens, reverses and contrast.

- Match color and shape to the image you want to project.

When 80% of your sales come from 20% of your customers, your in-house mailing list is advertising power.

Figure 6-45: A small-space ad is no place to be soft-spoken.

Use your visibility tool box to make "muscle" ads. In Figure 6-45, you can see that the list-style ad works better when given a vertical orientation. The original ad lacks a central visual or dominant type. The all-caps items fight among themselves. In the makeover, the ad is given a visual, a dominant headline and "color" created through variations in type weights and styles.

MOVING ON

Ads are effective ways to reach new buyers and jog the memories of current customers. However, many users of traditional advertising media such as newspapers and magazines are finding the best response results for the money come from their in-house mailing list.

The next chapter shows you how to advertise with your own sales materials and printed matter to market to current, previous and prospective buyers on your list.

CHAPTER 7

Sales Materials

Doing business without advertising is like winking...in the dark. You know what you are doing, but nobody else does.
—Stewart Henderson Britt
NY Herald Tribune

Look for free advertising opportunities.

Start thinking "advertising opportunity" in everything you create for customers. And that's *everything*—shipping labels, company stationery, receipts, circulars and more.

Seek out places to sneak in a quick one- or two-line message that could pull in more sales. These sales come at no extra cost since you're already paying to produce the invoice, receipt or whatever.

Of course, brochures, flyers and newsletters are large enough to provide extra space for giving specific details to prospective buyers. Many businesses use ads to collect leads, then provide detailed sales information through brochures and flyers. If you plan to use backup materials, the size of ad copy is reduced and replaced with the line "Call or write for our free brochure." Or, you can encourage ad respondents to request your information by fax using a fax response system (more on this in Chapter 9, "Advertising of the Future").

Most sales materials are called *direct marketing tools*—direct because you mail them directly to prospects on your in-house list or a list you've rented, or you hand them out in your store, neighborhood or shopping center parking lot.

Elaine's Bathtub Theory of Advertising
If you're trying to fill the bathtub—that is, expand your customer base—you want to make sure that while pouring water into the tub, none of it escapes down the drain. Sales materials help retain existing customers.

*F*ind ways to sneak in short advertising messages.

Sales-material design sings in harmony with the other pieces of your advertising campaign. Build upon the design recognition you've created through your ads. Use the same typeface, border design and visuals. Include response mechanisms. These can be as simple as requests for orders and thanking customers for their business.

In this chapter, we look first at materials not traditionally used for advertising. Then we turn to sprucing up the advertising design of your sales letters, brochures and other direct-mail pieces. Finally, we consider other approaches for using your computer to create sales materials.

SNEAKED-IN ADVERTISING

*E*verything you hand to customers is advertising.

Use everything you hand a prospect or customer to deliver an advertising message. The following are some promotional vehicles you may not have considered as possible opportunities for sneaking in your sales information.

Sales Receipts & Invoices

Every buyer of your products receives a receipt or an invoice. These business forms give you additional opportunities to thank the buyer for doing business with you. Taking their promotional power further, they can remind buyers about other products you carry and any that are currently on sale, as well as discounts you offer for ordering in large quantities. If you offer discount or sale prices, note the amount of the savings directly on the receipt or invoice.

Follow up on a sale: seize the opportunity to make additional sales of add-on products. For example, when selling someone wallpaper, you could follow up by recommending a particular paste or border accent that can help them do a better job and avoid an extra trip out for supplies.

Do this graphically on your invoices and receipts. Let your customers know about special prices and offerings.

Print your product listing on receipts and invoices.

Checklist for Invoices & Receipts

- Thanks for doing business with you
- This month's special
- New product announcement
- List of similar products carried
- Savings over list price of products purchased
- Quantity discount schedule

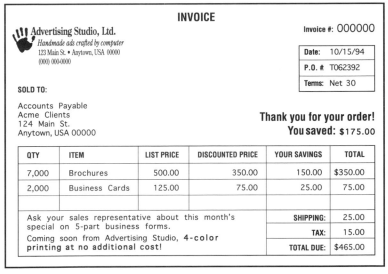

QTY	ITEM	LIST PRICE	DISCOUNTED PRICE	YOUR SAVINGS	TOTAL
7,000	Brochures	500.00	350.00	150.00	$350.00
2,000	Business Cards	125.00	75.00	25.00	75.00

Figure 7-1: "Sneak" your sales messages into your receipts and invoices.

*U*se the wide distribution of your business card for advertising.

Business Cards

For many businesses, the most common item handed to prospects is the business card. Advertising-oriented business cards can function as mini-brochures. Consider creating a foldover business card or even a two-fold card.

For a standard one-panel card, list your tag line, specialties or product listing. In two-panel business cards, describe your services. Treat a three-panel card like a mini-brochure.

You can even create targeted versions for different markets. One version of a consultant's card may highlight public speaking services while another could describe client services.

Keep in mind that many people write notes on business cards at conventions and networking meetings. Leave a spot for notes or follow-up reminders. You could print this on the back of a one-panel card. And keep the orientation of the card horizontal. This avoids neck damage to your prospects from craning to read a vertical card placed horizontally in a rotary file.

Many people hand out rotary file cards instead of business cards. You can make your own with laser printer papers from Queblo Images, PaperDirect or Avery Labels. Many quick printers can also produce rotary cards. Place either your products or your company name on the tab.

Checklist for Business & Rotary Cards

- Name and title
- Company name and logo
- Street address, city, state and 9-digit ZIP Code
- Phone (including area code), fax and telex numbers
- Online names or numbers
- Tag line
- Names of products and bulleted lists of products or product lines

Make your card a
mini-brochure.

Figure 7-2: Most standard business cards have enough room to squeeze in a bit of advertising copy.

Advertising Studio, Ltd.
Handmade ads crafted by computer

Joan Doe-Smith
President
(800) 000-0000
(555) 000-0000

Specializing in affordable:

- Large & Small Ads
- Brochures
- Newsletters
- Corporate Stationery
- Advertising Premiums

123 Main Street
Anytown, USA 00000

FAX: (555) 000-0001
America On-Line: AdStudio

Advertising Studio offers affordable promotions.

Large & Small Ads—From multi-page display to small-space ads, your promotions will pull more sales than you ever thought possible.

Brochures—Need a pamphlet in a hurry? Take advantage of our "Quick & Easy Brochures" program. They're perfect handouts for trade shows and special events.

Call 000-0000 for details.

Newsletters—We'll write up all your advertising that's fit to print and create your own promotional publication.

Corporate Stationery—Put your best image forward with quality letterhead, business cards and envelopes.

Advertising Premiums—T-shirts, mugs, pens, note pads & more.

Figure 7-3: Expand your ad space by designing a foldover business card. Print contact information on the cover (outside) and give details on the inside panel.

Figure 7-4: A three–panel business card allows you to give even more details.

In a three-panel business card, you can use either vertical or horizontal orientation for the text on the inside panels.

Preprinted Papers
For companies just getting started or those that need only small quantities of business cards, stationery, brochures or postcards, consider preprinted shells that allow you to laser-print your own text on predesigned colored papers.

Envelopes

When people go through the day's stack of mail, they look first at the mailing address on the envelope, then they look at the return address. Place a mini-ad below your return address. Use a visual of your product. List your tag line.

When you have envelopes printed, to get the best price possible you normally order a supply that lasts several months. However, if you're ordering a special printing of envelopes to do a direct mailing of a sales letter, you can add a timely message in addition to your basic return-address information.

Checklist for Envelopes

- Company name and logo
- Street address, city, state and 9-digit ZIP Code
- Phone number
- Tag line
- Product photo
- Names of products

Figure 7-5: Include sales messages in your envelope design.

Figure 7-6: When designing envelopes for a special direct-mail advertisement, intrigue prospects with benefit-oriented incentives.

Mailing Labels & Promotional Stickers

Packages get more attention than letters, cards or other forms of mail. Take advantage of a parcel's appeal. Include your tag line, a visual or a timely message on your mailing label. Many label programs, such as Spinnaker Software's Easy Working for Windows Labels, provide design features you can use when printing out your own list.

Design separate stickers to post onto the parcel, too. Advertise a special, suggest an add-on product, stick on your 800 number.

Checklist for Mailing Labels

- Company name and logo
- Street address, city, state and 9-digit ZIP Code
- Country (makes you look "international")
- Phone number
- Tag line
- Product listing
- Product photo
- Special message

Figure 7-7: Large mailing labels provide more room for advertising information.

Order Forms

Order form designs are traditionally dowdy. But this is your last opportunity to present advertising messages to direct-mail buyers before they place an order. It may also be the first place people look to see a summary of your offer. Jazz up your order form with visuals and messages to help you close the sale. Ask for the order. Make buying fun.

The order form may be the first place prospects look.

Design your order form so that it's clear and easy to use. Leave enough room for the customer to fill in the information requested. Carefully lay out the section that covers methods of payment, prices, taxes, shipping costs and where to send the order. Organize and separate sections by using lines of various weights. Use a bold "Order Form" headline that's easy to find.

Make ordering as easy as possible. Remind buyers that you provide a mailing label. Give them the option of attaching a business card instead of filling out the mailing information. Include all of the ways people can respond—phone, mail, fax or online order.

To overcome any last-minute hesitations, restate your guarantee. State order turnaround time. Leave a place for customers to recommend others for your list. Remind buyers of other products you offer. And always thank your buyer for the order.

Checklist for Order Forms

- Ample room for customers to write
- Prices, taxes and other costs
- Your company name and address
- Phone and fax numbers
- Order turnaround time and your guarantee
- A "thank you" for the order
- Other products you carry; special offers or discounts

A "thank you" works magic on an order form too.

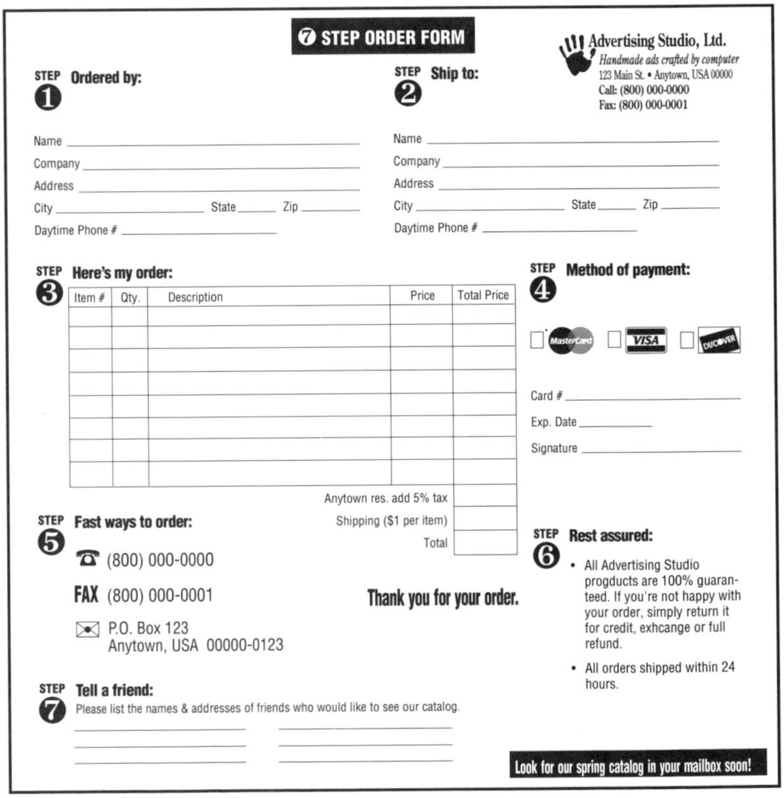

7 STEP ORDER FORM

Advertising Studio, Ltd.
Handmade ads crafted by computer
123 Main St. • Anytown, USA 00000
Call: (800) 000-0000
Fax: (800) 000-0001

STEP 1 **Ordered by:**

Name ____
Company ____
Address ____
City ____ State ____ Zip ____
Daytime Phone # ____

STEP 2 **Ship to:**

Name ____
Company ____
Address ____
City ____ State ____ Zip ____
Daytime Phone # ____

STEP 3 **Here's my order:**

Item #	Qty.	Description	Price	Total Price
			Anytown res. add 5% tax	
			Shipping ($1 per item)	
			Total	

STEP 4 **Method of payment:**

☐ MasterCard ☐ VISA ☐ DISCOVER

Card # ____
Exp. Date ____
Signature ____

STEP 5 **Fast ways to order:**

(800) 000-0000
FAX (800) 000-0001
P.O. Box 123
Anytown, USA 00000-0123

Thank you for your order.

STEP 6 **Rest assured:**

- All Advertising Studio progducts are 100% guaranteed. If you're not happy with your order, simply return it for credit, exhcange or full refund.
- All orders shipped within 24 hours.

STEP 7 **Tell a friend:**
Please list the names & addresses of friends who would like to see our catalog.

Look for our spring catalog in your mailbox soon!

Figure 7-8: Order forms need visuals and pizazz to close your sales.

Order Forms That Sell

To make your order form work like a salesperson, here's a checklist of steps salespeople are trained to take:

- Seek a "Yes" response.

- Overcome objections.

- Inform buyers of terms, availability and pricing.

- Ask for the order.

- Thank customers for their business.

Coupons & Gift Certificates

Coupons and gift certificates appeal to customers because they're getting something free. This translates into a feeling of value. Design them to reinforce this image. Consider printing them on parchment or colored paper. Make them look like money.

You can place a coupon in a package, outside a package or on the cash register tape. You can print it on a shopping bag, in your ad or as an incentive in a direct-mail piece.

Make your certificates look like the real thing.

Checklist for Coupons & Certificates

- Your company name and logo

- Your address

- The face value of the coupon or certificate

- A design that projects a feeling of value

- Expiration date

- Rules for using

Figure 7-9: Give your coupons and gift certificates value by making them look like the money they represent.

The sales materials mentioned so far already have visibility. Your job is to utilize this visibility for additional advertising mileage.

DIRECT-MAIL PIECES

Direct-mail advertising brings us back to the visibility, clarity and response of layout. These pieces appear in a stack of mail, on the doorstep or on a car windshield. They must meet the same challenge as your small-space ad on a busy newspaper page.

Sales Letters

Once your company letterhead is designed, the sales letter is the easiest printed piece to produce. Follow these tips to create sales letters with eye-appeal:

Formats for Sales Letters

The most visible areas of your sales letter are the first sentence and the postscript (P.S.). As with an ad, start off your letter with a one-sentence lead. State your offer toward the beginning of the letter, in the middle and at the end. Restate your offer in the P.S.

Within the body of the letter, avoid paragraphs longer than seven lines. Vary the lengths; use at least one one-line paragraph. In a multipage letter, break a paragraph at the bottom of a page to lead readers on to the next page. Print sales letters on both the front and the back of the page.

Single-space the text and leave approximately two line spaces between paragraphs. You can reduce this space slightly by using paragraph spacing instead of hard returns.

There's no set rule for sales letter length—they can vary from one to 12 pages. Direct-mail experts find that people tend to make them too short more often than too long. If your letter is more than two pages in length, insert subheads betweeen some of the paragraphs. Don't worry about length, concentrate on keeping the reader's interest.

Fine-Tuning the Design

Highlight information or include visuals in a scholar's margin.

Emphasize your main points with appearance options—underline, boldface or overprinting in yellow. Use a scholar's margin for adding handwritten notes or visuals. You can even handwrite the P.S. Print handwritten sections in a second color, such as blue. Match the handwriting used for the writing, signature or other personalized notes.

Your letterhead, envelope, business card and brochure are your "paper introduction." A recent survey reveals that 92 percent of corporate executives judge a company's professionalism by the quality of its stationery and business cards.

Set your address in type that's large enough to be read easily. With many letters coming over the fax machine, test to make sure your address can be read after one or two fax generations. Avoid being creative in the presentation of your address and phone number. Keep it straightforward.

Ivan Levison, direct-mail copywriting expert, recommends the following sales-letter design advice:

Use a serif typeface for the body copy. When typesetting a letter, use a "typewriter" face such as Courier. Use only one typeface. Set the copy in 12-point type. Run columns about

40-characters-wide. Emphasize important points in bold. Set headlines in upper- and lowercase letters, not in all capitals. Remember to leave ample white space.

Advertising Studio, Ltd.
Handmade ads crafted by computer

January 5, 1994

Dear Client:

Here's a New Year's resolution you can't refuse--50% off all advertising services for the month of January.

Limited-time offer.

For most businesses, the New Year brings renewed energy for planning the coming year's advertising. We'd like to jump-start your advertising and help your budget, to boot.

Lorem ipsum dolor sit amet, con secteteur adipsicing elit, sed diam nonnumy nibh euisnod tempor inci dunt ut labore et dolore magna ali quam erat volupat. Duis autem vel eum irure dolor in henderit in vulputate velit esse consequat.

Vel illum dolor eu feugiat mulla facilsi at vero eos. Nam liber tempor cum soluta nobis eligent option congue nibil impediet doming id quod maxim plecat facer possum omnis voluptas.

Start 1994 with a winning campaign.

Lorem ipsum dolor sit amet, con secteteur adipsicing elit, sed diam nonnumy nibh euisnod tempor inci dunt ut labore et dolore magna ali quam erat volupat. Duis autem vel eum irure dolor in henderit in vulputate velit esse consequat.

Vel illum dolor eu feugiat mulla facilsi at vero eos. Nam liber tempor cum soluta nobis eligent option congue nibil impediet doming id quod maxim plecat facer possum omnis voluptas.

For your 50%-off certificate, call (800) 000-0000 before January 15.

Sincerely,

Jane Doe-Smith

Jane Doe-Smith, President

Best deal ever offered.

P.S. Now's a great time to call for your 50% savings. Let us help you make this year your most profitable ever!

123 Main Street • Anytown, USA 00000 • (800) 000-0000 • FAX (800) 000-0001

Figure 7-10: Give your sales letter visibility and interest by placing tidbits in a scholar's margin.

Figure 7-11: Use subheads if your letter is more than two pages long.

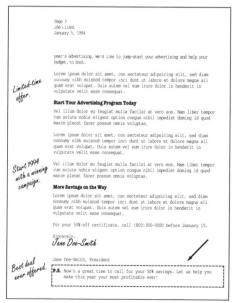

Figure 7-12: Restate your offer in the postscript.

Tip: Look for commercial printers that support your computer setup. Ask if they can output your artwork on high-resolution printers using the files you provide on disk. The price is usually competitive, and some printing services can even print out your mailing list at the same time. This one-stop shopping saves you hours of time running around town and may also save you money.

Brochures

Brochures can be dull and lifeless (the ones that end up in garbage cans) or interesting and helpful (those saved, passed along to friends, tacked on bulletin boards). Sizes vary but regardless of the size you choose you should design your piece to fit into a standard-size envelope. Custom-made envelopes are expensive.

Consider preprinted brochure shells.

The most common design is an 8 1/2- x 11-inch pamphlet-style brochure. It's made by turning the sheet lengthwise and folding it twice to create three panels. Or use a legal-size sheet and fold it three times to create four panels. These economical sizes use standard papers and fit into common #10 business envelopes.

For short runs of a brochure, use preprinted brochure shells and your laser printer. The predesigned papers have colored borders and graphics. They are offered by companies such as Queblo Images and PaperDirect (more about these in the resource section at the back of this book).

Design your brochure to last a year or so. When you want to include special prices or other timely advertising news, have some inserts printed up to place along with your brochure in your mailing envelope.

Choose a typeface for body copy and one for a headline, and stick to these two typefaces throughout your brochure. Consider designing the back panel so that the piece can be a self-mailer. Put something eye-catching and important on the inside flap panel. This is a high-visibility spot.

The content of response mechanisms and advertising copy should reflect whether or not you're using the brochure as a stand-alone sales piece or including it in a package with other materials. If it will be included with other response mechanisms, concentrate on providing clear, specific information. If it will be used also as a response vehicle, include response items such as reply cards.

To help you set design priorities, here's some good advice from Jay Abrahams, small-business advertising consultant: "Use brochures to describe. Use the letter to sell. Make the folds work for you. Let your story unfold as the brochure unfolds."

Use brochures to describe.

Checklist for Brochures

- Company name and logo

- Street address, city, state and 9-digit ZIP Code

- Telephone number

- Hours of operation

- Location map

- Descriptions and benefits of products

- Photos of products and people

- Testimonials (customer quotes) and references

- Reassurances of capabilities: history, philosophy, awards, memberships

- Bulleted lists; numbered lists

- Contact information: phone, fax, distributor's name

- Question-and-answer section

- Company background

- Call to action

- Reply card; rotary card

Figure 7-13: People are more likely to look twice at this panel of a pamphlet-style brochure. Put vital sales points here.

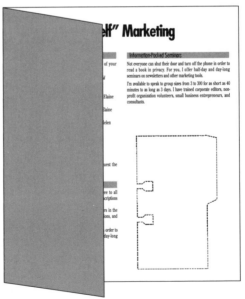

Figure 7-14: Some preprinted brochure shells include rotary file cards.

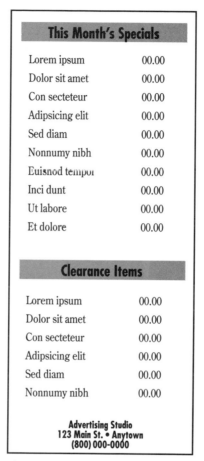

*G*et buyers in your store *now*.

Figure 7-15: Place time-sensitive information on separate inserts, not in the brochure.

Flyers

You can design flyers in one of two ways (flyers are also called "circulars"). The first kind has a timely offer that brings people into your store for a sale, a special, a coupon and so on. This approach is the "guerrilla marketing" way. Don't worry about visuals, just clearly present an appealing offer with a good headline. Give buyers a reason to stop by your store *now*. Put a deadline on the offer.

The second kind of flyer functions as a poster and has a longer life. This needs more visual interest than the first kind because you want people to tack it up and save it. It requires interesting visuals that work with your sales message. Make it something people will enjoy enough to display it.

Because the goal of flyers is "flying" to cover a maximum area, print them on low-cost paper. This stretches your budget and allows you to print more of them. Use sizes based on 8 1/2 x 11 inches. These can be full-size or a half, thirds or quarters of a sheet.

Adapt your flyer to your purpose: it can be a reprint of your ad that you hand out in your store. Or turn your circular into a poster or in-store display. Insert copies of them in shopping bags. Place them on counters, windshields and doorknobs.

P rint flyers on low-cost paper.

More *bon mots* from an authority on the subject, Jay Conrad Levinson, author of *Guerrilla Marketing*: "The main thrust of a circular should be a clear and simple offer—using a headline...get right down to the business of selling."

Checklist for Flyers

- Name, address, phone number
- Timely, irresistible offer
- Your business hours
- Credit cards accepted

Or:

- Interesting visual
- Curio headline or typography
- Timeless-appeal approach
- Popular-appeal approach

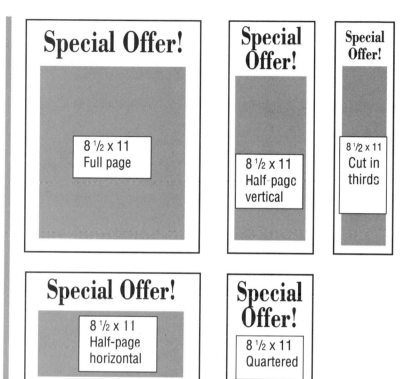

*S*tandard sizes cost less to print.

Figure 7-16: Design flyers for printing on standard 81/2- x 11-inch sheets.

Figure 7-17: Your flyer can contain a special offer.

Try a poster look
for your flyer.

What-cha-ma-callits, What-cha-ma-doodles, Thinga-ma-jiggers, Doo-hickies

Black Cow Hardware
125 Main St., Anytown
Open Mon–Sat., 9 am to 7 pm

If you know what-cha' need but don't know what it's called, we probably have it. Black Cow Hardware specializes in the hard-to-find, impossible-to-pronounce. What-cha waiting for? Stop by today!

Figure 7-18: Other types of flyers have popular appeal and are used as posters.

Novel Shapes

You aren't limited to squares and rectangles for printed pieces either. You can fold the piece in many directions to create different shapes. For example, you can fold a flyer for a charitable dinner into a triangular shape to simulate a dinner napkin.

Postcards

Postcards display their messages for all to see. Postcards save printing and mailing costs while attracting the attention of multiple readers, even the mail carrier. Readership exposure is high because people don't feel like they're violating anyone's privacy by reading a postcard. You also don't have to convince the recipient to open the envelope.

People peek at postcards.

The economies of printing and mailing postcards allow you to design an entire campaign instead of a one-shot mailing. The increased frequency results in greater response.

Include a good offer with an expiration date. Your postcard can be one panel only, front-and-back or a foldover design. The advantage of a foldover is that buyers can respond simply by folding the card in the opposite direction and mailing it back.

Consider using four-color postcards. Your local branch of a national printing service can print them in lots of 5,000 for $400 and also help you with color choices, design and typesetting. You can even put your newsletter on a postcard!

Checklist for Postcards

- An appealing offer with an expiration date
- A visible headline or visual
- Details that will ensure a response
- A call to action set in bold type
- Design consistency throughout your postcard campaign
- A foldover design that can double as the reply form

Figure 7-19: Include a good offer with an expiration date.

Use postcards to advertise special offers.

Figure 7-20: A postcard in the form of a foldover can serve as a reply card.

Card Decks

Growth in the card deck industry attests to the effectiveness of these little cards. Your design challenge is to fit in enough information on the card to encourage a response or sale.

Design the side of the card that appears face-up in the deck to stop people from flipping long enough to read your offer. Then, the design concept must continue onto the back side. This is where you close the sale. Tie your concept together using both sides of the card. They work as a unit.

You can offer one of three response options: print a business reply permit number so that your respondents don't have to use a stamp, request people to place a stamp, or request them to place the response in an envelope and mail it. The response rate decreases for every additional step you ask people to take. On the other hand, the quality of the lead increases for each step.

Card decks are most successful at collecting leads you can work from. Qualify your respondents. Don't mail back an expensive advertising package to all responses. Increase the quality of your leads by requiring people to list a phone number and place a stamp.

Collect sales leads with card decks.

Checklist for Card-Deck Cards

- Benefit-oriented, clear headline

- Good visual that backs up the headline

- Sell copy

- Request for an order or response

- Ample space for prospect's name, address and so on

- Uncrowded design

- Ease of mailing

- Postage requirement to qualify leads

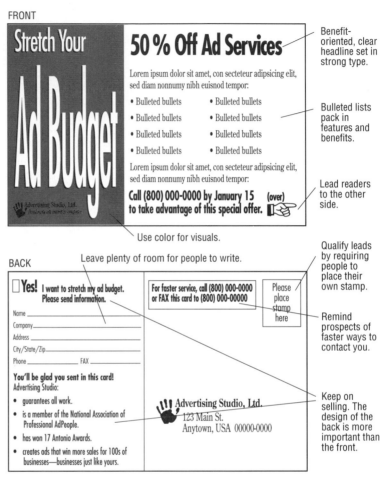

FRONT

Stretch Your Ad Budget

Benefit-oriented, clear headline set in strong type.

50 % Off Ad Services

Lorem ipsum dolor sit amet, con secteteur adipsicing elit, sed diam nonnumy nibh euisnod tempor:

- Bulleted bullets
- Bulleted bullets
- Bulleted bullets
- Bulleted bullets
- Bulleted bullets
- Bulleted bullets
- Bulleted bullets
- Bulleted bullets

Bulleted lists pack in features and benefits.

Lorem ipsum dolor sit amet, con secteteur adipsicing elit, sed diam nonnumy nibh euisnod tempor:

Call (800) 000-0000 by January 15 **(over)**
to take advantage of this special offer.

Lead readers to the other side.

Advertising Studio, Ltd.

Use color for visuals.

BACK

Leave plenty of room for people to write.

Qualify leads by requiring people to place their own stamp.

☐ **Yes!** I want to stretch my ad budget. Please send information.

For faster service, call (800) 000-0000 or FAX this card to (800) 000-00000

Please place stamp here

Name _____
Company _____
Address _____
City/State/Zip _____
Phone _____ FAX _____

Remind prospects of faster ways to contact you.

You'll be glad you sent in this card!
Advertising Studio:

- guarantees all work.
- is a member of the National Association of Professional AdPeople.
- has won 17 Antonio Awards.
- creates ads that win more sales for 100s of businesses—businesses just like yours.

Advertising Studio, Ltd.
123 Main St.
Anytown, USA 00000-0000

Keep on selling. The design of the back is more important than the front.

Figure 7-21: Dr. Jeffrey Lant, expert in card-deck design, advises, "Don't get cute. Get serious."

*S*hort one- or two-page newsletters are easy on readers and easy on you.

Promotional Newsletters

Providing ongoing information on technical products and services is a natural for a newsletter. The most effective format to achieve high readership and to make the project easy to implement on a regular schedule is what I call the "Quick and Easy" newsletter design.

These short one- or two-page formats are easy for busy people to skim while opening their mail, and they're easy on your time and budget as well. They're also aggressive advertising tools. Include order forms, reply cards, directions for passing along to other people and requests to add other names to the mailing list.

As you would with an envelope, place a small ad near the mailing area of your newsletter. Note how people are using your newsletter, and add graphic features that further encourage their direct involvement. Add check boxes near product articles if the newsletter is used as a direct-mail piece. In one of my newsletters, I noticed that customers were writing notes near the products telling their purchasing agent which books to buy and which ones they already had. In my next newsletter I added a check-box feature to accommodate readers who wanted to use it.

Checklist for Newsletters

- A teaser, ad or contents box near the mailing panel

- An attractive nameplate (the area containing the newsletter's name)

- A tag line or benefit statement in the nameplate

- Newsbriefs and short articles

- A minimum of three articles per page

- Product updates and announcements

- Organizational changes and advances

- Industry-related news

- How-to articles and customer testimonials or case histories

- Technical product specifications

- Call-to-action response information

- Complete contact information in the masthead

- An order form or inserted flyer

Figure 7-22: Include short articles and newsbriefs in your newsletter.

Figure 7-23: Note how people interact with your newsletter and provide graphic devices to encourage involvement.

> **Tip:** Deliver your advertising messages in the form of "news":
>
> - Pass along testimonials and tips from users, particularly about unusual ways they've used your products.
>
> - Report on product updates or changes and relate these to how the industry is changing.
>
> - Note anniversaries or milestones.
>
> - Mention awards and other recognition or comments from the press.
>
> - Use question–and–answer formats to discuss technical issues.

Reply Cards

*O*n your reply cards, list alternate ways you can be contacted.

Design your reply cards to return to your mailbox at boomerang speed. Present the benefit of returning the card in large type. Use an affirmative statement that includes the word "yes." Attract attention to your reply card by using visuals, benefit-oriented headlines and color.

Highlight the alternatives to mailing your offer. List your phone, fax and online numbers for people in a hurry (your best prospective buyers). Leave plenty of space to make it easy for respondents to fill in response information such as address, phone number and credit card or purchase order number.

Make the card easy to remove (if it's attached to another piece) and mail back.

Checklist for Reply Cards

- Affirmation of interest or benefit of returning the card

- Affirmation or benefit set in large, visible type

- Strategic use of color

- Illustration or photograph of product

- How to reach you, including phone, fax and online numbers

- Ample room for buyer to write

- Clear instructions for removing and returning

Qty	Title	Price	Total		
	Start building your resource library today:			Name:	
	The Gray Book	$22.95		Company:	
	Marketing With Newsletters	$24.95		Address:	
	Newsletters From The Desktop	$23.95		City/State/Zip:	
	The Newsletter Editor's Desk Book	$12.95		Phone: ( )	
	Editing Your Newsletter	$18.50			
	Looking Good in Print	$23.95			

Start building your resource library today:

Qty	Title	Price	Total
	The Gray Book	$22.95	
	Marketing With Newsletters	$24.95	
	Newsletters From The Desktop	$23.95	
	The Newsletter Editor's Desk Book	$12.95	
	Editing Your Newsletter	$18.50	
	Looking Good in Print	$23.95	

Shipping Charges: $3 for the first book, $1 each add'l book

Satisfaction guaranteed. Tax: OH & MO residents add 6%

Total Enclosed:

Name:_____
Company:_____
Address:_____
City/State/Zip:_____
Phone: ( )_____

Method of Payment:
☐ Check or Money Order ☐ American Express
☐ MasterCard ☐ VISA

Card #:_____
Expires:_____
Name on Card:_____

Ordering Made Easy!
Phone: (800) 264-6305 • FAX: (314) 647-1609
Mail: EF Communications, 6614 Pernod Ave., St. Louis, MO 63139-2149

Figure 7-24: Close the deal with a sales–oriented reply card.

INNOVATIVE APPROACHES

The list of possible ways to advertise is as unlimited as your creativity. For every business, there's a combination of approaches that work best. Experiment to find yours. But experiment in small-scale ways. Your laser printer and computer can help you create short runs for testing.

Stickers

How do you get your advertising message to your prospects at the exact moment when they most need your product? Stick 'em up!

Create stickers that customers can place in their home or office. For example, if you refill cartridges or provide other printer supplies, tell customers to place your sticker inside the lid of their printer where they can't miss seeing it. Another example: a plumbing business could distribute

Test your ad design in a short run.

stickers printed with the company name and the 24-hour emergency repair phone number for customers to place on the water heater, furnace and garbage disposer. A restaurant offering takeout or delivery could give customers stickers or refrigerator magnets.

Figure 7-25: Advertising on stickers and magnets helps customers reach you when they need you most.

Notes

Attract attention to direct-mail sales letter packages by sticking on a Post-It note. 3-M can print these handy stickers for you in sizes ranging from 1 x 2 inches up to 16 x 16 inches. The most economical sizes are 3 x 4 and 4 x 6. The price for printing 5,000 one-color 3-inch x 4-inch notes is around one cent each.

3-M can also print pads with your logo or sales message to give as gifts to your prospects.

The cost of printing Post-It notes is about one cent each, in quantities of 5,000.

Figure 7-26: Attract attention to your sales letter with a personalized Post-It note.

Advertising Premiums

Other gifts that will deliver your advertising message to a captive audience include coffee mugs, pens, notepads and T-shirts. Imagine the recognition power of your coffee mug sitting on a buyer's desk for all to see. Or your buyer's teenage kid wearing your premium T-shirt every day for a month.

Use the "poster formula," mentioned earlier: make premium designs decorative but simple, but include the essential information.

Advertising premiums keep your message in front of buyers.

Figure 7-27: When designing advertising premiums, follow the poster formula: headline, visual and response.

International Marketing

John Smith

Smith **Communications**
P.O. Box 126
(000) 000-0000   Anytown, USA 00000

Figure 7-28: Convert your traditionally designed business card into a mini–brochure.

MOVING ON

Your advertising designs have been hard at work in your ads, brochures, newsletters, postcards and more. You've created a lot of interest. Now potential customers are on the way to your store, trade show or meeting. When they arrive will they find an atmosphere consistent with your advertising image? The next chapter shows you how to make sure they do—how to continue advertising right up to the sale, and afterward as well.

CHAPTER 8

1N-STORE ADVERTISING

It pays to make your poster what Savignac called "visual scandal." But don't overdo the scandal or you will stop traffic and cause fatal accidents.

— David Ogilvy
Ogilvy on Advertising

*C*oncentrate on visibility when you're designing signs.

At last, all of your hard advertising work is paying off. Your potential customers are about to take the final step—entering your place of business. But you're not home free yet. When you and your customers meet face-to-face, your designs must go to work again in the form of in-store promotions: signs, posters, displays, packaging and shopping bags. These items do the follow-through work that cinches a sale—they can turn a "maybe" into a "yes."

When potential customers enter your business or store environment, this is the reality check, the real thing. Here they can see, hear, touch, smell and taste. This chapter focuses on these important advertising features that help you bridge the final gap between potential and real sales success. We'll talk about designing signs, displays, packaging and shopping bags and how your desktop computer can help you create them. Other in-store advertising media, such as multimedia presentations, your own in-store music commercials and hands-on displays are covered in the final chapter, Chapter 9, "Advertising of the Future."

To make effective and economical in-store advertising requires a bit of ingenuity. You're creating one or two signs, not printing hundreds of flyers or placing an ad that will be reprinted thousands of times. But the good news is that you have more freedom to work with color, size, shape and design.

Visibility—color, shape, visuals and key words—for in-store advertising materials will make the strongest impression and exert the greatest impact on sales.

BANNERS & SIGNS

The history of signs goes as far back as the history of business. Signs made up of symbols were used in olden times when the common people were virtually illiterate. Icons such as the red-and-blue-striped barber shop pole and the three golden balls hanging in front of a pawn shop effectively advertised the services offered within. Though most people are now able to read, effective use of symbolism still helps your sign communicate with busy passersby.

From peace signs to yellow ribbons—symbols are still with us.

Figure 8-1: Symbols and icons communicate to passing traffic.

Banners and window signs directed toward the street attract customers. Take advantage of your store location and its exposure to passing traffic. Exterior signs are a free advertising medium. If your business is on a busy street— even if you don't sell at the retail level— your window signs and banners tell people about your business. Use them to direct people into your store or create interest in your service or products.

A quick word of caution here. Most cities regulate the placement and duration of temporary exterior signs. Some require permits, and fines are steep if you hang a sign without a permit. Some shopping centers and landlords have additional restrictions on banners and window signs. Investigate the regulations before investing your time and money.

*W*indow space is a free medium for your advertising.

America on the Move
According to the U.S. Small Business Administration, each year 40 million people in the U.S. travel a total of 1 trillion-plus miles by automobile, and the number of people who change their address is close to 20 percent of the population. Exterior signs effectively reach mobile consumers.

Designing Banners & Signs

Banners and signs demand effective use of colors, shapes, visuals and key words. Design with strong, pure colors and bold sans-serif typefaces. Place no more than six words on a banner or window sign. Three or four is ideal. One element should dominate the design. People passing by must quickly get the message.

Treat your store window as you would a page layout. Balance shapes and colors, and choose colors that contrast with the background.

Figure 8-2: Simplicity gives your sign its advertising power.

*C*arry a camera in your car for quick snapshots of effec-tive sign designs.

Collect sign designs you like and make a file. Keep a camera in your car. When you see a sign that catches your eye, photograph and file it.

Sometimes you may need temporary exterior signs for special events. Hang banners for special events, such as sidewalk sales and open houses. Display your window signs year-round.

Tie sign design into your current campaign by using the same typeface, key words, colors and visuals.

*C*ontrast sign colors with those of the surrounding area.

Figure 8-3: To coordinate your campaign elements, use the same border designs and visuals in space ads and store signs.

Wave Your Own Banner

Good banner design involves the effective use of horizontal shapes. A horizontal orientation works best for text. Limit your visuals to decorative runners or simple lines. The design quickly gets crammed if you try to include too much information.

Use large text for your banner. If you include your signature, make it small. This allows you to size text as large as possible. Design with the high-visibility color combinations shown in Chapter 4. These are yellow on black, red on black, white on black, white on blue, white on red, black on white, green on white, red on white or blue on white. It's also important to consider how the colors you use will be affected by the area in which your banner will appear. Choose colors for your banner that contrast with surrounding elements.

Grand Opening

Figure 8-4: A text-only banner focuses on the message.

Figure 8-5: Banners can include simple graphics.

Many quick-print shops can print banners in black ink on a colored 18- x 48-inch paper (you'll usually have a variety of colors to choose from). A banner created for exterior use should be made of vinyl, or laminated for protection against the weather.

Window Sign Language

Coordinate window signs with your current campaign. Or perhaps window signs are your *entire* campaign. Possibilities for window signs include notice of a sale or the day's special, an announcement of special arrivals or a thought for the day. If you change your window signs often, people who pass by regularly are more likely to make a point of scanning your window to see what's new or different. Make it fun. Promote the same items seen in your ads.

Place your signs to face the majority of the oncoming traffic. Then switch them to face in the opposite direction at midday to take advantage of the afternoon traffic pattern.

Pay attention to what your signs say about you and your business.

Your Visibility Toolbox

Design your signs using your desktop-publishing and layout high-visibility tools:

- Attention-getting colors
- Dynamic shapes
- Dominant sizes
- Tall, dark typography
- Tilted text, lines or visuals
- Drop shadows

Figure 8-6: Side–by–side signs tie your message together.

Light your signs at night to broaden your reach.

When designing your signs, create sizes that occupy no more than 15 percent of the available window space. If you're using more than one sign, design each one to coordinate with all the others. Each can have a separate color but all should follow a common theme.

Consider nighttime lighting for your window signs, especially in the winter when days are shorter. This lengthens your period of advertising exposure.

Use visible colors, large type and graphic devices that attract attention. Tilted text, drop shadows and dynamic shapes also catch attention. For even more exposure and more impact, use side-by-side signs.

Note that people judge your store by its signs. The founder of a fast-food chain said he never put a "help-wanted" sign in the window. Help-wanted signs can imply that you're short of help or have a new, untrained staff. Signs spray-painted on kraft paper tell shoppers you're about to go out of business.

PosterWorks

If you create lots of interior or exterior signs, consider using PosterWorks. This program can produce a sign up to 10,000 square feet in size. You can either output the sign using your own PostScript printer or have it done by one of the more than 50 service bureaus across the country that print in full color on sheet sizes up to 3 1/2 x 12 feet.

T iling give you larger signs.

PosterWorks produces your design in "tiles" that you can print out on your laser printer, put together like puzzle pieces, and mount onto cardboard backing (using a glue stick) to create your poster or billboard. This program's tiling method is easier than the approach used in most publishing programs. It allows you to import your sign design from a desktop publishing program like Quark or PageMaker.

Figure 8-7: PosterWorks divides your composition into tiles.

Figure 8-8: Promote sale items in your window signs.

1n-store signs are your silent salespeople.

Sources for sign production are as high-tech as large-format service bureaus or as simple as your neighborhood quick-print shop. Many of these shops can now copy your standard-size original onto large-format 18- x 24-inch posters for around $5 each. They also copy banners onto 18- x 48-inch paper for around $10 each. For signs and banners, consider using the highly visible Astrobright colored papers, which provide greater visibility than white.

For design tips, study billboards up close. You'll notice that the visuals are stark and grainy; that's because they've been "posterized." Many photo retouch programs can do posterization, making screened halftones and high-quality output unnecessary.

Checklist for Sign Designs

- Color—Attractive combinations in strong, pure colors.

- Typeface—One or two simple, legible typefaces.

- Size—Coverage of 15 percent or less of the available space.

- Shape—Square or rectangular; rounded edges or cut-out polygons.

- Location—Eye level and facing the heaviest traffic.

- Message—Simple, clear copy stating one essential point.

IN-STORE SIGNS & DISPLAYS

*C*reate trade-show displays and kiosks on the desktop with PosterWorks.

You can include more copy on interior than exterior advertising media. Point-of-purchase displays can more intimately introduce products to your customers. Signs in the store can provide further information on products, overcome fears of buying and contribute to the overall image of your store.

Create point-of-purchase and in-store signs that repeat the messages of your advertisements. Lead customers to sale or advertised items. The better your displays, the more you will sell. Create in-store signs that function like salespeople. Direct customers and give more product information.

Tip: When using the four-color output from a large-format service bureau, ask for sample swatches of their colors. The colors you see on your computer screen may vary from the ones you see in the final print. Good communication with your service bureau allows you to adjust for the differences between screen colors and print colors.

Figure 8-9: In-store signs lead buyers to advertised items.

Many shoppers presold by advertising change their minds when they see the package.

Place signs in your dressing room or behind the cash register. Frame them or put them on easels. Reprint and frame copies of articles written about your business or products. Place them throughout your store, but particularly in the areas near your cash register.

PosterWorks helps
you make displays.

As seen in *The Anytown News...*

ANNUAL AD AGENCY SURVEY

Advertising Studio Chosen
Best Anytown Agency

Lorem ipsum dolor sit amet, con secteteur adipsicing elit, sed diam nonnumy nibh euisnod tempor inci dunt ut labore et dolore magna ali quam erat volupat. Duis autem vel eum irure dolor in henderit in vulputate velit esse consequat.

Vel illum dolor eu feugiat mulla facilsi at vero eos. Nam liber tempor cum soluta nobis eligent option congue nibil impediet doming id quod maxim plecat facer possum omnis voluptas.

Lorem ipsum dolor sit amet, con secteteur adipsicing elit, sed diam nonnumy nibh euisnod tempor inci dunt ut labore et dolore magna ali quam erat volupat. Duis autem vel eum irure dolor in henderit in vulputate velit esse consequat.

Vel illum dolor eu feugiat mulla facilsi at vero eos. Nam liber tempor

cum soluta nobis eligent option congue nibil impediet doming id quod maxim plecat facer possum omnis voluptas.

Lorem ipsum dolor sit amet, con secteteur adipsicing elit, sed diam nonnumy nibh euisnod tempor inci dunt ut labore et dolore magna ali quam erat volupat. Duis autem vel eum irure dolor in henderit in vulputate velit esse consequat.

Vel illum dolor eu feugiat mulla facilsi at vero eos. Nam liber tempor cum soluta nobis eligent option congue nibil impediet doming id quod maxim plecat facer possum omnis voluptas.

Lorem ipsum dolor sit amet, con secteteur adipsicing elit, sed diam nonnumy nibh euisnod tempor inci dunt ut labore et dolore magna ali quam erat volupat. Duis autem vel eum irure dolor in

henderit in vulputate velit esse consequat.

Vel illum dolor eu feugiat mulla facilsi at vero eos. Nam liber tempor cum soluta nobis eligent option congue nibil impediet doming id quod maxim plecat facer possum omnis voluptas.

Lorem ipsum dolor sit amet, con secteteur adipsicing elit, sed diam nonnumy nibh euisnod tempor inci dunt ut labore et dolore magna ali quam erat volupat. Duis autem vel eum irure dolor in henderit in vulputate velit esse consequat.

Vel illum dolor eu feugiat mulla facilsi at vero eos. Nam liber tempor cum soluta nobis eligent option congue nibil impediet doming id quod maxim plecat facer possum omnis voluptas.

Lorem ipsum dolor sit amet, con secteteur adipsicing elit, sed diam

Figure 8-10: Create in-store displays around favorable publicity you have received.

When you're visiting your neighborhood Kinko's to investigate their sign services, note how the store is organized with banners and in-store signs. You can learn about all of Kinko's services simply by looking around the store. Arrow-shaped banners suspended from the ceiling point to the item being promoted. Pick up a copy of their brochure. The design of the brochure follows the same look as the in-store signs and posters.

You can also use PosterWorks to create large in-store kiosks and displays. Using the large-format service bureaus, you can create full-color displays. Many service bureaus will cut out and mount your signs on foam board. PosterWorks includes templates from 13 different display manufacturers. These can also be used to create trade show displays.

Tip: To create visual interest in displays:

- Set typography to be readable from at least 10 feet away.

- Use contrast in color—bright against dark, warm against cool, pure color against gray.

- Highlight an object by placing it in focus against a film or shadow.

- Cut out an object and place it with open space surrounding it.

An excellent source of information about signs and displays is ST Publications, publisher of *Signs of the Times, Visual Merchandising & Store Display* and numerous books. The company is listed in the resources section in the back of this book.

Packaging can close the sale.

PACKAGING

Think of all the advertising effort that goes into getting your customers face-to-face with a package. And yet, statistics show that one-third of the shoppers who have been presold by advertising change their minds at the point of purchase. This proves that package design is vital to the effectiveness of your overall advertising efforts.

At the point of purchase, what's inside your package is secondary to the appearance of the package itself. It's impossible to overemphasize the importance of making the package appealing and interesting. Money spent on good packaging is good for your advertising efforts.

Design attractive packages by stating in bold, easy-to-read type the product name and the benefits of using it. From a distance, test your package design for visibility and legibility. Use solid colors in large areas and avoid screens. To make typography legible, use sans-serif type and avoid decorative typefaces. Show visuals of the product in use. Your package must convey a feeling of value and worth.

Figure 8-11: Create package designs that sell your product.

Another interesting statistic is that two-thirds of all purchases are unplanned; so your goal is to catch the eye of package skimmers, just as you do with newspaper ad skimmers. On the supermarket shelf, for example, a package has 1/25 of a second to grab attention. Set your package design apart from your competition. Use your own distinctive colors, visuals and typography.

Some colors are closely associated with types of products. Personal-care products use sans-serif type and cool or refreshing colors. Foods are packaged in warm colors. This practice is widespread. Originally it resulted from studies done by large manufacturers on the effects of color on sales. Assuming you don't have the budget of Proctor & Gamble, note trends in color packaging and copy them. Again, use your own distinctive colors but establish some general rules for your choices based on what others do.

While most campaigns last 10 to 13 weeks, package designs will stay around for much longer—usually from two to five years. If you need to design a temporary package, low-cost packaging methods include using gift bags, putting labels on plain boxes or shrink-wrapping the items. Note that in some cases custom-printed boxes are less expensive than plain ones.

Package designs are usually continued for two to five years.

Figure 8-12: For a low-cost packaging method, affix your own labels to ready-made bags or boxes, or shrink-wrap the products.

The Five Tasks of Package Design
1. Catch the eye with appealing color.

2. Evoke visual and emotional responses.

3. Use text, color and visuals to describe what's in the box.

4. Invite the customer to pick up the item and read the information.

5. Make the product look durable and easy to use.

Package designs can keep on advertising even after the sale.

Your package design will continue to advertise for you after the customer has taken the product home if you make sure the package is easy to open, handle, store and reopen. Reusable packaging, such as metal and plastic containers, can keep your advertising message visible for a long time, instead of ending up in the trash.

In addition, your package can sell your other products. I was thinking about this concept in the shower today when, low and behold, in front of me was a bottle of Suave shampoo (hey, I'm not rich). Printed on the bottle was a one-line reminder, "Try Suave Antiperspirant."

SHOPPING BAGS

Another way to keep your message in front of current customers is with shopping bags.

Shopping bags are walking advertisements for retail stores, restaurants, companies that attend trade shows and more. Your bags can be paper, plastic, canvas or vinyl. And you can increase your advertising mileage by including ads, coupons, order forms or special event announcements. Add longevity to your message by designing a canvas or vinyl bag that people find attractive enough to save and use for other purposes.

*D*urable canvas or vinyl bags lend longevity to your promotional message.

For special seasonal designs, particularly at Christmastime, choose colors that reflect the concept of the advertising; that can mean a simple one-color design or a four-color painting. For example, businesses that have a natural or simple appeal, like Eddie Bauer and The Body Shop, use kraft paper bags with designs in hunter green, harvest gold or autumn red to match their old-fashioned concepts.

Typically, shopping bags are designed with small type around a large logo or visual. Sometimes large display type replaces a visual. Most designs are square or slightly vertical and contain a border. Signature bags feature a prominent logo of the store or business.

Figure 8-13: The advertiser's logo is prominent in most shopping bag designs.

Mail in when
you run out.

Fresh Aire Cosmetics

Order Form

Product: _____
Quantity: _____
Name: _____
Address: _____
City/State/Zip: _____

Figure 8-14: Your shopping bag can serve as an order form for repeat purchases.

A "signature bag" is the most common shopping bag design.

When you're designing shopping bags, keep in mind the color of the bag you're printing onto. For example, when working with brown kraft paper, use ink colors that coordinate with the brown background, such as green, gold, brown, red and black.

Wear Your Own Sign

Every time you attend a business meeting, you wear a name tag. If networking is an important way for you to meet prospective buyers, you can use your computer to design your own name tag. Avery makes kits of labels to use with your laser printer. Include your name, company logo, product photo or a fun tag line that can serve as an icebreaker and help people remember you. Then run the labels through your printer, and whenever you need one, you can just slide it into a clear plastic sheath and wear it. If your name-tag design matches the business card you hand out, you've further increased your recognition power.

Open 24 Hours

For Your Convenience

For Your Convenience

OPEN 24 HOURS

Figure 8-15: Design exterior signs with large, strong typography so they're visible from the street. The design on the right can be read easily from a distance.

MOVING ON

Up to this point, we've been talking about advertising approaches—space ads, sales letters, brochures, signs—that have been around since the days of hot metal type. But technology is changing the way we advertise. With change, opportunity awaits those open to new ideas.

New horizons on the desktop include advertising via fax, multimedia and computerized bulletin boards. Ready yourself for a new adventure. It starts in the next chapter.

CHAPTER 9

ADVERTISING OF THE FUTURE

"What kills a skunk is the publicity it gives itself."

—*Abraham Lincoln*

Just as desktop publishing has encouraged and empowered you to design your own ads, other technology may soon expand your advertising capabilities.

Technology moves forward so rapidly that most of us find it a real challenge to keep up. It's hard to leave familiar, comfortable methods behind. Also, it takes a commitment to persevere until we absorb and master new concepts. And the final disincentive: it costs money to acquire the latest and greatest updates and technological innovations.

And speaking of costs, the price curve for any new technology takes the form of an exponential decay curve. Before you say, "Whoa, no math theory, please," take a look at Figure 9-1. It shows that when a new product is released it's relatively pricey. Once it has market acceptance and is mass-produced, the price plunges. For example, I spent over $5,000 on my first laser printer in 1984. A similar model now sells for under $1,000.

The newer the technology, the higher the price.

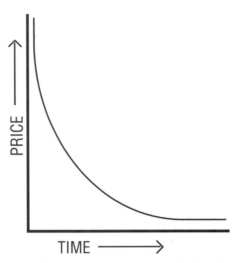

Figure 9–1: The cost of most new technologies is high at first, then it plunges and levels off quickly.

If you're like me, you wait until you see proof of how your business can profit from this new program or equipment before investing the time and money. For example, it makes no sense to create a multimedia presentation if a small-space ad sells just as well. Another example: the technology is available to put this book on disk and view it on a Sony DiscMan. But most people don't own a DiscMan. And besides, most of us are more comfortable acquiring information the old-fashioned way ("linearly") as you're doing now.

But it won't always be this way. Technology doesn't wait for us to catch up. As more electronic interactive media enter the market, we'll all be forced to learn in nonlinear form. We'll have to get used to the multimedia approach of pointing-and-clicking on the subject of interest.

So what's an advertiser to do? Take a practical approach: keep your eye on changing technologies and target audience expectations. But use the methods and media that work for the largest number of your customers.

Some of the techniques discussed in this chapter are expensive. Equipment for recording video is beyond the reach of many budgets. But advertising by fax isn't. So let's

Meet George Jetson...ta, ta, da, ta, ta, da.

A fax machine is a business-to-business advertiser's best friend.

start with fax materials. (This medium uses the desktop design tools you already have, and most businesses own fax machines.) Then we'll cover news releases on disk, customer bulletin boards, audio and multimedia.

JUST THE FAX

Fax technology has been around since the 1960s. The first fax machines weighed over 60 pounds and transmitted 10 pages per hour. Sending and receiving transmissions required two machines—one to send and another to receive. Today, lightweight, speedy fax machines are a business-to-business advertiser's best friend.

Just as frozen-food makers have adapted their recipes and added instructions for microwaving, your printed materials require some reformulation to make them fax-friendly. (But you don't have to worry about removing the foil.) And faxes provide advertisers with more visibility and convey more immediacy than mail. You can strike with advertising materials when the prospect is most interested.

*F*ax designs have certain requirements—but you don't have to remove the foil.

You want the design to be legible and inviting while making sure the piece doesn't take a long time to transmit. This saves money on long distance phone calls as well as being a courtesy to recipients.

Types of Fax Advertising

The pieces you design for faxing include cover sheets, brochures, price lists and order forms. These are sent one by one as requested, or in bulk via a broadcast fax system, or when a prospect calls your fax-on-demand system.

Broadcast fax systems store fax numbers in a database and transmit the same document to all numbers. It's basically like a bulk mailing, except that you're faxing the material.

Fax-on-demand (FOD) systems are used by catalog companies and space advertisers to provide brochures, price lists and additional information in response to inquiries. The way these systems work is that the advertiser lists the number

*f*ax-on-demand
systems work 24
hours a day.

people can call along with the document number for the specific product advertised. When a prospect calls, a recording offers options—for example, callers can request a complete index of all available documents or enter the numbers of particular documents they want sent to them. The inquirer uses a touch-tone phone to enter the document number along with the receiving fax number, then hangs up. Within a few minutes, the system sends the requested materials.

Need more information?
Call Advertising Studio's AdFAX
service at (800)000-0000 and
request document 2500.

Figure 9-2: List your fax-on-demand number along with the document number of the product advertised in your space ad.

Your FOD system can be accessed through an 800 number or a regular number. To avoid the cost of incoming and out-going calls, you can request prospects to call from their fax line. Once they enter the documents wanted, the transmission starts right away. If you use this approach, it's vital to keep documents short.

An alternative to purchasing the special hardware needed for a FOD system is to print a form that prospects fill in and fax. Then you return the documents requested. This way, you have the prospect's name and address for future mailings instead of just a fax number. Most FOD systems don't collect the requester's name.

Keep the fodder out of your fax-on-demand system by limiting transmissions to two pages per requested item.

Figure 9-3: Sample form for prospects to fax.

Fax-Friendly Designs

Your two goals when designing fax materials are maximizing legibility and minimizing transmission time. Because solid blocks of black or gray slow down transmission, avoid these design tools. Use 14-point or larger condensed sans-serif type (using condensed type allows you to fit more information on a page).

*f*ax-friendly type is 14 points or larger.

At first, a 14-point type size may seem too large to you. It did to me. But then I tested several fax-on-demand services. Not all used larger type. The special designs created for faxing worked much better than the ones that used mouse-sized italics in a serif typeface. Some surprisingly bad fax designs came from large, otherwise savvy, marketers.

> *While a 10-point serif italic looks fine on a printed piece...*
>
> ...a 14-point sans-serif typeface looks much better on a faxed piece.

Figure 9–4: Small italic type will be illegible on most fax transmissions. Large sans–serif type works better.

Because many logos include solid blacks, screens or detailed backgrounds, consider creating a special version of your logo for faxing. I discovered from a friend that my own logo doesn't transmit well. I removed the background behind the letters and created the fax version shown in Figure 9-5.

*B*eware of busy backgrounds.

Figure 9-5: A fax-friendly logo makeover.

Without the use of screens and solid blacks, you'll face the challenge of how to add "color" to your black-and-white designs. Remember that your other options for creating color include white space, type size, type style and leading. Use these design tools to create cover sheets, brochures, price lists and order forms.

The Facts on Fax Design

Here's a quick checklist to use when designing fax-friendly pieces:

- Use a sans-serif typeface for body copy.
- Keep body-copy type size at 14 points or larger.
- Condense type to allow more information to fit on a page.
- Minimize photos and screens.
- Use lines and borders to separate items.
- Simplify logos.
- Avoid solid blacks, including reverses.
- Avoid detailed backgrounds.

ƒaxes with simple, no-frills designs work best.

Fax Cover Sheets

When sending a fax to a company that's likely to be inundated with faxes, the cover sheet must sell the fax. Make it brief and to the point. Because many companies have strict policies on unrequested fax transmissions, be sure to note on the cover sheet that the fax was requested. Also, provide a number to call if the fax operator has problems or questions. Limit the number of pages per transmission to two plus the cover sheet. Consider using a half-size cover sheet to reduce transmission time.

Avoid using the predesigned fax sheets available in office supply stores and through some clip art manufacturers. These contain detailed graphics with blocks of grays and blacks that take too much time to transmit.

Follow your cover sheet with a brochure or a document index listing your fax-on-demand options.

!!! Advertising Studio, Ltd. *Handmade ads crafted by computer*	**IMPORTANT FAX MESSAGE**

To: _____

At: _____

Date: _____

From: _____

RE: _____

Memo:

Attention fax operator:

This fax was requested by the recipient. Please call (800)000-0000 if you have any questions.

Number of pages including cover: _____

Advertising Studio, Ltd. • 123 Main St • Anytown, USA 00000 • (800)000-0000 • FAX: (800)000-0001

Figure 9-6: A sample fax cover sheet.

Cover Sheet Checklist

- Recipient's name
- Recipient's fax number
- Date
- Sender's name
- Re: line (identifying subject of the fax)
- Memo space
- A note stating that the fax was requested
- The number of pages in the transmission

ADFAX RESPONSE SERVICE

Advertising Studio, Ltd.
Handmade ads crafted by computer

To: (000) 000-0000
Date: May 15, 1994
From: Advertising Studio

ATTENTION FAX OPERATOR:

This fax was requested by someone at your location.
Please call (800)000-0000 if you have any questions.

Number of pages including cover: 3

ABOUT ADFAX:

Advertising Studio's **ADFax Response Service** is designed to provide you with information on desktop advertising products and services. Available 24 hours per day, 7 days per week, the service is an efficient way to quickly serve you.

If you have further questions about the products discussed on the following pages, call our customer service department at (800) 000-0002. To place an order, call (800) 000-0000.

For a complete directory of ADFax options, call (800) 000-0003 and enter document number 0001.

Advertising Studio, Ltd. • 123 Main St • Anytown, USA 00000 • (800)000-0000 • FAX: (800)000-0001

Figure 9-7: Fax-on-demand cover sheets include more details on services offered. Also, the "fax requested" message is highlighted typographically.

A catchy cover sheet makes your fax stand out at the fax receiving station.

Fax Brochures

Fax brochures take on the form of fact sheets reduced to fit on standard-size paper (due to size limitations of the fax sheet and because the fax machine can't transmit folded sheets). The information can be formatted in a variety of ways—usually in one, two or three columns.

Organize and highlight the content using your desktop tools. Highlight with boldface type, and select typefaces in a variety of weights. Leave ample white space. Replace photographs with line art when possible. Remove any small type or detailed graphics—they'll just get muddied in the transmission and confuse your readers.

When designing a document index for fax-on-demand systems, add leading between the listings to make it easier for the reader to connect the document name with its corresponding number.

Use benefit-oriented titles.

Advertising Studio, Ltd.
Handmade ads crafted by computer

ADFAX RESPONSE SERVICE

DOCUMENT INDEX

You may request up to three documents per session. Use your touch-tone phone to select the desired document's corresponding number.

SPACE ADS

Small spaces that sell	**1025**
Display ad budget sheet	**1035**
Adv. Studio campaign results	**1050**
Ad insertion order form	**1067**
Ad design templates	**1075**

BROCHURES

Pamphlet-style design ideas	**1125**
Award-winning flyers	**1145**
Reply cards that work	**1156**
Content ideas	**1168**
Naming your brochure	**1175**

NEWSLETTERS

Content ideas	**1345**
Deadline-beating tools	**1355**
Nameplates for all seasons	**1367**
From ad to news	**1377**
Column guidelines	**1388**

POSTERS

Best-choice backgrounds	**1245**
Using banner services	**1255**
Windows that work	**1267**
Drive-by magic	**1277**

Advertising Studio, Ltd. • 123 Main St • Anytown, USA 00000 • (800)000-0000 • FAX: (800)000-0001

Figure 9–8: A document index for a fax–on–demand system.

*Y*our fact sheet follows the form of the fax sheet.

 **Advertising Studio, Ltd.**
Handmade ads crafted by computer

AdFax Response Service

NEWSLETTERS:

EDITORIAL PLANNING

Advertising Studio has ideas to fill your company newsletter for years to come. Here's a quick sample.

New Products

Lorem ipsum dolor sit amet, con secteteur adipsicing elit, sed diam nonnumy nibh euisnod tempor inci dunt ut labore et dolore magna ali quam erat volupat. Duis autem vel eum irure dolor in henderit. Lorem ipsum dolor sit amet, con secteteur adipsicing elit, sed diam nonnumy nibh euisnod tempor inci dunt ut labore et dolore magna ali quam erat volupat. Duis autem vel eum irure dolor in henderit.

Company News

Lorem ipsum dolor sit amet, con secteteur adipsicing elit, sed diam nonnumy nibh euisnod tempor inci dunt ut labore et dolore magna ali quam erat volupat. Duis autem vel eum irure dolor in henderit.

Industry News

Lorem ipsum dolor sit amet, con secteteur adipsicing elit, sed diam nonnumy nibh euisnod tempor inci dunt ut labore et dolore magna ali quam erat volupat. Duis autem vel eum irure dolor in henderit.

How-To Articles

Lorem ipsum dolor sit amet, con secteteur adipsicing elit, sed diam nonnumy nibh euisnod tempor inci dunt ut labore et dolore magna ali quam erat volupat. Duis autem vel eum irure dolor in henderit.

Your Editorial Board

Call Advertising Studio to make an appointment to discuss your newsletter further. We'll help you develop your full editorial schedule and budget for the year.

Call (800) 000-0000.

Advertising Studio, Ltd. • 123 Main St • Anytown, USA 00000 • (800) 000-0000 • FAX: (800) 000-0001

Figure 9-9: Brochure design for faxing.

Fax Price Lists

Often, prices can be included along with the brochure or fact sheet. In cases where many products, options and varying quantity discounts are presented, set up your price list in columnar form. Again, keep the type size to 14-point or larger. Organize the list into sections using white space or lines. Design your price list to match your cover sheet, brochure and order form.

Advertising Studio, Ltd.
Handmade ads crafted by computer

AdFax Response Service

Price List

Prices on certain projects vary. Please use this list for "ballpark" budgeting only. Call Advertising Studio at (800) 000-0000 for guaranteed pricing.

Space Ads

Copy Writing	$00.00
Design	$00.00
Illustration	$00.00
Placement	$00.00
Consultation	$00.00

Brochures

Copy Writing	$00.00
Design	$00.00
Illustration	$00.00
Consultation	$00.00
Printing	$00.00

Newsletters

Copy Writing	$00.00
Design	$00.00
Illustration	$00.00
Consultation	$00.00
Printing	$00.00

Posters

Copy Writing	$00.00
Design	$00.00
Illustration	$00.00
Consultation	$00.00
Printing	$00.00

Advertising Studio, Ltd. • 123 Main St • Anytown, USA 00000 • (800) 000-0000 • FAX: (800) 000-0001

Figure 9-10: Price list design for faxing.

Fax Order Forms

Keep order forms simple. The standard ordering information that you normally set in 8-point type must be enlarged. If you must include disclaimers and other details, place them on a separate sheet if the large type prevents them from fitting on the order form.

You may be surprised at how many people currently order by fax. I advertised in a card deck pack and was amazed to find over 60 percent of the respondents sending their orders via fax. The fax machine is a viable modern-day advertising medium.

Advertising Studio, Ltd.
Handmade ads crafted by computer

ADFAX RESPONSE SERVICE

ORDER FORM

ORDERED BY:

Name _____

Company _____

Address _____

City _____ State ____ Zip _____

Phone _____

FAX _____

SHIP TO:

Name _____

Company _____

Address _____

City _____ State ____ Zip _____

Phone _____

FAX _____

Item #	Qty	Description	Price	Total Price

Anytown res. add 5% tax _____

METHOD OF PAYMENT:

☐ VISA   ☐ MasterCard   ☐ Discover

Card # _____

Exp. Date _____

Signature _____

Shipping ($1 per item) _____

Total: _____

THANK YOU FOR YOUR ORDER.

Please fax this form to (800) 000-0001

or call (800) 000-0000.

Advertising Studio, Ltd. • 123 Main St • Anytown, USA 00000 • (800)000-0000 • FAX: (800)000-0001

Figure 9-11: Order form for faxing.

NEWS RELEASES ON DISK

Here's something that few companies do, but every editor I've mentioned it to raises an interested eyebrow. (If you've dealt much with the media, you know that editors' eyebrows are hard to raise!) When submitting desktop-produced news releases to newspapers, business journals and magazines, send them in printed form along with a disk. Place the text of the release along with scanned TIFF, CIF or PICT files containing visuals. Create two versions—one for the Macin-tosh and one for the PC. For best media relations, make sure all disks are virus-free.

*W*in media attention with news on a disk.

The trick to making a disk work for your media relations is to give your files accurate but intriguing titles, so that the recipient will be interested enough to take the time and trouble of firing up the computer and inserting the disk.

Use your desktop publishing skills and your laser printer to create an attractive label for the disk. Avery makes laser printer-compatible disk labels.

Figure 9-12: Disk label designs.

Peel-&-Stick Media Coverage
Create your own disk labels using your computer and laser printer. Include on the label:

- Your company name, address and phone number
- Your online name (most editors are online)
- The file name(s)
- The program used to create the file
- The file type and the format (DOS or Mac)

CUSTOMER BULLETIN BOARDS

Bulletin boards streamline ordering and customer support.

Over 50,000 public and private computer bulletin boards currently operate, and the numbers continue to grow. Approximately 70 percent of new bulletin boards are set up by businesses.

Bulletin boards provide business customers with an additional source for information such as brochures and newsletters and a place to ask technical questions and place orders.

Here, your fax design skills once again come in handy. Create and fax to your customers an instruction sheet on how to use your bulletin board. Include the modem settings, such as baud rate, that the customer will need to connect and communicate with your bulletin board.

Just today, I had what I call a "near tech" experience. I ordered slides of the cover of my book *Marketing With Newsletters*. Since the design exists electronically, I sent the file via the slide company's bulletin board along with my order form (and credit card number, of course). The slides will be printed and sent out tomorrow—the same day. The bulletin board saved me overnight shipping charges in sending the disk: it saved me a full day, allowing me to receive the slide via two-day service and still meet my deadline. In addition, it saved me errand time (and sometimes time is more valuable than money). The entire transaction was completed in about ten minutes right from my office! I will definitely use this service again—it's Slide Imagers, located in Atlanta.

Bulletin boards are multiuser or multitasking.

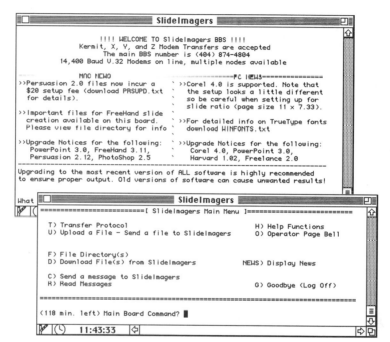

Figure 9-13: Here's the BBS I used to send my slide. They even provided online software news.

The hardware investment you'll need to set up your own bulletin board system (BBS) depends on the BBS software you purchase. Some packages, the *multiuser* bulletin boards, require you to have networking equipment and more than one computer. Others are *multitasking* and allow you to use just one computer. See the resources section in the back of this book for information on bulletin board packages for the PC and Mac.

The "Oldest Profession" Adapts, Too
When you start investigating bulletin board services, don't be shocked by the number of hanky–panky adult BBSes out there. As was the case with 900 phone numbers, the first marketers to discover the power of customer bulletin board systems served the "adult" market. In no way should this demean bulletin board advertising.

AUDIO RECORDINGS

How would you like to put together your own in-store music, complete with commercials for your products? The same tape could be used as background for telephone callers on hold. With clip tunes, recording and voice digitizing, you can record, edit and mix your own music on your computer. You can store it on disk or record the final product onto a standard cassette tape.

Digital sound and music takes the sound waves and converts them to numbers. This is the technology used to make music on compact disks.

If you own a Macintosh, you'll be happy to know that every Mac is equipped with the necessary hardware for audio production—a speaker, a standard sound file type and the hardware to digitize and play back sound. Newer Macintoshes even have an internal microphone. PCs can be upgraded with Microsoft's Multimedia Extensions for Windows 3.0, a compatible sound card, a microphone and an external speaker setup.

Audio software allows you to combine your own voice recordings with prerecorded music. Audio editing software available on the market includes Sound Edit Pro for the Macintosh and Wave for Windows for the PC. These and other products are listed in the resources section of this book.

With computerized audio you can adjust volume, and you can copy, cut and paste sounds. Music clips and sound effects are available for recordings much as clip art is for

Make your dream of becoming a disc jockey come true.

desktop publishing. Most sound libraries are stored on CD-ROM. The same audio technology is used to add voice-over narration to multimedia presentations.

Just as it's easier to start with graphics and word processing and then move into desktop publishing, it's easiest to start with audio then move into full multimedia.

MULTIMEDIA PRESENTATIONS & CATALOGS

Interactive demonstrations increase recollection.

Why would you ever want to get involved in anything so messy as multimedia? Because statistics show that it helps people remember you. People remember (short-term) 20 percent of what they *see*, 40 percent of what they *see and hear*, and 70 percent of what they *see, hear and do*. Interactive ads and point-of-purchase or point-of-information kiosks may dramatically increase your sales.

Although prices are still high and most of the software is created for either professional studios or hard-core hobbyists, multimedia will someday be on the computer of the average do-it-yourself advertiser.

Imagine being able to use the mass media techniques of television for niche marketing. Multimedia allows you to combine the targeting advantages of direct mailing with the strong attraction of video.

With the advent of AT&T's video phone, you could even have a service similar to a fax-on-demand system. Customers would call to see prerecorded presentations on your products—simply by selecting the number of the product on a touch-tone phone.

But getting back to the real world, current users of multimedia advertising use it to put catalogs on disks, for in-store point-of-sale (or point-of-information) presentations and for creating presentations to play at client sites.

Hardware needed to get into multimedia include a CD-ROM drive, an 8- or 24-bit video card, a sound digitizer and a video digitizer. In addition to the various other hardware tools, you need a minimum of 8mb of Random Access Memory (RAM) and a 150mb hard drive.

The least expensive way to get into multimedia is to add voice or music to the slide-style graphic overlays created in PowerPoint, Persuasion, HyperCard or SuperCard. These programs don't require all the extra hardware listed above.

*S*tart with slide–style graphic overlays.

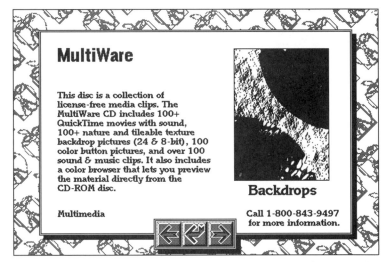

Figure 9-14: EduCorp's slide presentation showcases its products on a CD Sampler, a disk-based catalog; clip tunes accompany images.

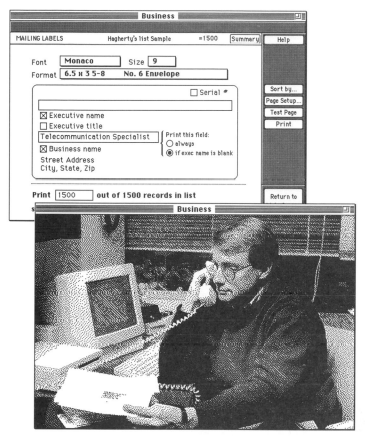

Figure 9-15: MarketPlace multimedia software shows how people use the product. Voice-over narration accompanies a slide-style presentation.

Make your mouse *roar* in the 90s.

UNTIL NEXT TIME...

The basics of advertising haven't changed since the "Roaring 20s." Though I was tickled as I was reading in old books about how magazines of the future would contain full color, I also thought as I wrote this chapter of someone seeing this 20 years from now and snickering, too.

Your challenge as a modern-day technologically aware advertiser is to see opportunity and adapt your messages to different media. Your computing power and skill will continue to grow and thrive and help your advertising win in the marketplace.

Reading this book is a good step toward broadening your ideas of how to use your computer to advertise (writing it certainly broadened mine). Our computer software industry is the most innovative in the world. New creativity software allows you to use your computer in entirely new ways. Next time you're confronted with an advertising challenge, ask yourself, "How can I do every step of this on my computer?"

The latest computerized advertising tools are now yours to use. So, grab your mouse and start advertising!

This book has truly been a joy to work on. My goal in writing it was to provide you with ideas that will help your business grow and prosper. If you have any comments, I would like to hear from you. Please send any ideas, comments, errors or omissions to me, in care of the publisher.

SECTION III

Helpful Resources

The best ad is a good product.
—Alan H. Meyer

SOFTWARE & SERVICES

He who dies with the most software wins! Okay, so even if you're not a software fiend, the right desktop tools make your job much easier. Here are the names and addresses of the companies that make the software we've mentioned in the book, plus a few others we either didn't have room for or have discovered recently.

PAGE LAYOUT PROGRAMS

Page layout programs vary greatly in price, approach and features. Some are designed for long documents, others for designing newsletters and brochures, and a select few for creating ads. See the "Advertising Software Features" resource section for a detailed feature listing on most of the following programs.

Aldus PageMaker 5.0
Aldus Corp.
411 First Ave. S.
Seattle, WA 98104-2871
(206) 628-2320
Mac, Windows

Aldus Personal Press
Aldus Corp.
411 First Ave. S.
Seattle, WA 98104-2871
(206) 628-2320
Mac, Windows

Easy Working Desktop Publisher
Spinnaker Software Corp.
201 Broadway
Cambridge, MA 02139
(800) 826-0706
Windows

Express Publisher
Spinnaker Software Corp.
201 Broadway
Cambridge, MA 02139
(800) 826-0706
DOS, Windows

FrameMaker
Frame Technology Corp.
1010 Rincon Cir.
San Jose, CA 95131
(800) 843-7263
(408) 433-3311
Mac, Windows

Microsoft Publisher
Microsoft Corp.
One Microsoft Way
Redmond, WA 98052
(800) 426-9400
(206) 882-8080
Windows

Multi-Ad Creator
Multi-Ad Services Inc.
1720 W. Detweiller Dr.
Peoria, IL 61615-1695
(800) 447-1950
(309) 692-1530
Mac

PagePlus
Serif Inc.
P.O. Box 803
Nashua, NH 03061
(800) 697-3743
(603) 889-8650
Windows

PFS: Publisher for Windows
Spinnaker Software Corp.
201 Broadway
Cambridge, MA 02139
(800) 826-0706
Windows

Publish It!
Timeworks Inc.
625 Academy Dr.
Northbrook, IL 60062
(708) 559-1300
Mac, DOS, Windows

Publish It Easy
Timeworks Inc.
625 Academy Dr.
Northbrook, IL 60062
(708) 559-1300
Mac

QuarkXPress
Quark Inc.
1800 Grant St.
Denver, CO 80203
(800) 788-7830
Mac, Windows

Ready-Set-Go (formerly DesignStudio)
Manhattan Graphics Corp.
250 E. Hartsdale Ave., Ste. 23
Hartsdale, NY 10530
(800) 572-6533
Mac

Ventura AdPro
Ventura Software Inc.
15175 Innovation Dr.
San Diego, CA 92128
(800) 822-8221
(619) 695-7891
DOS, Windows

Ventura Publisher
Ventura Software Inc.
15175 Innovation Dr.
San Diego, CA 92128
(800) 822-8221
(619) 695-7891
DOS, Windows

POWER WORD PROCESSING

Word processing programs have gradually evolved from being electronic typewritters to including such features as creating columns, importing graphics and rotating text. Though ad design requires more of these sophisticated features, these word processing programs will likely do the trick for designing simple brochures, newsletters and forms.

AmiPro
Lotus Development Corp.
55 Cambridge Pkwy.
Cambridge, MA 02142
(800) 345-1043
Windows

Microsoft Word
Microsoft Corp.
One Microsoft Way
Redmond, WA 98052
(800) 426-9400
(206) 882-8080
Mac, DOS, Windows

WordPerfect
WordPerfect Corp.
1555 N. Technology Way
Orem, UT 84057
(800) 321-4566
(801) 225-5000
Mac, DOS, Windows

WordStar
WordStar Intl. Inc.
201 Alameda del Prado
Novato, CA 94949
(800) 227-5609
(415) 382-8000
DOS

SPECIALTY PROGRAMS

The software industry continues to provide us with specialized solutions. Just when you think it would be nice if one of the tasks you have to do could be automated...poof!...out pops a solution. Here are some solutions that make specialized tasks easier.

Color Up!
Pantone Inc.
590 Commerce Blvd.
Carlstadt, NJ 07072-3098
(201) 935-5500

Provides predesigned, professionally coordinated color schemes to use in presentations. Color Up!'s color palettes can be exported into Aldus Persuasion, Aldus Freehand, Adobe Illustrator, Microsoft PowerPoint and Claris MacDraw Pro.

Certificate Maker
McMillan/McGraw Hill
220 Danieldale Rd.
DeSoto, TX 75115
(800) 442-9685
DOS

If you design certificates as an active part of your advertising, this package will make your task easier.

Easy Working for Windows Labels
Spinnaker Software Corp.
201 Broadway
Cambridge, MA 02139
(800) 826-0706
DOS

Customizes your mailing address to include graphics and a special advertising message. For all standard label formats.

PosterWorks
S.H. Pierce & Co.
Bldg. 600, Ste. 323
One Kendall Square
Cambridge, MA 02139
(617) 395-8350

All of the large-formatting tools you need to create posters, point-of-purchase displays, trade show exhibits and even billboards right on your desktop. You can create layouts up to 10,000 square feet and output them on a PostScript printer or have them produced by a PosterWorks large-format service bureau.

PrintShop
BannerMania
PosterMaker Plus
Broderbund Software Inc.
17 Paul Dr.
San Rafael, CA 94903-2101
(800) 521-6263
(415) 492-3200

The good news about Broderbund's software packages is that they are easy to use and include template-oriented options. The bad news is that fine-tuning—even adjusting leading and type size—is difficult to impossible. Most programs include clip art.

CREATIVITY SOFTWARE

Dig *way* back in your memory to Chapter 1 of this book. We mentioned using IdeaFisher as a way to automate brainstorming. Here's the information on IdeaFisher along with some similar products. All take a slightly different approach to creativity and problem-solving (probably because they all used their own software to develop the products!).

Decision Pad
Apian Software
P.O. Box 1224
Menlo Park, CA 94026
(800) 237-4565
(415) 694-2900
DOS

Lets you create "what if" scenarios for decision making. Works similar to a spreadsheet. Generates reports and graphs.

IdeaFisher Software
IdeaFisher Systems Inc.
2222 Martin St., Ste. 110
Irvine, CA 92715
(800) 289-4332
(714) 474-8111
Mac, Windows

"The Most Powerful Brainstorming System Invented."
Conceived and developed by Marsh Fisher, cofounder of
Century 21 Real Estate. Helps you generate ideas for marketing plans, ad concepts, advertising campaigns, new products,
product names and more.

Idea Generator Plus
Experience in Software
2000 Hearst Ave.
Berkeley, CA 94709
(800) 678-7008
DOS

Uses a problem-solving approach to guide you through the
brainstorming process. Focuses on problems and how to help
you achieve your goals by leading you through a series of
questions. Includes links to Decision Pad.

Inspiration
Inspiration Software
2920 S.W. Dolph Ct., Ste. 3
Portland, OR 97219
(800) 877-4292
(503) 245-9011
Mac

Idea development software that helps people plan visually.
Includes tools for creating mind maps, flow charts and
technical diagrams.

MindLink
MindLink Inc.
P.O. Box 247
North Pomfret, VT 05053
(802) 457-2025
Mac

Encourages users to take creative "excursions."

MAILING LIST DATABASES

These are the CD-ROM-based databases that we know of at this printing. We're sure to be adding more as this viable way to create lists takes hold.

American Business Information
5711 S. 86th Cr.
Omaha, NE 68127
(402) 593-4565
DOS, Windows

Information on over 9 million businesses on CD-ROM and through the company's online bulletin board system, Electronic Business Link.

MarketPlace Business
MarketPlace Information Corp.
Three University Office Park
Waltham, MA 02154
(617) 894-4100
Mac, Windows

MarketPlace is designed for business-to-business sales and marketing. It's a powerful resource for analyzing and identifying new market segments, generating data for research and surveys, and creating targeted mailing lists. CD-ROM required for use.

DATABASE & SPREADSHEET PROGRAMS

Assuming you've had your computer for a while, you probably already have a database for automating your mailing list. If not, here are the programs mentioned in the text of this book.

FileMaker
Claris Corp.
Box 58168
MSC 11
Santa Clara, CA 95052
(408) 727-8227
Mac, Windows

Lotus 1-2-3
Lotus Development Corp.
55 Cambridge Pkwy.
Cambridge, MA 02142
(800) 345-1043
Mac, DOS, Windows

Microsoft Excel
Microsoft Corp.
One Microsoft Way
Redmond, WA 98052
(800) 426-9400
(206) 882-8080
Mac, Windows

Panorama II
ProVUE Development
15180 Transistor Ln.
Huntington Beach, CA 92649
(714) 892-8199
Mac

MAILING SOFTWARE

Contact the information desk at the main branch of your post office for other certified programs that sort and code mail. According to Software Publishers (listed below), you can save up to 50 percent on a bulk-rate mailing by sorting to ZIP+4, bar coding, removing duplicates and verifying addresses.

AccuZip6
Software Publishers Inc.
P.O. Box 2705-253
Huntington Beach, CA 92647-0705
(714) 846-1908
Mac

Certified by the U.S. Postal Service, the program standardizes every address then adds carrier route, ZIP+4 and Postnet bar code to every deliverable address. Allows list merging and removes duplicate names.

ILLUSTRATION

Though my coauthor, Lee Wilson, can draw anything you can dream of, I've taken the approach in this book that most of you fall more into my category (stick-people specialists). The following programs help you modify existing clip art or draw simple to complex full-color illustrations.

Adobe Illustrator
Adobe Streamline
Adobe Systems Inc.
1585 Charleston Rd.
P.O. Box 7900
Mountain View, CA 94039
(800) 833-6687
(415) 961-4400
Mac, Windows

Aldus Freehand
Aldus Corp.
411 First Ave. S.
Seattle, WA 98104-2871
(206) 628-2320
Mac, Windows

CorelDRAW
Corel Systems Corp.
Corel Bldg.
1600 Carling Ave.
Ottawa, Ont., Canada K1Z 8R7
(613) 728-8200
Windows

CLIP ART

For my fellow stick-people specialists, here are some good collections of quality you can use "as is" or modify for your advertising visuals.

Ad Builder & SCAN
Multi-Ad Services Inc.
1720 W. Detweiller Dr.
Peoria, IL 61615-1695
(800) 447-1950
(309) 692-1530

This collection is an advertiser's dream. It includes frames, clip art and finished ad layouts for realtors, car dealerships and grocery stores. Available on disk and CD-ROM. Used by newspapers across the country, including the *Los Angeles Times* and the *Washington Post*. Organized and cataloged using Multi-Ad Search (see "Image Databases," and Multi-Ad Creator under "Page Layout Programs" in this section.

Art for the Church
Communication Resources
4150 Belden Village St., 4th floor
Canton, OH 44718
(800) 992-2144

Religious clip art, including special images for each season.

Artbeats
P.O. Box 1287
Myrtle Creek, OR 97457
(800) 822-0772

Backgrounds, dimensions, natural images, textures and beveled frames on disk and CD-ROM.

Arts & Letters
15926 Midway Rd.
Dallas, TX 75244
(214) 661-8960

Images include aerospace, arts and entertainment, cartoons, buildings and structures, holidays, household objects, nature, science and transportation.

ClickArt
T/Maker Co.
1390 Villa St.
Mountain View, CA 94041
(415) 962-0195

ClickArt series includes business, sports, transportation, animals, nature, holidays, symbols and more.

Cliptures
Dream Maker Software
925 W. Kenyon Ave., Ste. 16
Englewood, CO 80110
(800) 876-5665

Volume bundles include business, sports, flags and borders.

CorelDRAW
Corel Systems Corp.
Corel Bldg.
1600 Carling Ave.
Ottawa, Ont., Canada K1Z 8R7
(613) 728-8200

Includes sports, people, computers, business, landmarks, charts, animals, signs and homes—over 18,000 images on CD-ROM bundled with the illustration program.

Designer's Club, Electronic Clipper
Dynamic Graphics Inc.
6000 N. Forest Park Dr.
P.O. Box 1901
Peoria, IL 61656-1901
(800) 255-8800

Monthly subscriptions for images such as recycling, borders, nature and medical.

Gazelle Technologies Inc./EduCorp
7434 Trade St.
San Diego, CA 92121
(800) 843-9497
(619) 536-9999

Animals, camping, food, furniture, holidays, office, people, signs, sports and transportation. Humorous cartoons. On disk or CD-ROM.

Images with Impact
3G Graphics
114 Second Ave. S., Ste. 104
Edmonds, WA 98020
(800) 456-0234

Accents, borders, business, people, graphics and symbols available on disk and CD-ROM.

PFS: Power Album
Spinnaker Software Corp.
201 Broadway
Cambridge, MA 02139
(800) 826-0706

This graphic database package is bundled with 1,000 clip art images.

Volk Clip Art
P.O. Box 347
Washington, IL 61571-9982
(800) 227-7048

Subscription art service offering over 70 images per month including sports, seasonal, transportation, education, business and industry.

PHOTO RETOUCH

With the exception of Aldus Gallery Effects and Ofoto, these programs crop, flop, edit and change the brightness and contrast of your photographs. Photoshop and Aldus Gallery Effects let you give your photographs special effects. Ofoto automates the process of retouching color photos.

Adobe Photoshop
Adobe Systems Inc.
1585 Charleston Rd.
P.O. Box 7900
Mountain View, CA 94039
(800) 833-6687
(415) 961-4400
Mac, Windows

Aldus Digital Darkroom
Aldus Corp.
411 First Ave. S.
Seattle, WA 98104-2871
(206) 628-2320
Mac, Windows

Aldus Gallery Effects
Silicon Beach Software
A subsidiary of Aldus Corporation
3 Governor Park
5120 Shoreham Dr.
San Diego, CA 92122
(619) 558-6000
Mac, Windows

ColorStudio
Fractal Design Corp.
P.O. Box 2380
Aptos, CA 95003
(800) 647-7443
(408) 688-8800
Mac

Corel Photo-Paint
Corel Systems Corp.
Corel Bldg.
1600 Carling Ave.
Ottawa, Ont., Canada K1Z 8R7
(613) 728-8200
Windows

ImageStudio
Fractal Design Corp.
P.O. Box 2380
Aptos, CA 95003
(800) 647-7443
(408) 688-8800
Mac

Kodak PhotoEdge
Eastman Kodak Co.
343 State St.
Rochester, NY 14650
(800) 242-2424
Mac, Windows

Ofoto
Light Source
17 E. Sir Francis Drake Blvd., Ste. 100
Larkspur, CA 94939
(415) 461-8000
Mac, Windows

PhotoFinish
ZSoft
P.O. Box 2030
Shingle Springs, CA 95682
(800) 843-5514
Windows

Includes an AutoEnhance feature that adjusts contrast, brightness and color saturation automatically.

CLIP PHOTOS

When pricing stock photography, it used to be a painful process full of "youch," "what?" and "oooh." With photographs stored digitally, much of the pricing is becoming reasonable enough not to elicit such drastic reactions. Here are some of the companies offering high-quality clip photos.

CD Stock
3M
3M Center, Bldg. 220-9W-07
St. Paul, MN 55144-1000
(800) 447-1858
(612) 722-4895

Comstock Desktop Photography
Comstock Inc.
30 Irving Pl.
New York, NY 10003
(800) 225-2727
(212) 353-8600

Digital Photographics
Husom & Rose Photographics
1988 Stanford Ave.
St. Paul, MN 55105
(612) 699-1858

Gazelle Technologies Inc./EduCorp
7434 Trade St.
San Diego, CA 92121
(800) 843-9497
(619) 536-9999

Photo CD
Eastman Kodak Co.
343 State St.
Rochester, NY 14650
(800) 242-2424

PhotoDisc Inc.
2013 4th Ave., Ste. 403
Seattle, WA 98121
(206) 441-9355

PhotoLibrary
ZSoft
P.O. Box 2030
Shingle Springs, CA 95682
(800) 843-5514

DIGITAL CAMERA

Okay, it's in the software section and it's not really software. But I ran across this a few days ago and wanted to let you know about it. It's a portable digital camera that takes black-and-white pictures in 256 grays. The digital images are immediately captured, stored electronically and can be merged into photo retouch programs. This is a neat little gadget for anyone who takes photos often, particularly realtors, insurance investigators and even police.

Fotoman Plus by Logitech
Tiger Software
800 Douglas Entrance
Executive Tower, 7th Floor
Coral Gables, FL 33134
(800) 666-2562
Mac, DOS, Windows

Note: There are several other digital cameras available on the market, including Canon's Xapshot and Sony's Mavica.

IMAGE DATABASES

If you belong to my stick-people artists club and rely heavily on clip art and clip photos for your advertising visuals, sooner or later you're going to need an automated way to keep track of your collection. The following programs will help you set up a system.

Aldus Fetch
Aldus Corp.
411 First Ave. S.
Seattle, WA 98104-2871
(206) 628-2320
Mac, Windows

CorelMOSIAC
Corel Systems Corp.
Corel Bldg.
1600 Carling Ave.
Ottawa, Ont., Canada K1Z 8R7
(613) 728-8200
Windows

Kodak Shoebox
Eastman Kodak Co.
343 State St.
Rochester, NY 14650
(800) 242-2424
Mac, Windows

Multi-Ad Search
Multi-Ad Services Inc.
1720 W. Detweiller Dr.
Peoria, IL 61615-1695
(800) 447-1950
(309) 692-1530
Mac

PFS: Power Album
Spinnaker Software Corp.
201 Broadway
Cambridge, MA 02139
(800) 826-0706
Windows

TYPE MANAGEMENT, CREATION & LIBRARIES

It's not too far into our desktop publishing careers that most of us become type junkies. It's all about power (desktop power, that is). There's just nothing like the feeling you get when you select your "font window" and see a super-turbo-length list of typefaces to choose from. Here are some good sources for top-quality faces.

Adobe Type Libraries
Adobe Systems Inc.
1585 Charleston Rd.
P.O. Box 7900
Mountain View, CA 94039
(800) 833-6687
(415) 961-4400
Mac, Windows

Adobe Type Manager
Adobe Systems Inc.
1585 Charleston Rd.
P.O. Box 7900
Mountain View, CA 94039
(800) 833-6687
(415) 961-4400
Mac, Windows

Apple Font Pack
Apple Computer Inc.
20525 Mariani Ave.
Cupertino, CA 95014
(800) 776-2333
(408) 996-1010

Fontographer
Altsys Corp.
269 W. Renner Pkwy.
Richardson, TX 75080
(214) 680-2060

Microsoft TrueType Master Set
Microsoft Corp.
One Microsoft Way
Redmond, WA 98052
(800) 426-9400
(206) 882-8080

SPECIAL EFFECTS FOR TYPE & GRAPHICS

Though not recommended for every ad you create, on occasion you want to wrap type into a circle or create a page-jumping graphic. These programs can make your job easier.

Adobe Dimensions
Adobe Systems Inc.
1585 Charleston Rd.
P.O. Box 7900
Mountain View, CA 94039
(800) 833-6687
(415) 961-4400
Mac, Windows

Adobe TypeAlign
Adobe Systems Inc.
1585 Charleston Rd.
P.O. Box 7900
Mountain View, CA 94039
(800) 833-6687
(415) 961-4400
Mac, Windows

Make Up
Bitstream Inc.
215 First St.
Cambridge, MA 02142
(617) 497-6222
Mac

Pixar Typestry
Pixar
1001 W. Cutting Blvd., Ste. 200
Richmond, CA 94804
(510) 236-4000
Mac

StrataType 3d
Strata Inc.
2 W. St. George Blvd.
St. George, UT 84770
(801) 628-5218
Mac

TextAppeal
Spinnaker Software Corp.
201 Broadway
Cambridge, MA 02139
(800) 826-0706
Windows

ONLINE FORUMS & BULLETIN BOARDS

Log on to any of these bulletin boards and you'll soon have
friends in high-tech places. If you join America Online or
CompuServe, take advantage of their special forums on
advertising and desktop publishing. I was amazed by the
amount of help these folks were willing to offer.

America Online
8619 Westwood Center Dr.
Vienna, VA 22182
(800) 827-6364

Online community that has a special-interest group for
advertising, including information on software and
hardware.

CompuServe
P.O. Box 20212
5000 Arlington Centre Blvd.
Columbus, OH 43220
(800) 635-6225
(800) 848-8199 customer service

Worldwide service for business and personal information. Includes special forums for desktop publishing, marketing, graphics and small business.

SBA On-Line
U.S. Small Business Administration
(800) 859-INFO 2400 baud
(800) 697-INFO 9600 baud

Calendars of training programs, seminars, basic information on the SBA. Free of charge, 7 days a week 24 hours a day. Some reference information on advertising, marketing and business plans. Offers gateway to other online services.

BULLETIN BOARD SYSTEMS

If after reading Chapter 9 you're tempted to find out more about setting up your own customer bulletin board, here are some sources to try.

The Major BBS
Galacticomm Inc.
4101 S.W. 47th Ave., Ste. 101
Ft. Lauderdale, FL 33314
(800) 328-1128
(305) 583-5990
FAX: (305) 583-7846
BBS: (305) 583-7808
Multitasking
PC

PCBoard
Clark Development Co. Inc.
3950 S. 700 E., Ste. 303
Murray, UT 84107-2173
(800) 356-1686
(801) 261-1686
FAX (801) 261-8987
BBS: (801) 261-8976
Multinode
PC

Second Sight
FreeSoft Co.
105 McKinley Rd.
Beaver Falls, PA 15010
(412) 846-2700
Mac

Searchlight
Searchlight Software
P.O. Box 640
Stony Brook, NY 11790
(516) 751-2966
BBS: (516) 689-2566
Multinode
PC

TBBS
ESoft Inc.
15200 E. Girard Ave., Ste. 3000
Aurora, CO 80014
(303) 699-6565
BBS: (303) 699-8222
Multitasking
PC

Wildcat!
Mustang Software Inc.
P.O. Box 2264
Bakersfield, CA 93303
(800) 999-9619
(805) 395-0223
FAX: (805) 395-0713
BBS: (805) 395-0650
Multinode
PC

FAX-ON-DEMAND SERVICES

Current equipment for fax-on-demand systems is expensive and requires some customization and programming. Until the systems become more mainstream (it never takes too long in these high-tech times), consider using a service like this one.

Anserphone
Michael Holzberg
3925 N. I-10 Service Rd., Ste. 117
Metairie, LA 70002
(800) 872-8004
(504) 885-5300

Service bureau that provides fax-on-demand and broadcast fax services.

MULTIMEDIA

It's still difficult to separate the hype from the reality of what can truly be done with your existing hardware (always "the catch"), but multimedia is starting to come around. Here are some sources to call for more information for audio and audio-visual products.

Audio Recording & Editing

Alchemy
Passport Designs Inc.
100 Stone Pine Rd.
Half Moon Bay, CA 94019
(415) 726-0280
Mac

Audiomedia & Clip Tunes
Digidesign Inc.
1360 Willow Rd. #101
Menlo Park, CA 94025
(800) 333-2137
(415) 688-0600

Help hobbyists and professionals set up computer-base studios.
Mac, PC

MacRecorder Sound System Pro
SoundEdit Pro
MacroMedia Inc.
600 Townsend St., Ste. 310W
San Francisco, CA 94103
(415) 252-2000
Mac

Pro Audio Spectrum 16
Media Vision Inc.
47300 Bayside Pkwy.
Fremont, CA 94538
(800) 348-7116
(510) 770-8600
PC

SoundFX/CD, Loops, A Zillion Sounds, Grooves, AudioVisions
EduCorp
7434 Trade St.
San Diego, CA 92121-2410
(800) 843-9497
(619) 636-9999

Wave for Windows
Turtle Beach Systems Inc.
P.O. Box 5074
York, PA 17404
(717) 843-6916
PC

Multimedia Software

Action
MacroMind Director
MacroMedia Inc.
600 Townsend St., Ste. 310W
San Francisco, CA 94103
(415) 252-2000
Mac, PC

Aldus Persuasion
Aldus Corp.
411 First Ave. S.
Seattle, WA 98104-2871
(206) 628-2320
Mac, Windows

Aldus SuperCard
Silicon Beach Software
A subsidiary of Aldus Corp.
3 Governor Park
5120 Shoreham Dr.
San Diego, CA 92122
(619) 558-6000
Mac

Animation Works
Gold Disk Inc.
5155 Spectrum Way #5
Mississauga, Ont., Canada
(416) 602-4000
Mac, Windows

Curtain Call
Zuma Group
6733 N. Black Canyon Hwy.
Phoenix, AZ 85015
(602) 246-4238
Windows

Hollywood
Claris Corp.
5201 Patrick Henry Dr.
Santa Clara, CA 95052
(408) 727-8227
Windows

HyperCard
Claris Corp.
5201 Patrick Henry Dr.
Santa Clara, CA 95052
(408) 727-8227
Mac

Microsoft's Multimedia Extensions for Windows
Microsoft Corp.
One Microsoft Way
Redmond, WA 98052
(800) 426-9400
(206) 882-8080
Windows

Multimedia ToolBook
MediaBlitz
Multimedia Make Your Point
Asymetrix Corp.
110 110th Ave., Ste. 700
Bellevue, WA 98004
(800) 448-6543
(206) 637-1500
Windows

PowerPoint
Microsoft Corp.
One Microsoft Way
Redmond, WA 98052
(800) 426-9400
(206) 882-8080
Mac, Windows

Multimedia Upgrade Kits for PC

InterSept CDR
NEC Technologies Inc.
1255 Michael Dr.
Wood Dale, IL 60191
(800) 632-4636
(708) 860-9500

Multimedia Upgrade Kit Plus
Pro 16 Multimedia System
Media Vision Inc.
47300 Bayside Pkwy.
Fremont, CA 94538
(800) 348-7116
(510) 770-8600

Sound Blaster Multimedia
Creative Labs
1900 McCarthy Blvd.
Milpitas, CA 95035
(800) 998-5227
(408) 428-6600

Clip Media

EduCorp
7434 Trade St.
San Diego, CA 92121-2410
(800) 843-9497
(619) 636-9999

Digital video libraries include MediaClips, MultiWare, QuickTime Movies, ClipTime and more. Call for EduCorp's free catalog.

MacroMedia Inc.
600 Townsend St., Ste. 310W
San Francisco, CA 94103
(415) 252-2000
ClipMedia I

Animation clips, sound files, graphics and digitized video clips on CD-ROM.

Media Clip-Art
1879 Old Cuthbert Rd., Unit #10
Cherry Hill, NJ 08003
(609) 667-5044

$\mathcal{B}$OOKS &
PERIODICALS

Life is but an ongoing research project, and it's certainly most enjoyable when you have good sources. Here are some books and magazines we've run across that have made our lives easier.

BOOKS

Of course, I'm biased, but there's nothing like curling up with a good book on advertising to end a busy advertiser's day. The following books will help you expand your advertising realm. You'll be ready to jump out of bed in the morning and rush to your desktop computer to try out some of your new ideas.

Creativity

Goleman, Danie, Kaufman, Paul and Ray, Michael. *The Creative Spirit*. New York: Dutton Books, 1991.

Developed from the PBS series by the same name, this book explores the basics of creativity and applies them to children, adults in the workplace and the international community.

Ueland, Brenda. *If You Want to Write: A Book About Art and Spirit, 2d ed*. St. Paul, MN: Graywolf Press, 1987.

This book was originally written in 1938 and is still a true gem. Though its subject is writing, it's more a book about art, independence and spirit. Ueland explains, "Whenever I say 'writing' in this book, I also mean anything that you love and want to do or to make.... You must be *sure* that your imagination and love are behind it." Reading this book will change your ideas about the creative process forever.

Market Plans & Advertising Strategies

Antin, Brad and Antin, Alan. *Secrets From the Lost Art of Common Sense Marketing*. Clearwater, FL: The Antin Marketing Group, Inc.

The two brothers humorously share their marketing success in a straightforward how-to guide. The book is self-published and is a bit sloppy in its design, but the information is priceless. Presented as 12 secrets, each taking its own chapter, you'll learn how to study your strengths and use them to your marketing and advertising advantage.

Kaatz, Ron. *The NTC Book of Advertising & Marketing Checklists*. Lincolnwood, IL: NTC Business Books, 1988.

Painless reading from list-master Ron Kaatz, this book will help you focus on your goals and remember to list an expiration date on your megasavings coupon.

Lant, Jeffrey. *No More Cold Calls*. Cambridge, MA: JLA Publications, 1993.

If you like hard-hitting information, Dr. Lant gives it to you. *No More Cold Calls* includes all the ways to generate and close prospective sales, a helpful section on card-deck design and another section on how to screen leads.

Levinson, Jay Conrad. *Guerrilla Marketing*. Boston: Houghton Mifflin Company.

The book that made "guerrilla marketing" an office-hold word. Levinson covers market planning and programs, target marketing, direct mail, ads, signs and seminars. You can usually find it in the business section of most bookstores.

Levinson, Jay Conrad. *Guerrilla Marketing Weapons: 100 Affordable Marketing Methods for Maximizing Profits From Your Small Business.* New York: Plume Div. of Penguin Books USA, 1992.

Levinson lists often-overlooked low-cost methods for marketing and advertising your business. Keep it on your shelf and reread it from time to time.

McKenna, Regis. *The Regis Touch: Million-Dollar Advice from America's Top Marketing Consultant.* Reading, MA: Addison-Wesley Publishing Co., Inc., 1986.

The marketing man for Apple Computer shares his knowledge of product, corporate and marketing positioning and how to develop strategies and implement marketing plans.

Reis, Al and Trout, Jack. *Positioning: The Battle for Your Mind.* New York: McGraw-Hill.

This book is the classic on how to position your company and target customers. It's available in paperback in the business section of most bookstores.

Copy Writing

Bayan, Richard. *Words That Sell: The Thesaurus to Help Promote Your Products, Services and Ideas.* Westbury, NY: Asher-Gallant Press, 1987.

A thesaurus to help promote your products, services and ideas. Buy it *now*, and *save valuable* time. *You're guaranteed* to *love* it. (Sorry, just emphasizing some sell words.)

Provost, Gary. *Make Your Words Work.* Cincinnati: Writer's Digest Books, 1990.

A writing instructor and published writer, Gary Provost warmly shares his own hard-earned lessons of how to write "humanized" yet succinct advertising copy.

Design & Typography

Beach, Mark. *Graphically Speaking: An Illustrated Guide to the Working Language of Design & Printing.* Manzanita, OR: Coast to Coast Books, 1992.

An illustrated glossary of printing and graphics terms. Defines terms used in advertising, computer electronics, marketing, mailing, photography and publishing.

Beaumont, Michael. *Type: Design, Color, Character & Use.* Cincinnati: North Light Books, 1991.

This author's love of designing with typography shows in every example of this book.

White, Jan V. *Graphic Design for the Electronic Age.* New York: Watson-Guptill Publications, 1988.

Designing printed materials using your computer. Includes how to select and set type, work with visuals and create computer-friendly layouts.

Color

Baker, Kim and Baker, Sunny. *Color Publishing on the Macintosh: From Desktop to Print Shop.* New York: Random House, 1992.

Explains the technical details of taking your color design from the computer to the print shop. Discusses file formats, software programs, service bureaus and more.

Berry, Susan and Martin, Judy. *Designing With Color.* Cincinnati: North Light Books, 1991.

Shows how to use color to achieve the look and mood you want. Starts with an information-packed introduction to color, then moves into color combinations that show various moods—feminine, masculine, passive, active, natural, artificial, corporate, traditional, modern and more.

Binns, Betty. *Designing with Two Colors.* New York: Watson-Guptill Publications, 1991.

How to communicate concepts and feelings through effective use of two-color printing. Includes ways to mix two colors to achieve a multi-colored look.

Advertising

Burton, Philip Ward and Purvis, Scott C. *Which Ad Pulled Best?* 6th ed. Chicago: Crain Books, 1990.

Helps the business advertiser put layout, design and copy in perspective with each other. Sometimes the better designs don't pull better because of problems with the message. Highly recommended reading for all advertisers.

Adler, Bill. *Big Sales from Small Spaces.* New York: Facts on File Publications, 1986.

While the majority of books on advertising show you the famous full-page, megabucks ads, this wonderful book helps us regular folks write, design and place low-cost small-space advertising.

Ogilvy, David. *Ogilvy on Advertising.* New York: Vintage Books, a Division of Random House, 1985.

See how the big guys do it. The book includes sections on finding an agency job, how to run your own agency and direct marketing. Most examples are full-page print ads.

Wallace, Carol Wilkie. *Great Ad! Do-It-Yourself Advertising for Your Small Business.* Blue Ridge Summit, PA: TAB Books, 1990.

Entire advertising concepts, from business name, store decor, slogans, marketing plans, unique selling propositions, campaigns, media and more.

Watkins, Julian Lewis. *The One Hundred Greatest Advertisements, Who Wrote Them and What They Did*. New York: Dover Books, 1959.

Take a trip down the Madison Avenue of days gone by with 100 of the most successful ads in history.

Print Pieces & Direct Mail

Beach, Mark, Shepro, Steve and Russon, Ken. *Getting It Printed*. Cincinnati: North Light Books, 1986.

Tells how to work with printers and graphic arts services to assure quality, stay on schedule and control costs.

Bly, Robert W. *Create the Perfect Sales Piece: Catalogs, Fliers & Pamphlets*. New York: John Wiley & Sons, Inc., 1985.

Mr. Bly is an excellent writer who through this book informs and inspires the do-it-yourselfer. The book includes information on copy writing and how to choose which type of sales piece to use. It was the first time I ever knew that business books could be fun to read.

Floyd, Elaine. *Marketing With Newsletters: How to Boost Sales, Add Members, Raise Donations & Further Your Cause With a Promotional Newsletter*. St. Louis, MO: EF Communications.

Shows for-profit and non-profit organizations how to promote themselves. Includes information on newsletter content, writing and design, how to save money, survey readers and find subcontractors and volunteers.

Gosney, Michael, Odam, John and Benson, Jim. *The Gray Book: Designing in Black and White on Your Computer*, 2d ed. Chapel Hill, NC: Ventana Press, 1990.

This book offers you a wealth of great ideas for improving designs using black-and-white and the many shades of gray in between. Includes tips and techniques for screens, reverses, bleeds, drop shadows, 3D effects and backgrounds.

Parker, Roger C. *Looking Good in Print: A Guide to Basic Design for Desktop Publishing, 3d ed.* Chapel Hill, NC: Ventana Press, 1993.

How to use your desktop computer to produce attractive newsletters, advertisements, brochures, manuals and correspondence. Includes how to avoid the 25 most common design pitfalls.

Parker, Roger C. *The Makeover Book: 101 Design Solutions for Desktop Publishing.* Chapel Hill, NC: Ventana Press, 1989.

Before-and-after examples of how to use basic design tools to improve your printed pieces.

Parker, Roger C. *Newsletters From the Desktop: Designing Effective Publications With Your Computer.* Chapel Hill, NC: Ventana Press, 1989.

If you're using your computer to create your newsletter, you'll learn hundreds of practical ways for improving your publication—using layouts, typefaces and graphics.

Signs

Stevens, Mike. *Mastering Layout: The Art of Eye Appeal.* Cincinnati: Signs of the Times Publications.

Mike Stevens shares his experience as a sign painter and uses it to develop basic principles for sign design. Includes 84 examples of sign designs and lettering.

Ewald, William R., Jr., and Manelker, Daniel R. *Street Graphics and the Law,* 3d ed. Chicago: Planners Press, 1988.

A scientific look at how to design effective signs.

Specialty

Lichty, Tom. *America Online Membership Kit & Tour Guide.* (Mac, PC and Windows editions) Chapel Hill, NC: Ventana Press, 1992.

A warm and friendly journey into the wonderful world of online. You'll not only be demystified about online services, you'll plug in your sample disk right away and start your own voyage.

Rabb, Margaret Y. *The Presentation Design Book: Tips, Techniques & Advice for Creating Effective, Attractive Slides, Overheads, Screen Shows, Multimedia & More.* Chapel Hill, NC: Ventana Press, 1990.

This generic design guide reviews the essentials of creating good-looking slides, overheads, charts, diagrams and handouts. Alerts you to basic pitfalls of producing presentation graphics, and provides examples of how to choose the best medium and tailor it for your audience.

U.S. Small Business Administration. *The Small Business Directory.* Washington, DC: U.S. Small Business Administration.

Contact the SBA for a free copy of The Small Business Directory, which lists over 50 business booklets and products (most booklets cost around $3) at 800-827-5722.

PERIODICALS

You'll be amazed at how much the infusion of a few ideas every month will improve the quality of your work. So take a few minutes every month to skim through a couple of these magazines and newsletters.

Advertising Age
740 N. Rush St.
Chicago, IL 60611
(312) 649-5200

Tracks the happenings in the agency and big corporate advertising arena. Includes information on technology trends and how they affect advertising.

In-House Graphics
United Communications Group
11300 Rockville Pike, Ste. 1100
Rockville, MD 20852-3030
(301) 816-8950
(800) 929-4824

Concise, well-written monthly newsletter articles, including lots of makeovers and visuals, cover design techniques.

Inc.
P.O. Box 54129
Boulder, CO 80322
(303) 447-9330
(800) 288-7805

Great for small- to medium-size businesses, *Inc.'s* monthly issues cover marketing approaches and successes along with general management concerns.

Newsletter News: Ideas & Inspiration for Promoters & Editors
EF Communications
6614 Pernod Ave.
St. Louis, MO 63139
(314) 647-6788

This bimonthly publication focuses on newsletters but includes promotions and advertising. This is my favorite newsletter of all (okay, it's my newsletter).

Online Access
Chicago Fine Print
920 N. Franklin St., Ste. 203
Chicago, IL 60610
(312) 573-1700
(800) 366-6336

Published eight times per year. Includes BBS directory and product information.

Publish!
Integrated Media, Inc.
P.O. Box 5039
Brentwood, TN 37024
(800) 685-3435

Covers design techniques along with the latest hardware and software products for the desktop publishing market. Published monthly.

Signs of the Times
ST Publications
407 Gilbert Ave.
Cincinnati, OH 45202
(513) 421-2050
(800) 925-1110

The international magazine of signs and corporate graphics.

VM&SD
ST Publications
407 Gilbert Ave.
Cincinnati, OH 45202
(513) 421-2050

A monthly magazine of visual merchandising and store design.

Who's Mailing What
401 N. Broad St.
Philadelphia, PA 19108
(215) 238-5300

A pricey newsletter discussing up-to-date direct mail successes and failures.

ASSOCIATIONS, CONSULTANTS & TRAINING

If you need the face-to-face contact that books and magazines don't (yet) provide, here's a list of associations, consultants and other sources for information and training.

ASSOCIATIONS

The following associations help advertisers and retailers with their promotions. Some also provide conferences, training and/or other resources.

Direct Marketing Association
11 West 42nd St.
New York, NY 10036-8096
(212) 768-7277

National Retail Merchants Association
National Retail Federation
Sales Promotion Division
100 W. 31st St.
New York, NY 10001
(212) 631-7400

Annually publishes an advertising planning book containing charts, graphs, calendars and other information.

Point-of-Purchase Advertising Institute, Inc.
66 N. Brunt St.
Englewood, NJ 07631
(201) 894-8899

Retail Council of Canada
210 Dundas St. W, Ste. 600
Toronto, Ont., M5G 2E8
Canada

U.S. Small Business Administration
Small Business Answer Desk
401 Third St., SW
Washington, DC 20416
(800) 827-5722

Provides information to help small businesses "get started and grow strong": starting a business, defining a market, financing, counseling and training, management and marketing. (See "SCORE" in this section under "Advertising Consultants" and "SBA On-Line" in the "Software & Services" section.

Yellow Pages Publishers Association
340 E. Big Beaver Rd., 5th floor
Troy, MI 48083
(313) 680-8880
(800) 841-0639

ADVERTISING CONSULTANTS

Here are some top-notch advertising folks I've met while writing this book. Most of these professionals answer their own phones and are approachable as well as knowledgeable.

EasyCom
1032 61st St.
Downers Grove, IL 60516
(708) 969-1441
FAX (708) 515-8092
CompuServe: 76703,575

Technologies education and consulting services. EasyCom helps companies select and use computers for marketing and public relations.

Maurice Julien
Marketing Strategies
3706 N. Ocean Blvd., Ste. 303
Ft. Lauderdale, FL 33308
(305) 561-7505

Helps businesses of all sizes with market planning and implementation.

Dr. Jeffrey Lant
Publisher of the Sales & Marketing SuccessDek
50 Follen St., #507
Cambridge, MA 02138
(617) 547-6372

Expert in card deck design. Will send details on his card deck upon request. (See Dr. Lant's *No More Cold Calls*, listed in the "Books & Periodicals" section.)

Ivan Levison
Ivan Levison & Associates
14 Los Cerros Dr.
Greenbrae, CA 94904-1157
(415) 461-0672

Freelance advertising and direct-mail copy writing.

Gloria Moore
G&M Marketing Services
1933 Port Bishop Pl.
Newport Beach, CA 92660
(714) 640-0334

Complete marketing & communications. Helps merchants associations with special events, including signs.

Polly Pattison
5092 Kingscross Rd.
Westminster, CA 92683
(714) 894-8143

Publication design training and consultant.

Sheri Rosen
Consult Rosen
67112 Emerson St.
Mandeville, LA 70448
(504) 898-0904

Advertising, marketing, technical communications copy writer.

SCORE (Service Corps of Retired Executives)
U.S. Small Business Administration
Small Business Answer Desk
409 Third St., SW
Washington, DC 20416
(800) 827-5722

Offers free expert business management consultation. 13,000 volunteer counselors, who average 35 years' experience, are available from nearly 800 offices nationwide. Contact your local SBA, the SBA On-Line bulletin board (listed in "Software & Services") or the Small Business Answer Desk for more information.

Telesaurus Corporation
21832 Green Hill Rd.
Farmington Hills, MI 48335
(313) 477-0067
BBS: (313) 447-7351

Provides consultation; resells bulletin board software.

Bob Westenburg
95 Devil's Kitchen Dr.
Sedona, AZ 86351
(602) 284-1111

Writes a monthly newsletter called IMP printed on a 4" x 6" postcard. Call Bob to find out how he can customize IMP as a marketing tool for your business—he'll send a free copy.

TRAINING

Ask these companies to let you know when their seminars are scheduled in your area.

Dynamic Graphics Educational Foundation
6000 N. Forest Park Dr.
Peoria, IL 61614
(309) 688-8800
(800) 255-8800

Multimedia and desktop design courses.

Eastman Kodak's Center for Creative Imaging
Eastman Kodak Co.
343 State St.
Rochester, NY 14650
(800) 242-2424

Offers courses in multimedia production including design, video tools and corporate audiovisual presentations.

Padgett-Thompson
11221 Roe Ave.
Leawood, KS 66211
(913) 491-2700
(800) 255-4141

Courses on desktop publishing.

Thunder Lizard Productions
1619 8th Ave. N.
Seattle, WA 98109
(206) 285-0308

Promotional Perspectives
1829 W. Stadium Blvd., Ste. 101
Ann Arbor, MI 48103
(313) 994-0007

Courses on desktop publishing.

CATALOGS & PRINT SERVICES

NEAT CATALOGS FOR DESKTOP ADVERTISERS

Good software and paper catalogs keep you up-to-date on the desktop publishing industry without having to pay for a computer magazine. The following catalogs provide quality products and good service.

Avery's Laser Product Catalog
20955 Pathfinder Rd.
Diamond Bar, CA 91765
(909) 869-7711
(800) 252-8379

Includes name badge kits along with labels for disks, audio and video tapes, envelopes and binder tabs.

EduCorp
7434 Trade St.
San Diego, CA 92121
(619) 536-9999
(800) 843-9497

Includes CD-ROM bundles including encyclopedias, clip art, clip photos, multimedia sounds and animations, games, books and lots more fun stuff.

Pantone Color System Guide
Pantone, Inc.
590 Commerce Blvd.
Carlstadt, NJ 07072-3098
(201) 935-5500
(800) 222-1149

Here's your source for Pantone color swatch and color matching guides.

PaperCatalog
PaperDirect
201 Chubb Ave.
Lyndhurst, NJ 07071
(800) 272-7377

Resellers of papers for brochures, letterheads, business cards and other company communications. They also sell accompanying templates on disk for Quark, PageMaker, Microsoft Word, WordPerfect and other desktop publishing programs.

Queblo Images
1000 Florida Ave.
Hagerstown, MD 21741
(301) 739-4487
(800) 523-9080

Preprinted papers for laser printers and photocopiers including full-color shells for brochures, newsletters, envelopes, business cards and certificates.

Sales Promotion Today
Nelson Marketing
210 Commerce St.
P.O. Box 320
Oshkosh, WI 54902-0320
(414) 236-7272
(800) 722-5203

Helpful information on how to use premiums, such as bags, mugs, hats, pens, etc., to advertise your business.

Tiger Software
800 Douglas Entrance
Executive Tower, 7th Floor
Coral Gables, FL 33134
(800) 666-2562

This catalog takes an informative approach to selling multi-media and CD-ROM-based products. Each page describes the products and how to use them. Includes hardware products such as CD-ROM drives, modems, speakers, scanners and more.

The Working Library
ST Publications
407 Gilbert Ave.
Cincinnati, OH 45202
(513) 421-2050
(800) 925-1110

A collection of books and videos helpful to retailers. Includes information on signs, displays, merchandising and silk-screening.

PRINTERS

Here are the printing services mentioned in the chapters of this book, along with two more that accept files on disk for printing.

Kinko's
(Many locations)
(800) 743-2679

Color copies, oversized posters, banners. Most university areas have a Kinko's close by. If not, call the toll-free number above for a Kinko's near you.

Post-It Printing
3M
1650 Tower Blvd.
N. Mankato, MN 56003
(800) 328-2407

Slide Imagers
22 Seventh St., NE
Atlanta, GA 30308
(404) 874-6740
(800) 232-5411

Output for full-color slides and overhead transparencies.

Sonic Graphic Systems
1113 Union Blvd.
Allentown, PA 18103
Easton, PA 18042
(215) 437-1000
(800) 899-2595

Accepts electronic files on disk and provides bulletin board to modem files. Call for samples and current pricing on four-color printing. Also offers a guide to electronic imaging and printing on disk, which tells you how to send files and work with service bureaus and printers.

U.S. Press
1628A James P. Rodgers Dr.
Valdosta, GA 31601
(912) 244-5634
(800) 227-7377

Offers competitive prices on four-color printing of postcards, brochures and posters. Accepts files on disk from most desktop publishing programs including PageMaker and Quark.

ADVERTISING SOFTWARE FEATURES

The desktop publishing software business is very competitive, and the game of one-upmanship never ends. As certain popular packages add helpful features, the rest follow quickly. This list is as accurate as possible. But for up-to-the-minute information, you can contact any of the software publishers listed in "Software & Services" about features of a particular program you're thinking of buying.

Note that almost all desktop publishing programs require you to have a powerful desktop computer. If you're in the market to buy a PC or compatible and plan on running Windows, buy a 486 machine with at least 8mb of memory and a speed of 66mHz. If you're using or planning to buy a Macintosh, buy or upgrade your computer to at least 8mb of RAM and use System 7.1. This will require a Macintosh SE or better. For either type of computer, a hard disk size of around 200mb will come in handy.

Note that you can usually find a "street price" much lower than the prices given here. Use these list prices for comparison only and check direct-mail companies' ads in the popular computing magazines for competitive prices.

General

Program name:	**Express Publisher**
Version #:	3.0
Operating system:	DOS
Object-oriented or pasteboard format?	object
Disk space required for program & accessories:	12mb available space
RAM required:	560K
List price:	$99

Style Sheets & Templates

Style sheets:	yes
Export style sheets:	yes
Save as template:	yes
Includes templates:	yes
View as thumbnails:	no

Color & Output

Spot color:	no
Includes Pantone Color Picker:	no
Ability to mix two colors:	no
Process color:	no
Trapping:	no
Output resolution set by the program:	yes
Halftone screens set by program:	no
Accepts color-separated images:	yes
Maximum page size:	11" x 14"
Save page as EPS or print to disk:	yes
Create font lists for service bureau:	no
Supports imagesetters:	yes

Text

Type-size increments:	1 point
Minimum/maximum type sizes:	6-500
Horizontal type scaling:	yes
Minimum/maximum scaling:	20-999%
Automatic fractions:	no
Kerning & tracking support:	yes

Adjust spacing between paragraphs:	yes
Automatic drop caps:	no
Text wrap:	yes
Irregular-shape text wrap:	yes
Rotate text:	yes
Spell checker:	yes
Thesaurus:	no
Search/Replace:	no

Graphics

File formats for imported images:	TIF, PCX, GIF, MacPaint, NAM, IMG, EPS, CGM
Align objects:	yes
Center graphics:	yes
Automatic drop shadow:	no
Specify custom line weights:	yes
Coupon borders:	yes
Border styles:	yes
Round corners of boxes:	yes
Rotate graphics:	yes
Flip graphics horizontal:	yes
Flip graphics vertical:	yes
Group text and graphics:	yes
Freehand drawing tool:	no
Polygons (starbursts, etc.):	yes
Automatic starbursts, triangles:	yes
Graduated fills:	no
Radial fills:	no
Library feature:	thru subdirectories in DOS

Notable additional features: TextEffects type manipulation package included with Express Publisher for DOS. Onscreen layout advice is also included from Roger Parker's Layout Advisor.

General

Program name:	**Express Publisher**
Version #:	1.02
Operating system:	Windows
Object-oriented or pasteboard format:	object
Disk space required for program & accessories:	8mb
RAM required:	2-3mb
List price:	$99

Style Sheets & Templates

Style sheets:	yes
Export style sheets:	yes
Save as template:	yes
Includes templates:	yes
View as thumbnails:	yes

Color & Output

Spot color:	yes
Includes Pantone Color Picker:	no
Ability to mix two colors:	no
Process color:	no
Trapping:	no
Output resolution set by the program:	no
Halftone screens set by program:	no
Accepts color-separated images:	yes
Maximum page size:	5' x 5'
Save page as EPS or print to disk:	yes
Create font lists for service bureau:	no
Supports imagesetters:	yes

Text

Type-size increments:	.1 point
Minimum/maximum type sizes:	1 to 1,024 points
Horizontal type scaling:	yes
Minimum/maximum scaling:	unlimited
Automatic fractions:	no
Kerning & tracking support:	yes
Adjust spacing between paragraphs:	yes

Automatic drop caps:	no
Text wrap:	yes
Irregular-shape text wrap:	depends on graphic
Rotate text:	yes
Spell checker:	yes
Thesaurus:	no
Search/Replace:	yes

Graphics

File formats for imported images:	TIF, PCX, CGM, BMP, DRW, WMF, EPS
Align objects:	yes
Center graphics:	yes
Automatic drop shadow:	yes
Specify custom line weights:	in .1-point increments
Coupon borders:	yes
Border styles:	yes
Round corners of boxes:	yes
Rotate graphics:	yes
Flip graphics horizontal:	yes
Flip graphics vertical:	yes
Group text and graphics:	yes
Freehand drawing tool:	no
Polygons (starbursts, etc.):	yes
Automatic starbursts, triangles:	yes
Graduated fills:	no
Radial fills:	no
Library feature:	no

Notable additional features: Included in the package you'll find TextAppeal type manipulation software that allows users to curve, distort, give perspective to and add backgrounds and textures to type.

General

Program name:	**FrameMaker**
Version #:	3.0.1
Operating system:	Mac, Windows
Object-oriented or pasteboard format:	object
Disk space required for program & accessories:	15mb
RAM required:	2-4mb
List price:	$795

Style Sheets & Templates

Style sheets:	yes
Export style sheets:	yes
Save as template:	yes
Includes templates:	yes
View as thumbnails:	yes

Color & Output

Spot color:	yes
Includes Pantone Color Picker:	no
Ability to mix two colors:	no
Process color:	no
Trapping:	no
Output resolution set by the program:	set by printer
Halftone screens set by program:	no
Accepts color-separated images:	yes
Maximum page size:	40" x 40"
Save page as EPS or print to disk:	yes
Create font lists for service bureau:	no
Supports imagesetters:	yes

Text

Type-size increments:	.1 point
Minimum/maximum type sizes:	2-400 points
Horizontal type scaling:	no
Minimum/maximum scaling:	equation editor
Automatic fractions:	yes
Kerning & tracking support:	yes
Adjust spacing between paragraphs:	yes

Automatic drop caps:	no
Text wrap:	no
Irregular-shape text wrap:	no
Rotate text:	90° increments
Spell checker:	yes
Thesaurus:	no
Search/Replace:	yes

Graphics

File formats for imported images:	TIF, PICT, EPS, Windows-supported formats
Align objects:	yes
Center graphics:	yes
Automatic drop shadow:	no
Specify custom line weights:	yes
Coupon borders:	yes
Border styles:	yes
Round corners of boxes:	yes
Rotate graphics:	90° increments
Flip graphics horizontal:	yes
Flip graphics vertical:	yes
Group text and graphics:	yes
Freehand drawing tool:	yes
Polygons (starbursts, etc.):	yes
Automatic starbursts, triangles:	no
Graduated fills:	no
Radial fills:	no
Library feature:	no

Notable additional features: This program is designed to create large documents such as books, reports and manuals. It's used extensively by large corporations, universities and government agencies.

General

Program name:	**Microsoft Publisher**
Version #:	2.0
Operating system:	DOS, Windows
Object-oriented or pasteboard format:	pasteboard
Disk space required for program & accessories:	6-13mb
RAM required:	2-4mb
List price:	$139

Style Sheets & Templates

Style sheets:	yes
Export style sheets:	yes
Save as template:	yes
Includes templates:	yes (35)
View as thumbnails:	no

Color & Output

Spot color:	no
Includes Pantone Color Picker:	no
Ability to mix two colors:	no
Process color:	no
Trapping:	no
Output resolution set by the program:	yes
Halftone screens set by program:	default
Accepts color-separated images:	no
Maximum page size:	20' x 20'
Save page as EPS:	yes
Create font lists for service bureau:	no
Supports imagesetters:	yes

Text

Type-size increments:	.5 point
Minimum/maximum type sizes:	8-72 points
Horizontal type scaling:	yes
Minimum/maximum scaling:	unlimited
Automatic fractions:	no
Kerning & tracking support:	yes
Adjust spacing between paragraphs:	no

Automatic drop caps:	yes
Text wrap:	yes
Irregular-shape text wrap:	yes
Rotate text:	yes
Spell checker:	yes
Thesaurus:	no
Search/Replace:	yes

Graphics

File formats for imported images:	TIF, PICT, EPS, CGM, PCX, DRW, WMF, BMP
Align objects:	yes
Center graphics:	yes
Automatic drop shadow:	yes
Specify custom line weights:	yes
Coupon borders:	yes
Border styles:	yes
Round corners of boxes:	yes
Rotate graphics:	up to 90°
Flip graphics horizontal:	yes
Flip graphics vertical:	yes
Group text and graphics:	yes
Freehand drawing tool:	yes
Polygons (starbursts, etc.):	yes
Automatic starbursts, triangles:	yes
Graduated fills:	no
Radial fills:	no
Library feature:	no

Notable additional features: Includes PageWizard design assistant that uses interactive questions and automatic formats. Also has a layout checker that lets you leave notes to yourself, 125 clip art images, 100 border designs and the ability to automatically generate bulleted and numbered lists.

General

Program name:	**Multi-Ad Creator**
Version #:	3.5
Operating system:	Mac
Object-oriented or pasteboard format:	object
Disk space required for program & accessories:	4mb
RAM required:	3-4mb
List price:	$995

Style Sheets & Templates

Style sheets:	yes
Export style sheets:	yes
Save as template:	yes
Includes templates:	no
View as thumbnails:	yes

Color & Output

Spot color:	yes
Includes Pantone Color Picker:	yes
Ability to mix two colors:	yes
Process color:	yes
Trapping:	yes
Output resolution set by the program:	yes
Halftone screens set by program:	yes
Accepts color-separated images:	yes
Maximum page size:	48" x 48"
Save page as EPS:	yes
Create font lists for service bureau:	yes
Supports imagesetters:	yes

Text

Type-size increments:	.01 point
Minimum/maximum type sizes:	2-1000 points
Horizontal type scaling:	yes
Minimum/maximum scaling:	yes
Automatic fractions:	yes
Kerning & tracking support:	yes
Adjust spacing between paragraphs:	yes

Automatic drop caps:	no
Text wrap:	yes
Irregular-shape text wrap:	yes
Rotate graphics:	yes
Rotate text:	yes
Spell checker:	yes
Thesaurus:	yes
Search/Replace:	no

Graphics

File formats for imported images:	TIFF, PICT, EPS, RIFF, MacPaint
Align objects:	yes
Center graphics:	yes
Automatic drop shadow:	yes
Specify custom line weights:	yes
Coupon borders:	yes
Border styles:	yes
Round corners of boxes:	yes
Flip graphics horizontal:	yes
Flip graphics vertical:	yes
Group text and graphics:	yes
Freehand drawing tool:	yes
Polygons (starbursts, etc.):	yes
Automatic starbursts, triangles:	yes
Graduated fills:	yes
Radial fills:	yes
Library feature:	yes

Notable additional features: A full-featured publishing program for advertisers. Includes masking graphics to shapes, copyfitting, a complete set of coupon borders and other borders, a border editor, the ability to add notes to the publication or printer outside of the crop marks, an automatic layout feature and standard layout sizes automatically set up for newspaper, magazine and even Reader's Digest ads. Special effects for typography let you curve, fill with patterns and distort type.

General

Program name:	**PageMaker**
Version #:	5.0
Operating system:	Mac, Windows
Object-oriented or pasteboard format:	pasteboard
Disk space required for program & accessories:	6mb
RAM required:	4mb
List price:	$895

Style Sheets & Templates

Style sheets:	yes
Export style sheets:	yes
Save as template:	yes
Includes templates:	no
View as thumbnails:	yes

Color & Output

Spot color:	yes
Includes Pantone Color Picker:	yes
Ability to mix two colors:	yes
Process color:	yes
Trapping:	yes
Output resolution set by the program:	yes
Halftone screens set by program:	yes
Accepts color-separated images:	yes
Maximum page size:	42" x 42"
Save page as EPS:	yes
Create font lists for service bureau:	yes
Supports imagesetters:	yes

Text

Type-size increments:	.1 point
Minimum/maximum type sizes:	4-650 points
Horizontal type scaling:	yes
Minimum/maximum scaling:	5-250%
Automatic fractions:	no
Kerning & tracking support:	yes

Adjust spacing between paragraphs:	yes
Automatic drop caps:	yes
Text wrap:	yes
Irregular-shape text wrap:	yes
Rotate text:	yes
Spell checker:	yes
Thesaurus:	no
Search/Replace:	yes

Graphics

File formats for imported images: TIF, PICT, EPS, MacPaint, Windows-supported graphics

Align objects:	yes
Center graphics:	no
Automatic drop shadow:	no
Specify custom line weights:	yes
Coupon borders:	yes
Border styles:	yes
Round corners of boxes:	yes
Rotate graphics:	yes
Flip graphics horizontal:	no
Flip graphics vertical:	no
Group text and graphics:	no
Freehand drawing tool:	no
Polygons (starbursts, etc.):	no
Automatic starbursts, triangles:	no
Graduated fills:	no
Radial fills:	no
Library feature:	yes

Notable additional features: Automatic bullets and numbering when creating lists. Balances columns of numbers. Has wide support by service bureaus, computer stores and desktop publishing magazines.

General

Program name:	**PagePlus**
Version #:	2.0
Operating system:	Windows
Object-oriented or pasteboard format:	pasteboard
Disk space required for program & accessories:	6-8mb
RAM required:	2-4mb
List price:	$59.95

Style Sheets & Templates

Style sheets:	yes
Export style sheets:	yes
Save as template:	yes
Includes templates:	yes (60)
View as thumbnails:	no

Color & Output

Spot color:	yes
Includes Pantone Color Picker:	yes
Ability to mix two colors:	yes
Process color:	yes
Trapping:	yes
Output resolution set by the program:	yes
Halftone screens set by program:	yes
Accepts color-separated images:	yes
Maximum page size:	22" x 22"
Save page as EPS:	yes
Create font lists for service bureau:	no
Supports imagesetters:	yes

Text

Type-size increments:	.1 point
Minimum/maximum type sizes:	4-1500 points
Horizontal type scaling:	yes
Minimum/maximum scaling:	25-250%
Automatic fractions:	no

Kerning & tracking support:	yes
Adjust spacing between paragraphs:	yes
Automatic drop caps:	no
Text wrap:	yes
Irregular-shape text wrap:	yes
Rotate text:	yes
Spell checker:	no
Thesaurus:	no
Search/Replace:	no

Graphics

File formats for imported images:	PCX, BMT, EPS, TIF, CGM, DXF, DRW, Windows metafile
Align objects:	yes
Center graphics:	yes
Automatic drop shadow:	no
Specify custom line weights:	yes
Coupon borders:	yes
Border styles:	yes
Round corners of boxes:	yes
Rotate graphics:	yes
Flip graphics horizontal:	no
Flip graphics vertical:	no
Group text and graphics:	yes
Freehand drawing tool:	no
Polygons (starbursts, etc.):	no
Automatic starbursts, triangles:	no
Graduated fills:	no
Radial fills:	no
Library feature:	yes

Notable additional features: Supports all Windows standards (similar commands). More of the above features to be added in future releases.

General

Program name:	**Publish It! Easy**
Version #:	3.0
Operating system:	Mac
Object-oriented or pasteboard format:	object
Disk space required for program & accessories:	2-4mb
RAM required:	1mb
List price:	$99

Style Sheets & Templates

Style sheets:	yes
Export style sheets:	yes
Save as template:	yes
Includes templates:	yes
View as thumbnails:	yes

Color & Output

Spot color:	yes
Includes Pantone Color Picker:	no
Ability to mix two colors:	yes
Process color:	no
Trapping:	no
Output resolution set by the program:	default
Halftone screens set by program:	no
Accepts color-separated images:	yes
Maximum page size:	40" x 40"
Save page as EPS:	yes
Create font lists for service bureau:	no
Supports imagesetters:	yes

Text

Type-size increments:	.01 point
Minimum/maximum type sizes:	4-127 points
Horizontal type scaling:	yes
Minimum/maximum scaling:	12-800%
Automatic fractions:	no
Kerning & tracking support:	yes
Adjust spacing between paragraphs:	yes

Automatic drop caps: no
Text wrap: yes
Irregular-shape text wrap: yes
Rotate text: yes
Spell checker: yes
Thesaurus: yes
Search/Replace: yes

Graphics
File formats for imported images: TIFF, PICT, EPS, MacPaint

Align objects: yes
Center graphics: yes
Automatic drop shadow: no
Specify custom line weights: yes
Coupon borders: yes
Border styles: yes
Round corners of boxes: yes
Rotate graphics: yes
Flip graphics horizontal: yes
Flip graphics vertical: yes
Group text and graphics: yes
Freehand drawing tool: yes
Polygons (starbursts, etc.):   yes
Automatic starbursts, triangles: diamonds
Graduated fills: yes
Radial fills: no
Library feature: no

Notable additional features: Includes File It! graphic database and image retrieval. Publisher's pack includes clip art and templates. Allows you to make a slide show from the page layout. With the minimum install feature, the program can take as little as 450kb of hard disk space. This program is widely used on notebook computers because it runs from RAM, taking little effort from the hard disk and saving batteries.

General

Program name:	**QuarkXPress**
Version #:	3.11
Operating system:	Mac, Windows
Object-oriented or pasteboard format:	object
Disk space required for program & accessories:	4.5mb
RAM required:	2-4mb
List price:	$895

Style Sheets & Templates

Style sheets:	yes
Export style sheets:	yes
Save as template:	yes
Includes templates:	no
View as thumbnails:	yes

Color & Output

Spot color:	yes
Includes Pantone Color Picker:	yes
Ability to mix two colors:	yes
Process color:	yes
Trapping:	yes
Output resolution set by the program:	yes
Halftone screens set by program:	yes
Accepts color-separated images:	yes
Maximum page size:	48" x 48"
Save page as EPS:	yes
Create font lists for service bureau:	yes
Supports imagesetters:	yes

Text

Type-size increments:	.01 point
Minimum/maximum type sizes:	2-720 points
Horizontal type scaling:	yes
Minimum/maximum scaling:	25-400%
Automatic fractions:	yes

Kerning & tracking support:	yes
Adjust spacing between paragraphs:	yes
Automatic drop caps:	yes
Text wrap:	yes
Irregular-shape text wrap:	yes
Rotate text:	yes
Spell checker:	yes
Thesaurus:	no
Search/Replace:	yes

Graphics

File formats for imported images:	TIF, PICT, EPS, MacPaint, others for Windows
Align objects:	yes
Center graphics:	yes
Automatic drop shadow:	no
Specify custom line weights:	yes
Coupon borders:	yes
Border styles:	yes
Round corners of boxes:	yes
Rotate graphics:	yes
Flip graphics horizontal:	no
Flip graphics vertical:	no
Group text and graphics:	yes
Freehand drawing tool:	yes
Polygons (starbursts, etc.):	yes
Automatic starbursts, triangles:	no
Graduated fills:	no
Radial fills:	no
Library feature:	yes

Notable additional features: Wide support by service bureaus. Most advertising agencies use this program. Additional utilities called "extensions" are available from other companies. Good handling of color and trapping. Lets you preview a graphic before placing it on the page.

General

Program name:	**Ready-Set-Go (formerly DesignStudio)**
Version #:	6.0
Operating system:	Mac
Object-oriented or pasteboard format:	object
Disk space required for program & accessories:	3mb
RAM required:	3mb
List price:	$395

Style Sheets & Templates

Style sheets:	yes
Export style sheets:	yes
Save as template:	yes
Includes templates:	yes
View as thumbnails:	yes

Color & Output

Spot color:	yes
Includes Pantone Color Picker:	yes
Ability to mix two colors:	yes
Process color:	yes
Trapping:	yes
Output resolution set by the program:	yes
Halftone screens set by program:	yes
Accepts color-separated images:	yes
Maximum page size:	99" x 99"
Save page as EPS:	yes
Create font lists for service bureau:	yes
Supports imagesetters:	yes

Text

Type-size increments:	.01 point
Minimum/maximum type sizes:	1-367 points
Horizontal type scaling:	yes
Minimum/maximum scaling:	25-250%
Automatic fractions:	yes
Kerning & tracking support:	yes
Adjust spacing between paragraphs:	yes

Automatic drop caps: yes
Text wrap: yes
Irregular-shape text wrap: yes
Rotate text: yes
Spell checker: yes
Thesaurus: no
Search/Replace: yes

Graphics

File formats for imported images: TIFF, EPS, PICT, MacPaint
Align objects: yes
Center graphics: yes
Automatic drop shadow: no
Specify custom line weights: yes
Coupon borders: yes
Border styles: yes
Round corners of boxes: yes
Rotate graphics: yes
Flip graphics horizontal: yes
Flip graphics vertical: yes
Group text and graphics: yes
Freehand drawing tool: no
Polygons (starbursts, etc.):   yes
Automatic starbursts, triangles: no
Graduated fills: yes
Radial fills: yes
Library feature: yes

Notable additional features: Includes automatic copyfitting, foreign language dictionaries, up to 26 left and right master pages, ability to import QuickTime movies, and control of the ragged zone of unjustified text.

General

Program name:	**Ventura AdPro**
Version #:	1.1
Operating system:	DOS, Windows
Object-oriented or pasteboard format:	object
Disk space required for program & accessories:	3mb
RAM required:	2mb
List price:	$695

Style Sheets & Templates

Style sheets:	yes
Export style sheets:	yes
Save as template:	yes
Includes templates:	no
View as thumbnails:	yes

Color & Output

Spot color:	yes
Includes Pantone Color Picker:	yes
Ability to mix two colors:	yes
Process color:	yes
Trapping:	yes
Output resolution set by the program:	yes
Halftone screens set by program:	yes
Accepts color-separated images:	yes
Save page as EPS:	yes
Create font lists for service bureau:	yes
Supports imagesetters:	yes

Text

Type-size increments:	.1 point
Minimum/maximum type sizes:	6-255 points
Horizontal type scaling:	yes
Minimum/maximum scaling:	unlimited
Automatic fractions:	no
Kerning & tracking support:	yes
Adjust spacing between paragraphs:	yes
Automatic drop caps:	yes

Text wrap:	yes
Irregular-shape text wrap:	yes
Rotate text:	yes
Spell checker:	no
Thesaurus:	no
Search/Replace:	no

Graphics

File formats for imported images:	DGS, EPS, PCX, TIF, WMF, TGA
Align objects:	yes
Center graphics:	yes
Automatic drop shadow:	yes
Specify custom line weights:	yes
Coupon borders:	yes
Border styles:	yes
Round corners of boxes:	yes
Rotate graphics:	yes
Flip graphics horizontal:	no
Flip graphics vertical:	no
Group text and graphics:	yes
Freehand drawing tool:	no
Polygons (starbursts, etc.):	yes
Automatic starbursts, triangles:	yes
Graduated fills:	no
Radial fills:	no
Library feature:	yes

Notable additional features: Provides an extensive collection of arrows, coupon borders and bezier curves.

General

Program name:	**Ventura Publisher**
Version #:	4.1.1
Operating system:	Mac, DOS, Windows
Object-oriented or pasteboard format:	pasteboard
Disk space required for program & accessories:	less than 10mb
RAM required:	6-8mb
List price:	$795

Style Sheets & Templates

Style sheets:	yes
Export style sheets:	yes
Save as template:	yes
Includes templates:	yes
View as thumbnails:	no

Color & Output

Spot color:	yes
Includes Pantone Color Picker:	yes
Ability to mix two colors:	yes
Process color:	yes
Trapping:	no
Output resolution set by the program:	default
Halftone screens set by program:	no
Accepts color-separated images:	yes
Save page as EPS:	yes
Create font lists for service bureau:	no
Supports imagesetters:	yes

Text

Type-size increments:	.5 point
Minimum/maximum type sizes:	6-255 points
Horizontal type scaling:	no
Minimum/maximum scaling:	N/A
Automatic fractions:	yes
Kerning & tracking support:	yes
Adjust spacing between paragraphs:	yes

Automatic drop caps:	yes
Text wrap:	yes
Irregular-shape text wrap:	no
Rotate text:	90° increments
Spell checker:	yes
Thesaurus:	no
Search/Replace:	yes

Graphics

File formats for imported images:	TIF, EPS, CGM
Align objects:	no
Center graphics:	no
Automatic drop shadow:	no
Specify custom line weights:	yes
Coupon borders:	yes
Border styles:	yes
Round corners of boxes:	no
Rotate graphics:	no
Flip graphics horizontal:	no
Flip graphics vertical:	no
Group text and graphics:	yes
Freehand drawing tool:	no
Polygons (starbursts, etc.):	no
Automatic starbursts, triangles:	no
Graduated fills:	yes
Radial fills:	no
Library feature:	no

Notable additional features: Ventura Publisher is a powerful program that is helpful for publishing long documents such

LOSSARY

Ascender   The part of a type character that extends above the body (the x-height) of the letter. The letters t, l, h, b, k, f, d contain ascenders.

Audience   *See* Target market.

Bitmap   A graphic image translated into pixels or dots for storage in a computer file.

Bleed   Printing an ad, illustration or photo to the edges of a page without leaving a page border or margin.

Body copy   The text portion of an ad, brochure, newsletter or flyer as distinguished from the headline, signature or other isolated text element.

Body type   The typeface (font) you use for your text.

Boldface   A heavier version of a typeface; the thickened strokes and serifs call attention without increasing the type's point size.

Border   A continuous line that extends around the text or a rectangular, oval or irregular-shaped visual in an ad.

Brainstorming   Generating as many ideas as possible in a short amount of time.

Broadcast fax   Automatically sending out the same fax transmission to several different fax machines.

Bulletin Board Service (BBS)   A central computer system, accessed by modem, designed for sharing information and exchanging messages.

Callout   A descriptive label referenced to a visual element.

Campaign   A coordinated effort of advertising and promotions designed to last a specific length of time and achieve set sales objectives.

Caption   Text that accompanies and describes a photograph or illustration. Also called *cutline*.

CD-ROM   A device used to store large amounts of data. Files are permanently stored on the device and can be copied to a disk but not altered directly. ROM stands for Read-Only Memory.

Circular   Advertising that's printed out on a sheet of paper and mailed, handed out or stuffed in other printed materials, packages or shopping bags.

Clip art   Predrawn illustrations sold in electronic format (on disk) for use in ads, newsletters, brochures and so on.

Clip photos   Photographs scanned and stored on disk for use in ads, newsletters, brochures and other documents.

Closing date   The last day (or minute) a publication will accept your ad artwork for inclusion in a specific issue.

CMYK   An abbreviation for the colors cyan, magenta, yellow and black used in four-color separations.

Color separation   The process used to produce full-color ads: color images are broken down into four parts—cyan, magenta, yellow and black—and each color is transferred onto a separate printing plate.

Concept   The idea or theme used to guide the advertiser in designing copy and visuals selected for an ad.

Condensed type   A narrowed, or slenderized, version of a typeface. Type appearance can be controlled in some desktop publishing software by using *scaling*, *condensing*, or *stretching* commands.

Copy   The advertising message, or text, including the headline, deck, subheads and body copy.

Database   An electronic information file set up in a way that makes it easy to quickly sort and retrieve data.

Deck   Text placed between the headline and the beginning of the body copy, usually in a type size smaller than the headline but larger than the body type.

Demographics   The various social and economic character-istics of a group of people, including age, sex, income and number of members in the household.

Descender   The part of a letter that extends below the body (the x-height) of the letter. The letters y, p, g and j contain descenders.

Direct response   Advertising that solicits a direct sale or inquiry by announcing a toll-free number or address.

Display ad   Print media advertising that is set apart from the masses of small items in the classified ad section of a publication.

Display type   The large type in a headline, deck or other attention-getting area.

Downstyle   A headline style in which only the first letter and any proper names in a headline are capitalized, while all other words start with a lowercase letter.

Drop cap   An initial capital, in a large point size, set into a block of text so that the top of the cap aligns with the tops of the other letters in the same line.

Drop shadow   A solid black or gray screen placed "behind" a visual, giving the effect of a shadow.

Duotone   The separation of a black-and-white photograph into black and a second color. This effect enriches the look of the photograph.

Environment   Everything your customers can hear, see, smell, touch and taste when they call or visit your place of business.

EPS   A file format used for storing a visual. Short for Encapsulated PostScript.

Expanded type   A widened version of a typeface design. This and other type effects can be created in some desktop publishing software using *scaling*, *condensing* or *stretching* commands.

Fax on Demand   A system that allows a caller to automatically request that a specific document (brochure, price list or order form) be sent directly to the caller's fax machine.

Fill   *See* Screen tint.

Flop To make a mirror image of visuals such as photographs or clip art. Also called flip.

Flush-left The formatting of text so that all lines of text in a column align on the left column margin.

Flush-right All text in a column aligns on the right column margin.

Font A font is the complete collection of all the characters (numbers, uppercase and lowercase and, in some cases, small caps and symbols) of a given typeface in a specific point size.

Forum Online clubs composed of people with similar interests such as desktop publishing or advertising.

Frequency The average number of times an audience sees your advertising message over a given period of time.

Graduated screen A fill pattern that goes from dark to light or light to dark.

Gutter The space formed by the inner page margins in a two-page spread—in other words, where the right margin of a left-hand page joins the left margin of a right-hand page.

Halftone A reproduction process in which a screen transforms the tones of a photograph into dots of various sizes to prepare the photo for printing.

Headline A title or other eye-catching words set in large type and designed to attract the attention of readers.

Hue The essence of a color, such as yellow, red or blue.

Image The tone, character or personality your business projects to the public. The ideal way you want your customers to perceive you.

Imagesetter A high-resolution output device (1200 dots per inch and above), such as a Linotronic, that prints camera-ready paper or photographic film masters.

Initial cap A large capital used as the first letter of the first word in a block of text.

Insertion order The set of instructions—including the publication date, ad size and requested placement on the page—that functions as a purchase order when placing an ad in a publication.

Italics A version of a typeface, designed with letters slanted to the right to resemble handwriting.

Justified type Type formatted so that text aligns on both the left and the right margin of a column or page.

Kerning Automatic or manual adjustment of space between two letters in a word in order to improve appearance and readability. *See also* Letterspacing.

Key word A word or benefit that's been proven successful in attracting the attention of your best prospects.

Kicker A short text item that introduces an advertisement, usually set in smaller type and placed above the headline.

Kiosk A cylindrical display booth or area for displaying posters and buyer information. (Kiosks were made popular in Europe and are now making inroads in the U.S. retail market.)

Landscape The shape of an ad whose width is greater than its length (or height). *See also* Portrait.

Layout The placement of ad elements—headline, visuals, body copy and signature—to fit the size of the area the advertiser purchases.

Leading   The space between two lines of type.

Letterspacing   The space between the letters within a word. *See also* Kerning.

Line art   A drawing or piece of artwork with no halftone screening.

Line screen   The number of lines per inch used when converting a photograph to a halftone.

Logo   Usually, a small image, consisting of graphics and text, that represents a business. A logo provides a distinctive "signature" and helps to establish recognition of the advertiser's name and product.

Lowercase   The uncapitalized letters of the alphabet.

Marketing plan   Strategies and a timetable for achieving sales objectives. Includes the positioning of your company and products, possible advertising campaigns, your budget and your target market.

Mask   To conform the shape of a photograph or illustration to another shape such as a circle or polygon.

Masthead   A listing in a magazine, journal, newspaper or newsletter (usually set off in a box or borders) that lists publisher information such as names, addresses, frequency of publication and staff members.

Media   All of the places you can place your advertising messages, such as newspapers, magazines, trade journals, television, radio, signs, direct mail, fax machines and more.

Merchandising   The advertising and promotions used in your place of business to make your products noticeable, attractive and salable.

Modem   A device that allows two computers to share data via a regular phone line by converting digital information to audio and back again.

Mouse type   Text set in small type, usually at the bottom of an ad or the end of a print piece, that cites trademarks, copyrights, disclaimers and other legal information and restrictions.

Multimedia   The combination of sound, video images and text to create a "moving" presentation.

Nameplate   The area, usually at the top of the first page, containing a newsletter's name in decorative type.

Oblique   The slanted version (usually at a 12-degree angle) of a typeface.

Online   The state of a computer when it is connected to another computer via a modem.

Pantone Matching System   (Also called PMS) A system for specifying colors by number; used by print services and in color desktop publishing to assure uniform color matching.

PICT   A file format that supports bitmapped as well as object-oriented images.

Point   A unit of measurement used to specify type size. There are 72 points to an inch.

Point-of-purchase   The place where the customer comes to see and buy the product.

Portrait   Refers to the shape of an ad whose width is greater than its length (or height). The shape of an ad that is longer than it is wide. *See also* Landscape.

Position   A specific section of a newspaper or magazine page where an ad may appear.

Preferred position   A requested location in a periodical. Most advertising media charge a higher rate for granting preferred positions.

Premiums   Customer gifts such as T-shirts, coffee mugs and pens that display your logo and advertising message.

Rate card   A card or sheet listing available ad sizes along with prices for each size and frequency. Usually also specifies how and when ad artwork should be submitted.

Readership   The number of people who actually read a publication.

Resolution   The number of dots per inch of a printer or output device. The higher the resolution, the crisper the output.

Reverse   The opposite of the conventional black objects on a white background—for example, white type on a black background.

RGB   The colors—red, green and blue—used by computer monitors to display the full spectrum of color.

Roman type   The normal, unslanted version of a typeface.

Runaround   *See* Wrap.

Sans-serif   A typeface without serifs.

Scaling (type)   Condensing or expanding a typeface in order to achieve a particular graphic effect.

Screen tint   In printing, the result of a solid color being broken up (screened) into dots to simulate a lighter color or shadow.

Serif   A typeface with small strokes at the ends of its letterforms.

Service bureau   A business that provides imagesetting services to desktop publishers. Some service bureaus also provide scanning, consulting and design work.

Signature   Your logo and tag line or slogan, usually placed at the bottom of an ad. Sometimes includes your address and phone number.

Silhouette   To remove part of the background of a photograph or illustration, leaving only the desired portion.

Slogan   A sentence or phrase used consistently to describe and sell a company's products or philosophy.

Small caps   A type style in which lowercase letters are replaced by capital letters set in a smaller point size.

Split run   A technique used in direct-mail advertising whereby two versions of a mailing piece and two prospect lists are created to test which piece results in more sales or inquiries.

Spot color   A color not created by CMYK separations, usually specified by a Pantone swatch number.

Stretch (type)   To expand or condense a typeface.

Subhead   A secondary-level heading used to organize body text. Sometimes called topic headline.

Target market   A group of people identified by either demographic or psychographic profile as a company's best prospective buyers to solicit with advertising messages.

Theme   The central idea you base most of your advertising around. Usually coordinates with your store image, campaigns and concepts.

TIFF   *Tagged image file format*, used for bitmapped images such as photographs.

Twin-color process   A method of separating a four-color photograph into two Pantone colors supported by photo editing programs such as Photoshop.

Type family   A set of typefaces created from the same basic design but in different weights, such as bold, light, italic, book and heavy.

Typeface   A design, or style, of type such as Helvetica or Times Roman.

Uppercase   The capital letters of a typeface as opposed to the lowercase, or smaller, letters.

Visual   A photograph, illustration, piece of clip art or graph used to attract attention in an advertisement.

Weight   The thickness of the strokes of a type character: type weights include light, book and ultra (thin, medium and thick strokes respectively).

Word spacing   The amount of space, determined by your text alignment choice and other parameters you select, that your desktop publishing software inserts between words.

Wrap   Type set on the page so that it wraps around the shape of a visual, either to the right side, the left side or both sides.

x-height   The height of the letter *x* in a given typeface. Also know as the *body size* of the type.

¹NDEX

A

Ad design formulas
  checklist-style 190
  choosing 207
  comparison and
    before-and-after 195-197
  editorial-style 189-193
  food 200-201
  how-to 190-191
  image 201-202
  the Ogilvy 180-184, 201
  price shopper 198-200
  question-and-answer 192
  storyboard 193-194
  testimonial 193-194
  two-page spreads 202-205
  visual reigns 184
  See also Small-space ads—
    design formulas
Addresses *See* Response devices
Adobe products
  Adobe Illustrator 41, 97
  Adobe Photoshop 38, 97, 143
  Adobe Streamline 42, 47
  Adobe Type Manager 64
Ads
  before-and-after 109
  borders for 123
  buying or placing 162
  color in 134, 137, 152-153, 163
  common mistakes 177

  components 1
  design of 161-208
  display 161-208
  editorial style 51, 115, 152, 189-193
  on envelopes 245-246
  increasing response 178
  insertion orders for 170
  in magazines 163-164
  in newsletters 265
  in newspapers 162-163, 167
  overview 1
  rate cards 169-170
  reprints of 258
  sizes of 163, 169-170
  text only 106, 149
  tracking performance 127, 209
  visibility 161-162
  in Yellow Pages and
    directories 162, 164-166
Ads, small-space *See* Small-space ads
Advertising agencies 2
Advertising premiums *See* Premiums
Advertising research findings
  before-and-after ads 197
  captions 30
  color 134, 155
  corporate stationery 251
  electronic bulletin boards 310
  food ads 200
  headlines 66
  indents 77

initial caps   52
multimedia   313
packaging   286-287
quotation marks   68
single-product ads   22
Aldus products
Aldus Fetch   38, 43
Aldus Freehand   41
Aldus Gallery Effects   44
Aldus PageMaker
companies using   97
kerning in   63
overview of   95-96
Library feature   19
PosterWorks support   281
Aldus Persuasion   314
America Online   4
Amoebas   36, 100
Ascenders   55, 69
Astrobright papers   282
AT&T video phone   313
Audience
attracting desired   20, 161-164, 173-174
demographics   8
psychographic profile   8
surveys   10
Avery Labels
disk labels   309
name tags   292
rotary cards   242

B

Backgrounds   8, 204, 230-231, 301
BannerMania   95
Banners
ad messages in   16
colors of   144, 151
design of   275-278
example of   18

Bar code (Postnet)   10
Benefits
in card deck cards   263
concepts and   12
graphically highlighting   24, 31, 93
in reply cards   267
visuals showing   171
Birren, Faber   133, 153
Bitmaps
converting files   42
disadvantages of   42
file formats   41
Bleeds   109, 180, 187, 216, 223
Body copy
in ads   174-175, 221
centering   75
color of   73, 78, 104
consistency in   19
editing   115, 175
justification of   75-76
overview of   1
paragraph spacing   77
in sales letters   251-253
shape of   75-76
typefaces for   73-75
varying   126
in Yellow Pages ads   165
Boldface   *See* Type styles
Borders and frames
in ads   199, 210-211, 218, 232
in brochures   123
clip art for   84
consistency in   18-19
in faxes   302
line weights of   83, 218-219
overview of   1, 82-83
spacing and   123, 218
styles   83-84
use of   83, 123
white space as   84, 219
See also Boxes; Lines

Boxes
    drop shadows   87, 231
    graduated screens   89
    overview of   82, 86
    rounded corners   83
    See also Borders
Brainerd, Paul   27
Brainstorming   12, 14-15
Broadcast fax systems   297
Brochures
    borders in   123
    via bulletin boards   310
    business cards as   242-244
    campaigns and   16
    checklist for   255
    colors for   144
    design of   254-257
    drop caps in   52
    as faxes   304-306
    name tags and   292
    overview of   238
    quality of   251
Bulletin boards   310-312
Bullets   *See* Lists
Business cards
    checklist for   242
    design of   242-244
    makeover of   271
    overview of   242
    quality of   251
    rotary file cards as   242
Business communications   *See* Sales materials
Business reply mail   263

C

Call to action
    See Response devices
Callouts   191
Campaigns
    components of   24-25
        concepts in   12, 16, 24
        design of   18-19, 134, 150-151
        magazine ads and   164
        newspaper ads and   163
        overview   16
        postcards and   261
        sales materials and   240
        signs and banners and   276
        tracking performance   127
Captions
    in ads   116, 171-172, 180
    in flush-right type   77
    brand name in   30
    visuals and   30
Card decks   263-264
Cards, business   *See* Business cards
Cataloging programs   *See* Image databases
Catalogs   16, 313
CD-ROM
    clip art on   3, 43
    film developed on   38
    mailing lists on   10
    multimedia on   3
    sound libraries on   313
    thesauruses and encyclopedias on   16
Centering type   75-76
Certificates   *See* Gift certificates
Check lists   *See* Lists
CIF   309
Circulars   *See* Flyers
Classified ads   236
Clip art
    borders   84
    on CD-ROM   3
    in CorelDRAW   43
    custom vs.   44-45
    drop caps and initial caps   51
    file formats of   44
    modifying   44
    for newspaper advertising   163
    sources of   43
CMYK   136-138, 140

Color
    in ads   134, 164, 211-212, 215-216, 229-230
    backgrounds   152-153
    black-and-white as   79, 88, 103-106, 215, 301
    choosing   135, 138, 144-156
    and computers   135-143
    cost of   156
    in logos   6
    mood and   135, 139-140
    in packaging   287-288
    photographs, black-and-white versus   133-135
    placement of   117, 120-121, 139-140, 149-150, 154-155
    in postcards   261
    properties of   138
    as recognition tool   18, 135
    in response devices   128, 155-156, 267
    in sales letters   251
    the senses and   133-134
    and shape   146-147
    on shopping bags   290-291
    on signs and banners   277-278
    software for   95
    of typography   79, 81, 152-153
    two-color   *See* Spot color
    visibility of   94, 102-103, 134, 144-152
Color wheels   138-140
Complementary colors   138
Compressing type   *See* Type—condensing and expanding
CompuServe   4
Concepts
    campaigns and   1, 16
    design and   1, 24, 104-105, 108
    developing and following   27
    overview   12
    visuals for   28-30, 41
Condensed typefaces   *See* Type—condensing and expanding

Corel products
    CorelDRAW
        clip art in   43, 45
        illustrations using   41
    CorelPHOTO-PAINT   38
    CorelMOSIAC   43
Coupons   *See* Response devices
Creativity   12, 14-15
Credit card logos   *See* Response devices
Cropping photographs   *See* Photographs

D

Dashes   *See* Punctuation
Databases
    demographic   9
    image   38, 43
    mailing lists   10
    software programs   10
Decks   1, 175, 177, 229
Demonstrations   313-314
Descenders   5, 69
Design
    attracting audience   20
    color and   144-156
    consistency
        in campaigns   16-17, 24, 276
        as recognition tool   18
        in sales materials   240
        using templates for   19
    contrast in   105, 126, 229
    eye movement in   113-114, 117-122, 127-128, 154-155, 180, 218, 227
    first impression   19, 118-119
    headlines   66
    improving   27
    integration of parts   93, 113-125
    layout and   93-131
    proportion of elements   98, 115
    shape of elements   100-102, 107-108, 213-215

starting with sketches   93-94, 97-100
unifying   114, 123-125
See also Color
Desktop publishing software
choosing   95-97, 137
and color   135-143
influence on design   27
object-oriented format   96
overview of   94-95
pasteboard-style format   96
simple illustrations using   42-43
Digital Darkroom   38
Dingbats   50, 52
Direct mail
advantages of   237-238
color and   155-156
envelopes for   246
order forms and   247
overview of   239
See also Sales materials
Display typefaces   56
Displays
color in   152
design of   283-286
multimedia and   313
overview of   273
repeating ad message in   16
Drop caps
in ads   175, 180
clip art for   51
as visuals   51
words spelled by   52
Drop shadows
boxes   87
in illustrations   107
in signs   279
the white fence and   231
Dulling spray   39
Dun & Bradstreet   10
Duotones   142-143
Dwiggins, W.A.   27, 123

E

Easy Working for Windows Labels   246
EduCorp   314
Edwards, Dr. Charles   23, 93
Effects   *See* Special effects
80/20 rule   10
Ellipses   *See* Punctuation
Em dash   68
Encyclopedias   16
Envelopes
for brochures   254
design of   245-246
quality of   251
EPS format
bitmap to   42
clip art in   4
illustration software   41
logos in   47
Express Publisher   95

F

Faxes
advertising with   297
brochures   304-306
bulletin board instructions   310
cover sheets   302-304
design tips   300-302
order forms   307-308
price lists   306-307
type sizes for   251, 300-302
Fax-on-demand systems   239
cover sheets for   304
document indexes for   304-305
overview of   297-299
FileMaker   10
Flush-left type   75-76, 85
Flush-right type   75, 77, 85
Flopping   33-34, 121

Flyers
    checklist for   258
    design of   257-60
    in newsletters   265
    overview   239
    shapes of   260
Focoltone   140
Folds
    in business cards   242-243
    in postcards   261-262
Fontographer   56
Fonts   *See* Typefaces
Four-color   *See* Color
Fractions   72-73
FrameMaker   95

G

Gallup   197
GIF format   41
Gift certificates   249-250
Graduated fills or screens
    attracting attention   82
    black-and-white   103
    colored   154
    desktop publishing   89
    unifying with   124-125
Graphic design   *See* Design
Graphics   *See* Illustrations; Visuals
Gutters
    avoiding placement near   166, 168-169,
        175
    overlapping   203

H

Halftone screens
    color separations   137
    on glossy paper   37
    in magazines   37-38, 163

    in newspapers   37-38, 163
    overview   37
    setting   37
    on uncoated paper   37
    in Yellow Pages ads   165
Handwriting   251
Headlines
    in ads   64, 172-175, 221, 227, 232
    capitalization   64, 66-67
    color of   104
    condensing and expanding   70-71, 172
    consistency of style   18-19
    in flyers   257-258
    kerning   70-71, 172
    leading   70-71, 172
    legibility of   98
    length   66-67, 70, 172, 180
    letter spacing   70
    overview of use   64
    punctuation in   67-69
    in sales letters   252
    screening   106
    shape of   67-68
    reverse type in   106
    rotated type in   225
    typefaces   64-65
    visibility of   102-103, 113-114
    word spacing   70
    in Yellow Pages ads   165
Help-Wanted signs   280
Hours   *See* Response devices
Hue   138
HyperCard   314
Hyphenation   76

I

IdeaFisher   3-5, 12-14
Illustrations
    buying   41
    clip art   *See* Clip art

clip art vs. custom   44-45
consistency in style   18
file formats   41
layout hints   113-125
overview   39
photographs vs.   29, 33, 39, 40
See also Visuals
Image
ad design for   201-202, 207
of borders   82-83
of certificates   249-250
of colors   139-140, 145-146, 150-151, 153-154
creating and building   17
formal   20, 118
of headlines   65, 67-68
informal   20, 35, 119
illustrations and   39-40, 41
justification and   75
packaging and   287
of shapes   100-101
typography and   54-56
Image databases   38, 43
ImageStudio   38
Indents   73, 77
Information graphics   193
Initial caps   51, 52
Insertion orders   170
Invoices   240-241
Italics   *See* Type styles

J

Justified type   73, 75-76

K

Kerning   *See* Type—kerning, tracking and letter spacing

Key words
in ads   227
highlighting   53, 172-173
visibility of   94
visual associations   12-13
as visuals   47, 113
Kickers   174-175, 177
Kinko's   285
Kiosks   *See* Displays
Kodak products
Kodak PhotoEdge   38
Kodak Shoebox   38, 43
Photos on CD-ROM   38

L

Labels
ad messages on   16
checklist for   246
design of   246-247
for disks   309-310
overview of   246
packaging and   288
Landscape orientation   213-214, 232
Lant, Dr. Jeffrey   264
Laser printers   64, 115
Layout   *See* Design
Leading
color and   59, 75
default   59, 69
in faxes   301, 304
in headlines   69, 172
italic type and   75
legibility and   59, 75, 79
in mouse type   81
overview   59
paragraph spacing   77
in reversed type   80
sans-serif typefaces and   59, 79
serif typefaces and   79

Letterheads   250-251
  See also Sales letters
Letters   *See* Sales letters
Letter spacing   *See* Type—kerning, tracking
  and letter spacing
Levinson, Jay Conrad   201, 258
Levison, Ivan   251-252
Library feature   19
Lighting of signs   280
Lincoln, Abraham   295
Line spacing   *See* Leading
Lines
  in ads   87
  colored   147
  contrasting   126-127, 229
  in faxes   302
  overview of   82, 86-87
  styles   83, 86
  weights   40, 83, 86, 163, 165, 218
  See also Borders
Lists
  in ads   189, 192
  in brochures   255
  on business cards   242
  in card deck cards   264
  design of   23
  information in   22
  on invoices   241
  tabs, setting   73, 78
  in Yellow Pages ads   165
Logos
  changing or updating   6, 46
  colors in   6
  EPS format and   47
  in faxes   301
  first impressions   6, 46
  making negative of   46
  as recognition tool   18, 46
  scanning   39, 46
  on shopping bags   290-291
  in signatures   45

Lotus 1-2-3   10
Luminance   138

M

Magazine advertising
  advantages and disadvantages of   164
  color in   163
  ideal placement in   166-168, 209
  the Ogilvy formula   182
  production of   164
  rate cards   169-170
  screens   88
Mailing information   *See* Labels
Mailing lists   10, 237-238, 247, 254
Map, location   23
Margins   123, 252
  See also Borders; Gutters; White space
Marketing plan   1, 4-7
MarketPlace   10-11, 315
Mastheads   265
Media mix   7
Microsoft products
  Microsoft Excel   10
  Microsoft Word   94
Multimedia Extensions for Windows   312
Monitors (color)   136-137, 140-141
Montages   43
Mouse type   81-82, 178
Multi-Ad Services products
  Multi-Ad Creator   95
  Multi-Ad Search   43, 163
Multimedia
  overview of   295-296
  uses for   313-315

N

Name tags   292
Nameplates   265

National Retail Merchants Association 134
News releases 309
Newsletters
 borders in 123
 via bulletin boards 310
 checklist for 265
 content checklist 265, 267
 design of 264
 drop caps in 52
 overview of 264
 on postcards 261
Newspaper advertising
 advantages and disadvantages of 163
 placement of 163, 166-167, 236
 producing 163
 screens and line weights 40, 88
 visuals for 40, 89
 See also Ads; Small-space ads
Numbers
 in response devices 71
 as visuals 47, 49-50, 191
 white space around 52

O

Ogilvy, David
 on body copy 175
 on captions 30
 on indents 77
 on initial caps 52
 layout formula 120-121, 180-184, 201
 on posters 273
 on quotation marks 68
Online services 4
Optical center 115-118, 123, 175
Order forms
 ad messages 16
 checklist for 248
 design of 247-249
 in newsletters 265

 overview of 247
 on shopping bags 291
Outline formats 41-42

P

Packaging
 colors of 144, 151, 153-154
 coupons in 249
 design of 286-289
 overview of 273
 stuffers in 7
PageMaker *See* Aldus products
PagePlus 95
Paint programs 41
Pamphlets *See* Brochures
Panorama 10
Pantone Matching System 139-141, 143
PaperDirect 242, 254
Paragraph breaks and lengths 73, 78, 126, 175, 250-251
Paragraph spacing
 in ads 175
 indents vs. 77
 readership, increasing 77
 in sales letters 250-251
Patterns, background 231
Pauling, Linus 14
Percentages 73
Periods, in ad headlines *See* Punctuation
Phone numbers *See* Response devices
Photographs
 before-and-after 31, 109
 benefits and 31
 black-and-white 216
 bleeds of 216, 223
 captions for *See* Captions
 of children 32
 choosing 31, 33, 104
 clip photos 30
 color vs. black-and-white 133-135

contrast and brightness   33, 36-37
cropping   33-34, 111
duotones   142-143
emotion in   29
in faxes   302, 304
flopping   33-34, 121
of food   28, 31
halftone screening   165
illustration vs.   29, 32
masking   36
movement of   121-122
organizing   38
of people   29-30, 31, 103
of products   30, 103, 245
scanning   38-39
silhouetting
    attracting attention with   103, 111,
      215
    overview   33
    partial   35
    software for   35, 102
software for editing   33, 38, 282
sources of   32
special effects with   33, 36-37
twin-color process   142-143
PICT   309
PMS   *See* Pantone Matching System
Point size   57
Point-of-purchase display   *See* Displays
Polygons   42, 100
Portrait orientation   213-214, 233-235
Postcards   18, 261-262
Poster formula, the   221-222, 270
Posterization   282
Posters
    colors in   138, 144, 151
    as flyers   258-260
    shape of   108
    See also Signs
PosterWorks   95, 281, 285
Post-It notes   269
PostScript (P.S.)   250, 253

PowerPoint   314
Premiums   269-270
Prices
    in ads   71
    in brochures   254, 257
    buyers, attracting   20, 128
    designs for   72-73, 199
    lists of   240-241, 257, 306-307
    on order forms   247
    overview of   125
Printing
    banners   278
    black-and-white   103
    certificates and coupons   249
    color   136-137, 140-143
    of flyers   258-260
    high-resolution   27, 115, 164, 254
    labels for disks   309
    laser printers   64, 115
    name tags   292
    on Post-It notes   269
    on preprinted papers   242, 244, 254, 256
    quality   155
    saving money on   7, 245, 254, 261
    signs   281-282
    See also Laser printers
Proofs   115
Publicity   285, 309-310
Publish It!   95
Punctuation
    dashes   68-69
    ellipses   68-69
    exclamation points   68-69
    headlines and shape   67
    question marks   68-69
    quotation marks   68-69

Q

QuarkXPress
    companies using   97

kerning using   63
library feature of   19
overview of   95-97
PosterWorks support   281
Queblo Images   242, 254
Question marks   *See* Punctuation
Quotation marks   *See* Punctuation

R

RAM   314
Rate cards   169-170
Receipts   240-241
Recipes   200-201
Recognition
    building   17
    color's role in   150
    design elements for   18
Repetition   16-18
Reply cards   267-268
Response devices
    addresses   128
    in ads   177-179, 221
    in brochures   255
    in business cards   242
    in card deck cards   263-264
    color in   128, 155-156
    coupons   125, 128-129, 178, 181, 235,
        249, 257
    credit cards   178
    design of   125-129
    800 numbers   9, 125, 246
    in envelopes   245
    expiration dates   249, 261-262
    in flyers   257-258
    graphic emphasis of   24, 94
    guarantees   103, 128, 178
    highlighting   127-128
    hours of operation   9
    limited supplies   125, 128
    logos   *See* Logos

    in newsletters   265-266
    in order forms   125, 247-248
    overview   1-2, 23-24
    phone icons   29, 128, 178
    phone numbers   45, 71-72, 126, 128, 178
    in postcards   261-262
    in premiums   270
    prices   *See* Prices
    in reply cards   267-268
    sales dates   71, 125, 128
    signature   45-46
    in Yellow Pages ads   166
Reverse type and visuals
    in ads   187, 195-197
    color and   88, 104, 215
    in faxes   301-302
    guidelines for   75, 79-81, 175-176
    problems with   216-217
RGB   136-138, 140
RIFF   41
Rough layouts   98-99
Rounded corners, of boxes   83
Rotary file cards   242, 255-256
Rotating type and graphics
    attracting attention with   82, 89-90, 103,
        111-112
    decks   29
    movement of   117, 120
    in small-space ads   224-225
    in signs   279-280
    in Yellow Pages ads   165
Rules   *See* Lines

S

Sales letters   251-253
Sales materials
    brochures   254-257
    business cards   242-244, 271
    card deck cards   263-264
    coupons and gift certificates   249

envelopes 245-246
flyers 257-260
labels and stickers 246-247, 268
newsletters 264-267
order forms 247-249
overview of 239-240
postcards 261-262
Post-It notes 269
premiums 270
receipts and invoices 240-241
reply cards 267-268
sales letters 250-253
Sans-serif type
in faxes 300, 302
in headlines 65, 70
leading and 59, 79
letter spacing and 70
in mouse type 82
overview 55
in packaging 287
in reverses and screens 80
in signs and banners 275
Saturation (color) 138, 148
SBA Online 4
Scanning
avoiding 38
colors 136
logos 46-47
tips for 39
Scholar's margin 252
Screens
in ads 215, 229-230
color and 88, 103, 105-106, 141-142, 148
in faxes 301
in magazine ads 164
in newspaper ads 163
percent fill 88, 163
type set over 75, 79-81, 88
uses of 82, 88-89, 123
in Yellow Pages ads 145, 165

Serif type
in ads 189
classical 80
in faxes 300
in headlines 64-65
modern 79
overview 55
in sales letters 251
Service bureaus
choosing 137, 254
color matching and 283
for displays 285
lists of typefaces for 64
PosterWorks 281-282
using 115
Shadows *See* Drop Shadows
Shopping bags
coupons on 249
design of 289-291
flyers in 258
overview of 273
Signatures
components of 45
consistency of 46
in Ogilvy formula 180, 182, 223
overview 1, 6
shape of 46
on shopping bags 290
Signs
exterior
design of 275-283
history of 274
makeover of 292
overview of 273-275
regulations for 275
in-store 283-286
Signs of the Times 286
Silhouetting *See* Photographs—silhouetting
Slide imagers 310-311
Slogans 5, 242, 245, 261-262
Small Business Administration 4, 275

Small-space ads
    backgrounds in   154
    borders in   82, 123, 210-211
    design of   209-246
    drop caps in   52
    formal balance   118
    headline typefaces in   51
    paste-up test for   220
    placement of   167, 209, 236
    shape of   211-215, 232-235
    teasers   222
    test marketing with   162, 209
    white space in   84, 228
Small-space-ad design formulas
    backgrounds   230-231
    circular visual   224
    flanked borders   232
    frames   229-230
    headline reigns   227
    landscape   232-233
    the Ogilvy   223
    photo bleeds   223
    portrait   233-235
    question-and-answer   228
    tilting   223-225
    two-page spread   235
    visual reigns   226-227
    white fence   231
    white space   228
Sony DiscMan   296
Sound Edit Pro   312
Sound libraries   312-313
Spacing
    See Leading; Paragraph spacing;
        White space
    See also Type
Special effects   48
    See also 3D
Spinnaker Software   246
Spot color
    duotones   142-143
    overview   141

Pantone colors   136
    in sales letters   251
    screening   141-142
    software supporting   95
Spreads, two-page-ad
    color in   154
    design of   202-205
    small-space ads and   235
ST Publications   286
Starbursts
    attention and   89
    in design   102
    overuse   89
    overview   1
    price shoppers and   21
    in publishing software   42, 82
Stickers   246, 268-269   *See also* Labels
Storyboard ads   193-194
StrataType 3D   48
Strategic Planning Module (of IdeaFisher)   5
Stretching type   *See* Type, condensing
    and expanding
Subheads
    in ads   175, 189
    overview   1
    in sales letters   251, 253
    use of   126
SuperCard   314
Surveys   10
Symbols   274

T

Tabs   73
Tag lines   *See* Slogans
Target marketing   9, 161-164, 173-174, 179,
    242, 313
Telephone numbers   See Response devices—
    phone numbers
Testimonials   193-194, 255, 265, 267
Text   *See* Body copy

Text typefaces 56
Textures, background *See* Backgrounds
Thesauruses 16
3D effects
    audience for 8
    example of 44
    extruded type 48
    movement of 103, 120
    as visuals 28, 107
3-M 269
Thumbnails
    overview of 97-98
    viewing file as 38, 98
TIFF format
    clip art in 4
    photographs in 32, 309
    software using 41
Tiling 281
Tilting *See* Rotating type and graphics
Tints *See* Screens
Tracking *See* Type—kerning, tracking
    and letter spacing
Trumatch 140
Twin-color process 142-143
Two-color *See* Spot color
Type
    color and 103-104, 152-153
    condensing and expanding
        in body copy 61
        dingbats 50
        in faxes 300
        in headlines 60, 70-71, 172
        legibility and 60
        modifying 61
        overview 59
        phone numbers 178
        saving space 60
        taking space 60-61
        as visuals 47
        white space around 52

distortion on 53
extruding 48
faces *See* Typefaces
families *See* Type families
filling 48
fitting to shape 53
horizontal scaling *See* Type—
    condensing and expanding
kerning, tracking and letter-spacing
        in body copy 62-63, 79
        default 62-63
        dingbats 50
        in headlines 62-64, 70-71, 172
        keyboard commands 63
        overview 62
        phone numbers 178
        as visuals 53
    reversing and screening 79-81, 88
    rotating 47, 82
    screening 106
    size *See* Type sizes
    textures 48
    weights 58, 237
    word spacing
        awkward 76
        color and 79
        in headlines 70
        increasing 62
        reducing 62
    wrapping 53, 85, 123
Type families 58, 175
Type libraries 63-64
Type sizes
    in ads 57, 221
    in body copy 57, 115, 175
    in faxes 251, 300-301
    in fractions 73
    in headlines 57, 173
    in letterheads 251
    in mouse type 81-82

in reply cards   267
in sales letters   251-252
in Yellow Pages ads   165
See also Type
Type styles
bold   57, 75, 80, 251-252
italic   57-58
oblique   58
Roman   75
shadowed   178
underline   57, 251
Typefaces
Avant Garde   62
in brochures   254
choosing   54, 61, 74-75, 79-80
classical   55-56, 74
consistency in   18
creating or modifying   56
decorative   51-52
dingbats   *See* Dingbats
display   56
in fax messages   300, 302
formats of   63
Helvetica   56, 58, 82
investing in   27, 54
lists of, generating   64
modern   55-56, 75
personality of   54-56
pudgy   61
Sonata   51
Stencil   51
text   56
Tiffany   62
Times Roman   56
typewriter-style   251
x-height
See also Type libraries
Typestry   48

V

Value (color)   139-140, 152
Ventura AdPro   95
Visual Merchandising & Store Display   286
Visuals
in ads   171-172, 221
audience and   6, 8-9
choosing   29, 109-110
clip art   43
color and   141, 146-156
concept and   3, 28-30, 41, 104-105, 108
cropping   111
decorative caps   51
decorative typefaces   51
dingbats   50
in flyers   258
gray shades   105
grouping   186
improving design with   27
key words as   47, 113
layout tips   113-125, 226
movement of   121-122, 226-227
numbers   49, 191
overlapping   124, 175-176, 183, 217
overview   1, 28
in packaging   287
perspective   111-112
in reply cards   267-268
for scanning   39
shape of   107-108, 213-215, 224, 233
sizing   115, 184-188, 198
software for   41
sources of   30
subjects of   30, 32
tilting   111-112
tone of   30
type as   47-53
visibility of   94, 102, 134
wrapping type around   85
in Yellow Pages ads   165-166

W

Wave for Windows   312
Which Ad Pulled Best?   174
White, Jan V.   58, 80
White, as text color   *See* Reverse type
   and visuals
White fence   219-220, 231
White space
   awkward   76, 84-85
   basic use of   84-85, 123
   in bulleted lists   78
   color and   148
   consistency in   18
   decorative type and   52
   effect of   115
   expensive products and   20-21
   and eye movement   117
   in faxes   301, 304
   headlines and   65-66
   in image ads   201
   paragraphs, between   77
   in sales letters   252
   in small-space ads   218-220, 228
   in Yellow Pages ads   165
   See also Margins
Windows
   Adobe Type Manager   64
Window signs   *See* Signs—exterior
Word   *See* Microsoft products—
   Microsoft Word

Word processing software   94
Word spacing   *See* Type—word spacing
WordPerfect   94
Wrapping type   53, 83, 85, 123

X

x-height
   in body copy   74-75
   in headlines   65
   leading and   79
   overview   55
   in reverses   80

Y

Yellow Pages ads
   content checklist   166
   designing   165, 169
   ideal placement in   166-169, 168-169
   listing products in   22
   overview of   164
   red ink in   145, 165
Young, Frank   219

Z

ZIP Codes   10

olophon

Advertising From the Desktop was created on a Quadra 700 using Aldus PageMaker 5.0. Page proofs were printed on a LaserWriter Pro 603 and a LaserWriter IIG, while final film was output from a Linotronic 330 imagesetter.

Chapter titles and heads are set in DTC TF Forever, initial caps in DTC Shamrock and body text in Adobe Palatino.

Graphics were created using a variety of programs, including Adobe Illustrator 5.0, Adobe Photoshop, Multi-Ad Creator, Aldus PageMaker 5.0, Aldus FreeHand 3.1.1 and Quark-XPress 3.1. The color chapter was separated using Aldus PageMaker 5.0.

the
Ventana Press

Desktop Design Series

To order these and other Ventana Press titles, use the form in the back of this book or contact your local bookstore or computer store. Full money-back guarantee!

Return order form to:
Ventana Press, P.O. Box 2468, Chapel Hill, NC 27515
☎**919/942-0220; Fax 919/942-1140**

Can't wait? Call toll-free, 800/743-5369!

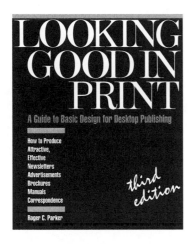

Newsletters From the Desktop
$23.95
306 pages, illustrated
ISBN: 0-940087-40-5
Now the millions of desktop publishers who produce newsletters can learn how to dramatically improve the design of their publications.

The Makeover Book: 101 Design Solutions for Desktop Publishing
$17.95
282 pages, illustrated
ISBN: 0-940087-20-0
"Before-and-after" desktop publishing examples demonstrate how basic design revisions can dramatically improve a document.

Advertising From the Desktop
$24.95
345 pages, illustrated
ISBN: 1-56604-064-7
Advertising From the Desktop offers unmatched design advice and helpful how-to instructions for creating persuasive ads. This book is an idea-packed resource for improving the look and effect of your ads.

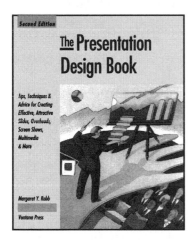

Looking Good in Print, Third Edition
$24.95
424 pages, illustrated
ISBN: 1-56604-047-7
With over 200,000 copies in print, **Looking Good in Print** is looking even better, with a new chapter on working with color, plus sections on photography and scanning. For use with any software or hardware, this desktop design bible has become the standard among novice and experienced desktop publishers alike.

The Presentation Design Book, Second Edition
$24.95
320 pages, illustrated
ISBN: 1-56604-014-0
The Presentation Design Book is filled with thoughtful advice and instructive examples for creating presentation visuals that have the power to communicate and persuade. For use with any software or hardware.

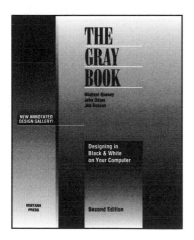

The Gray Book, Second Edition
$24.95
272 pages, illustrated
ISBN: 1-56604-073-6
This "idea gallery" for desktop publishers offers a lavish variety of the most interesting black, white and gray graphics effects that can be achieved with laser printers, scanners and high-resolution output devices.

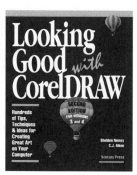

DESKTOP PUBLISHING WITH WORD FOR WINDOWS, Second Edition
Tom Lichty
ISBN: 1-56604-074-4
$21.95
352 pages

With hundreds of illustrations, step-by-step examples and lots of design advice, *Desktop Publishing With Word for Windows* is your key to creating attractive newsletters, brochures, ads, proposals and reports, business correspondence and more. Covers Word for Windows through Version 6.

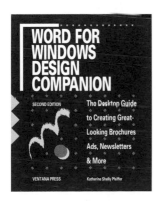

WORD FOR WINDOWS DESIGN COMPANION, Second Edition
Katherine Shelly Pfeiffer
ISBN: 1-56604-075-2
$21.95
473 pages

Gain the design know-how to create attractive documents! Learn the basics of good design with step-by-step instructions from one of the world's foremost desktop designers. Filled with innovative design advice and creative examples for getting the most from your Word investment. Covers Word for Windows through Version 6.

DESKTOP PUBLISHING WITH WORDPERFECT FOR WINDOWS 6
Richard Mansfield
ISBN:1-56604-068-8
$24.95
389 pages

Discover WordPerfect for Windows's powerful desktop publishing capabilities! Desktop design guru Richard Mansfield offers you expert advice on implementing WordPerfect's desktop features to create effective, well-designed documents.

TO ORDER additional copies of *Advertising From the Desktop* or any other Ventana Press title, please fill out this order form and return it to us for quick shipment.

	Quantity		Price		Total
Advertising From the Desktop	_____	x	$24.95	=	$_____
Newsletters From the Desktop	_____	x	$23.95	=	$_____
The Makeover Book	_____	x	$17.95	=	$_____
Looking Good in Print, Third Edition	_____	x	$24.95	=	$_____
The Presentation Design Book, Second Edition	_____	x	$24.95	=	$_____
The Gray Book, Second Edition	_____	x	$24.95	=	$_____
Desktop Publishing With WordPerfect for Windows 6	_____	x	$24.95	=	$_____
Desktop Publishing With WordPerfect 5.0 & 5.1	_____	x	$21.95	=	$_____
Desktop Publishing With Word for Windows, Second Edition	_____	x	$21.95	=	$_____
Desktop Publishing With WordPerfect 6	_____	x	$24.95	=	$_____
Word for Windows Design Companion, Second Edition	_____	x	$21.95	=	$_____
Looking Good With CorelDRAW!, Second Edition	_____	x	$27.95	=	$_____

Shipping: Please add $4.50/first book, $1.35/book thereafter; $8.25/book "two-day air," $2.25/book thereafter. For Canada, add $6.50/book.   − $_____

Send C.O.D. (add $4.50 to shipping charges)   = $_____

North Carolina residents add 6% sales tax   = $_____

                                                          Total   = $_____

Name _____

Company _____

Address (No PO Box) _____

City_____ State_____ Zip_____

Daytime Telephone _____

___ Payment enclosed ___VISA ___MC Acc't # _____

Expiration Date_____ Interbank # _____

Signature _____

Please mail or fax to: **Ventana Press, PO Box 2468, Chapel Hill, NC 27515**
☎ **919/942-0220, FAX: 919/942-1140**
CAN'T WAIT? CALL TOLL-FREE ☎ 800/743-5369!